Praise for Meg Meeker, M.D.

Strong Fathers, Strong Daughters

"Dr. Meeker's conclusions are timely, relevant, and often deeply moving. No one interested in what girls experience growing up in our culture today—and the impact that parents, especially fathers, have on the experience—can afford to miss reading this book."

—ARMAND M. NICHOLI, JR., M.D., professor of psychiatry, Harvard Medical School

"Reassuring and challenging . . . a helpful roadmap for concerned fathers [that] tackles difficult issues."

—*National Review*

Boys Should Be Boys

"If you want to raise a boy you'll be proud of, read *Boys Should Be Boys*."

—DAVE RAMSEY, author of *The Total Money Makeover*

"Filled with inspirational vignettes, *Boys Should Be Boys* empowers parents to stay involved and protect their sons' innocence. It's a wonderfully written and eye-opening book—a must-read."

—NEIL BERNSTEIN, PH.D., author of *There When He Needs You*

The 10 Habits of Happy Mothers

"Offers practical ways to help you let go of 'mom guilt' in order to become a happier, healthier woman."

—*Parent & Child*

"A compassionate discussion of the joys of parenthood and the 'gritty' nature of love."

—*Kirkus Reviews*

"Just about any mom, or dad, can find useful wisdom in this book."

—Associated Press

BY MEG MEEKER, M.D.

Strong Mothers, Strong Sons

The 10 Habits of Happy Mothers

Strong Fathers, Strong Daughters

Boys Should Be Boys

Strong Mothers, Strong Sons

Strong Mothers, Strong Sons

Lessons Mothers Need to Raise Extraordinary Men

MEG MEEKER, M.D.

 Ballantine Books · New York

2015 Ballantine Books Trade Paperback Edition

Published in the United States by Ballantine Books, an imprint of Random House, a division of Random House LLC, a Penguin Random House Company, New York.

BALLANTINE and the HOUSE colophon are registered trademarks of Random House LLC.

Originally published in hardcover in the United States by Ballantine Books, an imprint of Random House, a division of Random House LLC, in 2014.

ISBN 978-0-345-51810-1
eBook ISBN 978-0-345-51811-8

Printed in the United States of America on acid-free paper

www.ballantinebooks.com

12 14 16 18 19 17 15 13

Book design by Jo Anne Metsch

This book is dedicated to six beloved and strong women in my life:
Beth, Granmere, Mary, Charlotte,
Laura, and Ainsley Grace

Contents

Introduction

Janie was, to the outside world, the perfect mother. As an imperfect one, I envied her calm demeanor, her unflappable personality, and her devotion to her two children. She was the kind of mother who baked chocolate zucchini cake for her boys, boys who loved it because she'd taught them to eat and enjoy healthy foods. She packed their lunches every day, with organic snacks. She worked part-time in a bookstore, but got home each afternoon before school let out so she would be there when her sons Jason, thirteen, and Drew, eleven, arrived home. She volunteered at her sons' school for recess duty and as room mother, and even canned her own vegetables. She was the kind of mom the rest of us love to hate.

I will never forget the tormented expression on Janie's face that early January morning in 2005. She came alone to my office to talk about her son Jason, despite the heavy snow, which always made driving in northern Michigan a harrowing experience. But she was desperate.

When I opened the exam room door, I was startled by her ashen face. She looked exhausted. Not the usual "I just had a terrible night's sleep" exhaustion, but a fatigue that had set in over many months. Something was clearly terribly wrong at home.

"What's going on?" I immediately asked.

"It's Jason," she said apologetically. "He's out of control. Jim can't handle him and neither can I. I just don't know what to do."

He was thirteen at the time. I had known Jason since he was two and he had always been a handful—spirited, curious, and volatile. Janie and Jim had adopted him through an open adoption from his young birth mother, and had graciously cared for her during the first three months of his life. Even as an infant, Jason was one of those boys who just seemed to be wired a bit differently. He was cute, cuddly, and affectionate but also slightly unpredictable, prone to occasional explosions of his temper. At eight, a psychiatrist and education specialist diagnosed him with ADHD and I reluctantly went along with medicating him with a small dose of a stimulant. I wasn't quite convinced that ADHD was the reason for his behavior problems, but I thought that a trial of a stimulant might not hurt. He took the medication and it seemed to help—at least for several years.

"I just don't understand his behavior," Janie told me. "One minute he'll be joking with us at dinner, then the next minute he erupts! He'll jump up from the table and start yelling at me or his dad for no reason. We've tried grounding him and taking privileges away from him but nothing seems to work. Two nights ago, he snuck out of the house in the middle of the night and got caught by the police drinking beer with some guys in the Walmart parking lot."

Janie began to cry. Her son—the apple of her and his father's eye—was suddenly a "troubled kid," like the sullen, angry teenage boys depicted on highway billboard ads for drug and alcohol rehabilitation centers. The trouble was, Jason didn't look like that kid on the outside. He was clean-cut, always nicely dressed (no tattoos or piercings), and he addressed his parents' friends politely. He was an outstanding hockey player. He went to church regularly, even attended a few youth groups, and once went on a trip with a local church to help families in New Orleans after Hurricane Katrina hit. His parents loved him, spent a lot of time with him, and seemingly attended to all of his needs.

"Where did I go wrong?" Janie wailed. "Tell me and I'll fix it. Please, tell me. I need to know because I can't go on like this any longer. How could this little boy who I've poured my heart into for thirteen years suddenly hate his father and me so much? I've tried, but there's nothing left. And the worst part is he scares me. When his dad's not around and he flies off the handle, he gets physical. One time he pushed me hard up against the kitchen wall! I think it was an accident, but who knows; all I know is that I was really scared. He's twice my size."

We sat together for many minutes and I wondered whom or what Janie was crying harder for: Jason, herself, or the loss of the beautiful thirteen-year-old boy she had always envisioned that her son would become, but hadn't.

That day, I tried to help her sort through the gnarled complexity of Jason's emotions and hers so that, while she couldn't fully understand them as yet, she (we) could at least devise a plan. She needed to have a plan so that she could move forward. She needed to be able to find hope in the midst of this anguish, which was making her feel as though her life was collapsing around her. And I do believe that I helped Janie find hope. After all, helping her was the best way I could help my patient, her son.

―――――

Janie would tell you that particular day in January was a turning point in her life. It was the day she realized that Jason wasn't who she really wanted him to be; but even more important, that she wasn't the mother she wanted to be. It was a day that began a significant new freedom for her. It was the day that Janie recognized that she not only had one problem on her hands—whatever was driving her son's out-of-control behavior—but equally important, that she had her own issues to face, the demons within her, that had festered for over thirteen years, the ones that were embryonic even as she finished college. But where would she start, with his pain or hers? Her new freedom felt exhilarating, but also overwhelming. I suggested that if she were to understand her son, she would have to start by understanding herself. And as it turned out, she had a lot of emotional baggage she brought to her role as mother.

Shortly after that visit, she began seeing a counselor who meticulously unraveled the hidden anger Janie harbored toward men, anger that she'd been carrying around for years. When she was in her early teens, she had been assaulted by a male neighbor and told no one— not her parents, her husband, or even her best friend. She hated the man for what he did and, for a number of complex reasons, she blamed herself for what happened. When Jason hit puberty, something triggered that pent-up rage in her and she subconsciously took her hurt out on him. In hindsight, she realized her own behavior had changed. She'd become sarcastic and demeaning and secretly felt a sense of disgust toward her own son. She was aware of that disgust, but was so appalled by it that she persisted in pushing it away and trying to ignore it, neither of which stopped the feeling from persisting.

Jason was not immune to the secret war his mother was having with herself. While he didn't know the cause, he understood enough to assume it had something to do with him. What he felt coming from his mother was anger toward him. At times, he felt she was ashamed of him. In response to these feelings, he fought back verbally, determined to prove to his mother that he didn't need her and that he could make her life as miserable as she seemed to be making his. Until Janie sought some answers, this vicious cycle just kept escalating until she found herself scared of her own son.

Both Jason and Janie received the help they each needed in order to restore the sanity and joy to their relationship. When both were schooled about their feelings and their behaviors and how the two intertwined, only then were they able to begin changing. But the process took a lot of time. Janie, in particular, was determined to revive her relationship with Jason because she never once wavered in the intensity of her love and adoration for him.

She learned to interact with him differently. She changed her language, her tone of voice, and even guarded her body language. And then, by continually putting these changes into practice, her feelings toward her son began to evolve. She peeled the hatred she felt toward her old neighbor off her young son and the stranglehold those feelings had on her relationship with Jason broke. Both mother and son felt a new warmth and intimacy. And Jason began getting along better with his younger brother.

Jason is currently finishing his senior year at a very good college.

He is excelling at school and he no longer lashes out at his mother and dad. Shortly after her initial visit with me in which we first addressed Jason's problems, his parents enrolled him in a local residential school for troubled kids. He spent eighteen months there learning to live in a very tightly scheduled and demanding environment. Jason and his parents spent hundreds of hours counseling with the school's psychologist and Jason learned to understand himself, his emotions, and their power—but most important, he learned how to take responsibility for his feelings and his behaviors. And Janie learned to understand how she projected her own suppressed anger onto her young son. More important, she learned how to keep her long-hidden anger toward her past abuser out of her relationship with him.

Janie and Jason are the lucky ones. How many other mother-son dyads exist, fraught with untold pressures and tensions, that don't get enough help? That is why I felt compelled to write this book, for all the mothers of boys who love their sons but are confused about how to be good mothers *to* their sons. And for sons who face inordinate pressures to be the embodiment of the mother's greatest hopes, something they can neither envision nor understand, and who end up enduring a vortex of internal tensions that can lead to an explosion.

The mother-son dyad is complicated by the opposition of gender. Neither mother nor son can fully understand what it is like to be the other half of the equation. Boys face challenges because, as males, they feel responsible in many ways for their mothers' welfare, which can lead to tension and anger within the relationship. Furthermore, mothers can too often subconsciously rely on sons for the kind of support they might look for from an adult. And the reality is that boys, simply because they are male, face trials in our culture that can easily overwhelm them, while mothers face stresses and place expectations on themselves that can become equally overwhelming. Put the two together and disaster can ensue.

But here's the good news. Disaster is not an ordained outcome. Yes, young men today are experiencing what some professionals like myself call a "boy crisis." As psychologist and author Dr. James Dobson writes in *Bringing Up Boys,* "Boys, when compared to girls, are six times more likely to have learning disabilities, three times more likely to be registered drug addicts, and four times more likely to be diagnosed as emotionally disturbed. They are at greater risk for schizophrenia, autism, sexual addiction, alcoholism, bed-wetting and all forms of antisocial and criminal behavior. They are twelve times more likely to murder someone, and their rate of death in car accidents is greater by fifty percent. Seventy-seven percent of delinquency-related court cases involve males."[1]

In discussing Dr. Michael Gurian's *The Wonder of Boys,* Dobson describes the academic troubles that many boys face. He cites that boys receive lower grades than girls from elementary through high school. He tells us that eighth-grade boys are held back 50 percent more frequently than girls, and that two-thirds of the students in special education classes in high school are boys. Finally, he says that boys are ten times more likely to suffer from "hyperactivity" than girls and that boys account for 71 percent of all school suspensions.[2]

There are more troubling numbers to cite regarding the current crisis that boys in America face, but the point here is that the means to resolving this crisis often lie in the mother's hands. We are the ones who can help reverse these trends for our sons. And I believe that we mothers can not only enjoy raising our sons in the process, but also help them thrive amid the pressures they face. We can teach them to rise above the problems and flourish. I know this because I've seen great mothers parent their sons through difficulties over and over in my twenty-five years of pediatric practice. I've seen single mothers duke it out with their sons and become closer than ever. I've watched married mothers with stable home lives struggle with sons who have become involved with drugs and alcohol and pull them through to healthy adulthood. With help and encouragement mothers and sons can find a way to survive and thrive.

———

If we tease apart the unique dynamics of this most wonderful relationship, we see that mothers have their own set of pressures, separate from those their sons experience. It is critical that we understand both sets: the pressures unique to boys and the pressures unique to mothers. Sometimes the two intertwine, sometimes they don't. I will explore these sets in detail. First, I will attend to the issues mothers face, because research shows that the surest way to help a boy is to help whoever has the greatest influence over him. For millions of boys, that means mom.

What are the specific stresses mothers contend with? First, there is the common triad, which every mother in America feels at some point: guilt, fear, and anger. Mothers in the postfeminist culture feel internal pressure to be everything to everyone. In fact, I have yet to meet a mother who feels that she is good enough at the job. Working women feel that they must perform equally well both in the office and in caring for their home, husband, and children. Mothers feel that they must counsel their boys, cook for them, pay for college tuition, provide opportunities commensurate with their sons' friends' opportunities, and, on top of all that, they must be calm and upbeat at all times. They think they must be wholly sensitive and nurturing to their sons, yet tough enough to be a surrogate when dad is absent. Some mothers have husbands who are either too busy or preoccupied to be involved with their sons. Other mothers who are divorced parent sons whose fathers can't or won't be involved in their lives. The truth is, many of the 14 million single mothers in the United States feel that they must be both mother and father to their sons because the son's real father isn't in the home.

Clearly, they need encouragement and some help, because no mother can live up to the expectations that she (and others around her) puts on herself. Every mother lives with a mental picture of what she should look like and act like as the perfect mother to her son (or daughter). And every day we get up in the morning and try desperately to be just like that perfect version of ourselves. But we never get there. This book is about helping every mother understand and *accept who she is and who she isn't*. I believe that if each of us mothers can come to this point, freedom ensues. The freedom that allows us to accept that we are good enough, just the way we are, for our sons.

Boys have their own pressures, both powerful and potentially destructive. They face confusion regarding the role of masculinity in a rapidly changing world, a role that morphs under their feet even as they learn about what it means to be a man. Consider the trends in boys and education, a very important part of healthy male development. Boys are falling behind girls. Fewer boys graduate from high school and college than girls.[3] Dr. William Pollack of Harvard Medical School cites that "there is a gender gap in academic performance, and boys are falling to the bottom of the heap." He says that much of this stems from the fact that boys lack confidence, in addition to an inability to perform.[4] We can see a vicious cycle among boys emerging; many fail to graduate from high school or college and their self-esteem and productivity fall.[5] As this happens, their sense of being strong men plummets and they become less motivated to excel.[6]

This is a deeply disturbing trend.

Clearly, we need to develop new approaches to raising our boys. Research shows that mothers in any household still bear the lion's share of daily parenting responsibilities and household chores. It also shows that on an average day, 20 percent of men engage in housework—such as cleaning or doing laundry—compared with 48 percent of women. Thirty-nine percent of men participate in food preparation or cleanup, compared with 65 percent of women.[7]

And of course, for single mothers, all of the household responsibilities fall on their shoulders. Many of these single mothers are also the primary income earners for their families. According to a recent Pew Report, 63 percent of the "breadwinner mothers" were single mothers.[8] And currently, 24 percent of American children live with single moms. So we can see that the workload on American women is enormous.[9]

The burden on mothers is great, and many feel that it is simply too much when it comes to raising sons. For the most part, daughters seem easier; they are much less mysterious to mothers because of their shared gender—after all, every mother was once a young girl. But though it might be tough mothers cannot give up on their sons.

What this book offers is a road map to help mothers become "good enough" to raise extraordinary sons. It gives encouragement and practical advice, such as the need for mothers to exercise courage and be gutsier with their boys; the means by which mothers can express love in healthy ways to boys in order for them to learn to love women better as they mature; and the importance of hard work, service, and a well-developed inner life. In short, the topics I have chosen are the core issues I've seen mothers contend with as they raise their sons.

I also write about the unique needs all boys have. Once mothers learn to understand their boys better, they can help meet those needs, parent more effectively, and ultimately enjoy a more peaceful home life. On the surface, the topics may appear simple, but the reality is that homing in on the simple components of the mother/son relationship is the key to strengthening them.

This is a survival manual for mothers who adore their sons. Good mothers like Janie, who feel that their efforts never match up to their expectations. It is a tool mothers can use to come to grips with who they really need to be for their sons, and who they don't need to be. I intend this book to be the gateway to becoming the mother you want to be—a sounder, healthier, less stressed mother—and to raising a boy you can be proud of.

Strong Mothers, Strong Sons

CHAPTER 1

You Are His First Love
(But Never Tell Him That)

The moment that little bundle of pink, squirming flesh slips into our arms, love touches us. We feel it, not just in our hearts, but also on our skin. He is there. Our son. He is the one who will teach us what male love is like in its purest form. He will be devoted to us and care for us as no other man will.

In my practice, I've seen something extraordinary, almost spiritual, in the eyes of young mothers who hold their sons for the first time. It's as though we know we have to hold on tightly, while we can, because deep down, we realize that we can't keep them. They will grow up, fall in love, and another will take our place. At that point, sons must leave their mothers. We can't be in the middle of those relationships. Our daughters, on the other hand, don't need to leave us in the same way; somehow, we can maintain an intimacy with them even when they are grown and have fallen in love. We are connected to our sons by the same deep love we have for our daughters, but there is a different makeup to the mother-son relationship. One day, when he falls for someone, the nature of his bond with us will shift; we will no longer be his first love. And the moment he is born, our deep sensibilities know this.

For your infant son, you represent nurture and safety. You are the giver of joy, food, trust, love, and all good things. The moment he hears your voice and smells your skin he knows he will be taken care of. He intuitively believes that you will not go away, that you will always be there for him.

As he matures into his toddler years, he watches your face to see what you are feeling. He doesn't watch you because he is interested in you; rather, he watches because he wants to know what you think about him. If he reads your face and concludes that you are happy with him, then he will feel good about life. He needs your attention: He needs to know where you are and what you are doing. When he is unhappy or scared, he may even get mad at you because you are the one who should prevent these negative feelings, and if you haven't, he expects you to fix it. In his mind, you are his whole world.

Fathers are critical to the healthy emotional, physical, and intellectual development of boys, but their role is different, particularly when boys are young. It is generally true that mothers are more emotionally tuned in to children than are fathers. It's mom who gives the child his emotional and psychological vocabulary. It's mom who provides the physical and emotional nurture.

From the moment your son is born, he knows that you are different from him—not just because you are an adult, but because you are female. Even as a tiny infant, he realizes on some level that you are his introduction to female love. When you respond to him kindly when he is an infant, he learns to associate kindness with females. If you soothe him when he is afraid, then females are trustworthy. In a very real sense, you lay the foundation for how he will relate to women for the rest of his life. You set a template over his heart that will guide his actions from his earliest years through adulthood.

You are his world for the first few years of his life, but equally important, you are the prism through which he will see all women. If you are trustworthy, he can trust his sister, his grandmother, his teacher, and yes, his wife. As you love him he realizes that being loved by a woman feels good. Then, as he grows older, he will love and be loved by other female figures in a healthy way.

On the other hand, if he has perceived that you are unpredictable in your love, he will learn to protect himself very early on. He will withdraw from women and refuse to open his heart to them for fear of being hurt again. If he has felt rejection from you, he will believe that other women will reject him as well. Depending on how deeply a boy has been hurt, he may well recoil from all women throughout his life. Many of us have encountered men who can't trust women, either because they have been hurt by a woman they loved or, quite often, because the woman who was their first love (mother, grandmother, or any female who cared for them as an infant and toddler) emotionally abandoned them. Being a boy's introduction to female love is no small responsibility.

SHOWING THEM WHAT A WOMAN CAN BE

When John was ten years old, his father died of pancreatic cancer. As the oldest of three children, he immediately assumed the role of "man of the house." This wasn't something that his mother told him to do, he later recalled. He simply assumed it because that's what he believed his father would have wanted. John and his siblings were thrown into what felt like a black hole, he said. His father left the family financially drained because he had gambling debts and no life insurance. When his father was alive, his mother had worked outside the home as a housekeeper for several families, but only part-time so that she could be there when her children came home from school. After his father died, all of that changed. Not only did his mother now have to work full-time as a housekeeper, but she also took an evening job at a local restaurant waiting tables to pay the bills and clean up some of her husband's debt.

John described those years to me as "hell on earth." As a ten-year-old, he was feeling the rumblings of puberty along with his all-consuming grief. He couldn't study and his grades plummeted. When this happened, he felt guilty because he desperately didn't want his mother to feel disappointed. He tried harder at school and dropped out of sports in order to bring his grades up. In the evenings, he couldn't study because as the oldest child, he spent that time taking care of his siblings while his mother was at the restaurant. He helped them with their schoolwork and fed them dinner. And in addition to taking care of everyday chores, he assumed a more important role of protecting his younger siblings. He made sure that the doors were locked at night. But as a child himself, he too felt afraid. Keeping watch over his young siblings was frightening for him, especially because he felt insecure as a protector. "I don't know what it was," he told me, "but I was so afraid for them. I was scared that something bad would happen to them, too, and I would be responsible. I just remember sitting so many nights alone frightened and feeling overwhelmed."

When John first told me his story a year ago, he was a grown man with a family of his own. But as he recalled those nights trying to care for his younger siblings, I saw the fear he experienced as a child come alive in him. The frightened little boy inside the adult man began to speak for him, and I wanted to reach over to him and hug that small boy. The pain of those troubling days was still present and raw, and sitting next to him, I could feel it, too.

"It seemed like my teen years lasted twenty. I was so lonely for my mother. I was lonely for my dad, too, but I remember feeling mostly angry toward him. Not only was I mad at him for dying, and feeling guilty that I felt that way; I was mad because he hurt us so badly. My dad gambled and his debt forced my mother to have to leave us in order to work, but he drank a lot while he was alive. I hated him for that. In a way, I guess that you could say he left us before he died. He spent a lot of time drunk. I worried about my mother even before he died."

As John spoke, I wondered how he had managed to process his anger and grief so well that now, at age thirty-eight, he was able to speak so openly about the pain. Had he been to a grief counselor when he was a child? I queried. "Oh no," he said. "That would have been good, I suppose, but how would I have done that? I didn't drive and the other kids were home after school. They were all I had."

"So," I began, "how did you make it through? I mean, if you couldn't see your mother much and you really had no one to talk to, how did you get past the grief and move forward with your life?"

"It was really tough. But I have to say, my mother saved me. No, I didn't get much time with her, but I could watch her. I took in everything that she said when she was around and I watched every move she made."

I had to interrupt him because I couldn't help thinking that he must have felt neglected. So I asked him, "Didn't you feel neglected by your mother? She spent so much time working out of necessity."

He looked at me quizzically. "Never. I know that she was doing the best she could. Plus, she realized that my father's death was a terrible strain on us. She would ask us how we were doing. She took us out sometimes on weekends to the park or to do something fun. She would tell us that we needed to just be kids. I think hearing that validated our desires to sometimes live like 'normal' kids who had two living parents. Mostly, I never felt neglected because my mother showed us how to work together as a unit. We all had extra chores because my dad wasn't around and we all did them together. She was extraordinary and she led us by example. She worked harder than anyone I had—or still have—seen, and her refusal to give up on life kept us all going. I saw how much she was doing, just to take care of her kids. And she was always happy—or at least it seemed that way to me. When I saw how much she loved me and how hard she worked for me and my sister and brother, I loved her all the more. I always felt loved by my mother, even though she wasn't around all the time. She really showed me how to be a strong, good adult."

━━━━

As mothers, we want all our children to be happy. We rush to quiet their cries when they are infants because we don't want them to be uncomfortable or sad. When they are first playing sports or going to school, we watch to see how their peers treat them so that we can help if they are rejected or bullied. Sometimes we spoil them with games and treats and sometimes we give in to their whims far too easily because we don't want to say no. We want our sons to be happy; therefore we don't want to disappoint them by telling them that they can't do something or that we won't give them something that they desperately want. We mothers are pleasers. We are willing to sacrifice our desires in order to meet the needs of our kids. This is good, but there are times when we cross a line and cause problems down the road for our sons because we are simply too nice. This is a natural trap for loving mothers to fall into, but there are some very concrete ways of avoiding it and instead behaving in a way that results in true, long-lasting happiness for our sons.

Love Him When the Going Gets Tough

As mothers, we know that feeling loved brings our sons deep satisfaction, contentment, and a sense of security that they will take with them into adulthood. When they are born we ogle over them and wonder how we can feel such intense love for one human being. But as our boys grow older, that perfect love can become complicated by the realities of day-to-day living. Sometimes our sons make us mad, or they disappoint us. Sometimes it feels as though they don't appreciate us. Gone is the little boy who trusted us as his entire world, and in his place is a toddler who tells us that we don't know what we're talking about because after all, we're just "Mom." With our daughters, it's easier to talk things out and get at the emotional core of the issues that arise. But girls are communicators and most boys aren't. Though exact statistics vary among research, the number of words that females use per day is in the order of thirteen thousand more than men per day.[1] Boys see through a different lens than we do and often it is hard to understand one another. In fact, many times when we try to make amends by discussing our feelings with our sons, we can be met with further rejection because boys don't always want to talk things through. And then, hurt, we often end up pulling back, which creates unnecessary distance between us without solving the problem.

But it is important to remember that no son can be genuinely happy unless he knows deep in his soul that his mother loves him. Remember earlier when I said that mom represents safety? For our children, their mother's love has to be nonnegotiable and constant. That's why it sometimes seems that they take our love for granted; they do. We are the ones who won't change. We won't leave, run out, or withhold love. At least, that's what they want to feel, deep down inside. So what are we to do when the going gets tough and our natural ways of communicating—talking, analyzing, exploring our feelings—don't work with our sons?

When Aristotle wrote that men find complete happiness and contentment when life leaves them nothing else to be desired, he was not talking about material possessions.[2] He was talking about living with a sense of such deep satisfaction that nothing feels lacking. Not that video game, or that toy or those cupcakes. This is a contentment wherein the soul itself feels satisfied.

St. Augustine put a theological bent on this when describing happiness. He taught that "perfect happiness belongs to the immortal soul, completely at rest in the beatific vision, for in the vision of God the soul is united to the infinite good by knowledge and love. In the divine presence and glory all the natural desires of the human spirit are simultaneously satisfied—the intellect's search for truth and the will's yearning for the good."[3]

As mothers, our job, if we believe what both Aristotle and Augustine tell us, is to help our sons seek knowledge and truth, because these are the things that bring true satisfaction of the soul. If we are serious about helping our sons find happiness, we must challenge them to differentiate good from evil and right from wrong. We must also encourage them to make decisions on moral and ethical issues. If Aristotle is correct (and I believe that he is), then our sons literally cannot be happy without learning to live with virtues, because it is virtues, he says, that help regulate the choices that people make. What are these virtues? Specifically, they are: courage, temperance, justice, prudence, wisdom, and chastity. And what mother would not want her son to have any of these? We all would. And since Aristotle claims that having virtues is the primary means through which humans achieve happiness, we have more motivation to teach these to our sons.

Some mothers are hesitant to teach virtues, however, because they see them as outdated and unnecessary in modern-day society, with all its sophistication and complexity. But think for a moment. Courage is the ability to have the strength to do what is right regardless of what others think. Temperance is having the willpower to enjoy all pleasures in moderation by exercising self-control over one's bodily appetites and pleasures. Justice is righting what is wrong and treating others fairly. Prudence requires that one live with a "practical wisdom," utilizing caution. Wisdom, of course, is being able to make smart choices when required to do so, and chastity involves having control specifically over sexual desires.

So if our goal is to help our sons be genuinely happy, our first job as mothers is to begin to teach them the five virtues from an early age.

The second thing we must do in order to help them be happy is to teach them to have love. They must give it and receive it. And since we are our sons' first loves, the burden is upon us to show them love and to continue to teach them about love, even as they grow older and our relationship with them becomes more complicated. We often concentrate more on working for our kids, shuttling them around and paying for their activities, than on showing them they are loved. In our minds, of course, driving them to soccer, buying them the equipment they need, and volunteering at their school are all ways we express our affection. But in a son's mind, these tasks don't always equal demonstrations of love. This is a very important point because in order to help our sons be happy, we need to know exactly what makes them feel loved and what doesn't. Remember John's mother showed her sons love by working hard to keep food on the table and to pay heating bills—but she also knew that she needed to *tell* them she loved them in order for them to feel loved.

I have listened to many boys over the years tell me that the only way they can get attention from their mothers is to play sports, because during games, their mothers will come and clap, yell, or jump up and down. But when they see their mothers paying attention in this way, it can make them feel they must continue to perform in order to keep that attention. Mothers should attempt to prevent their kids from forming that idea, because it can be dangerous. Sons who feel that they must keep running, scoring, or pleasing their coaches in order to have their mother's eye understand themselves as puppets, not sons. They feel like showpieces, not regular boys who are loved merely for being who they are.

How do we show them love? We spend time with them, and not just when they are performing. This means quality time outside of the minutes spent driving them to an event, cheering them on the playing field, or taking them shopping. We need to spend the type of quality time with our sons that is centered around just having fun— playing a card game, watching a movie, throwing a ball outside, or riding bikes around the neighborhood. Time where we are paying attention to them and not just to what they are doing.

And it's not just our sons; we mothers have all become conditioned to feel that we, too, must "perform." We want to buy the right things for our boys, make sure they are attending the right school, cook the right foods, get them to play the best sports; the list goes on. But in all this, we have forgotten the fundamental truth that usually our sons just want to be with us. That's it. Sons don't want us to do more for them; they want us to be with them more and show them that we enjoy their company. When we perform less, they will, too. And this works well for both of us because when our sons are performing and we are doing the same, ultimately neither party feels particularly well loved or satisfied.

In their first days, when they are small and cuddly, we love our sons freely. We hug them, play with them, and kiss them frequently. We pour the love on. In the second phase of their lives, as they enter middle school, we pull back because we are afraid that what they need as boys we can't adequately provide, or we try to provide it only to be rebuffed. But by doing this, we begin to fail in showing them that we love them, and we cannot do that. We must love them as intentionally when they are eighteen as when they are eight days old. First we love them. Then we love them again and again. We say it, we show it through affection, and we show it by challenging them in meaningful ways.

Lara learned this when Elijah was twelve. Lara was married with three children, and Elijah was the middle child. She told me that the two of them were always close and that Elijah was her most sensitive child. As a toddler, he got his feelings hurt more easily than his sisters, and when he played poorly in a hockey game, he told her that he felt badly because he let his coach down.

When Elijah started sixth grade, he moved from the middle school building to the junior high school building. This was particularly tough for him, Lara told me, because his junior high school was much larger than the middle school. His entire fifth-grade class had thirty-two students; his sixth-grade class had 215. Elijah told his mother that he felt as though he had entered a whole new universe when he started junior high.

For the first three months, Elijah seemed to fare well. Lara said that he usually came home in a good mood and that his grades were solid. As the semester wore on, however, she noticed that he was changing. His normal bubbly demeanor soured and he began to snap at her. She chalked up his moodiness to hormones and let it pass. But after several months, she said, Elijah began to withdraw from her. He also seemed to change friends frequently and he rarely brought any of them home.

It was at this point that Lara came to chat with me. "We fight all the time. I just don't understand," she said. "He was so loving, so much fun to be with, and now, to be honest, I can't stand being in the same room with him."

I asked her how she handled his anger outbursts. "I'm embarrassed to say that I just yell back and tell him to go to his room," she replied. "I don't know what else to do. This makes the whole situation worse, of course, because he just yells louder, runs to his room, and starts throwing things around. I just don't know what to do with him."

I asked if Lara knew what was going on in Elijah's life. She wasn't sure what was happening at school, she said, because he told her that he was old enough to handle his work and his teachers. Since he didn't seem to be getting into any trouble, she honored his feelings and didn't try to pry or interfere. Was he having friend issues, I wondered? She said she didn't think so, though he didn't seem to have any close friends. And what about family life, I asked—any changes, deaths, even the death of a pet? "Nope," she said.

We talked for a time and I encouraged Lara to ask Elijah to do some things with her on the weekends that he might enjoy. I also told her to listen more than she talked and to try not to take his outbursts personally. That way, she wouldn't be so easily drawn into fights. She told me she would try.

I ran into Lara in the grocery store a few months later.

"How are things going with Elijah?" I asked.

"Really well," she said, much to my relief. "We're getting along so much better."

"What changed?" I asked her.

"After I saw you, I began to pay more attention to Elijah. I had been so angry with him that I had actually started avoiding him, and I decided to stop that because he was staying away from me the more I stayed away from him. When I reached out to him and asked him to go to a movie or swimming or whatever, he refused at first. But after a while, he began saying okay. When we were together I just tried to ask a question here or there and then listen without interruption to his answers. He started to open up and after a few weeks, I found out that he had overheard a couple of the boys in his class making fun of his size. He has always been self-conscious about being shorter than most of his friends, but I think that when he hit junior high, with all of the boys that are so much larger than him, he had a crisis in his self-confidence," she said.

"So what did you say to him?" I asked.

"Well, I recruited help from his father. I figured that he would understand since he was small, too. I asked him if he would spend more time with Elijah and just talk to him. He said that he would and since then, the two of them have been doing more things together. I think it's really working. Elijah now feels like someone understands how tough junior high can be."

When I originally spoke with Lara, she had told me she was worried that Elijah might be taking drugs, drinking, or being bullied. She saw such a sudden change in her tenderhearted son that she was sure something terrible was going on. But once she rolled up her emotional sleeves and decided to move toward him rather than away from him, she gained a different perspective. She shifted from avoiding him to gently approaching him and the troubles that were weighing on his mind, and in so doing she made him feel more loved. He had picked up on her avoidance and had felt that she was rejecting him, and this amplified his low self-confidence. Once she reached out to him and really began to listen to him, Lara realized that his issues weren't that major (at least compared to what she had been afraid of). She and his father were able to help bring Elijah out of his funk.

Often, loving our sons means getting over our own feelings of rejection and worry and taking the first steps toward them. Loving them in meaningful ways means acting beyond our comfort zones, like disciplining ourselves to listen without interrupting, tackling frustrating conversations, or offering to spend more time with our sons doing relaxing things like going to a movie or riding bikes. We must remember that as the adult, we bear the burden of initiating gestures of love to our sons. The great news for us moms is that when we do these hard things for our sons, the rewards are immeasurable.

DON'T BE AFRAID TO LOVE HIM

When our sons are first born, we become protective and possessive of them. This is natural because we don't want anything bad to happen to them. Part of us wants to build a safe cocoon for them so that we can keep them to ourselves and ensure that no one can come between us. But this will result in a stunted man, a man who hasn't been made ready to contribute to and benefit from a loving relationship with an adult partner.

Our love for our sons has to adjust in order to accommodate the changes that will come. That's the key that will make our bond with our son survive. This is especially true of physical affection. When they are toddlers we can hug them without them blushing or turning away. How wonderful it feels to be allowed to love them so openly. When preschool comes, so too does a gentle sense that they are more grown-up and thus less dependent upon mom. They might withhold physical affection in public, but then be grateful for it at bedtime. By the time our sons hit junior high, we must learn to be creative in showing them physical affection. Our boys feel awkward with their maturing bodies and this is reflected in their demeanor with us as well as with their friends and peers. Many boys wonder if they are still attractive. Their changing voices make them self-conscious. And those boys who haven't reached puberty feel as awkward as those who have. Boys are competitive and are keenly aware of how their peers are maturing. If a boy's friend shaves and he doesn't, then he feels immature. On the other hand, if he does shave and his friend doesn't, a boy may feel self-conscious about that. No matter what their stage of puberty is, the truth is that most boys feel uncomfortable with how they are growing. And so we must be sensitive to their discomfort.

One of the best gifts that we can give our boys is an increased ease with their bodies. This is a challenge because, as noted above, many sons become more uncomfortable with affection from their mothers when they begin puberty. But remember that since they still need affection from us, we must help them through their awkward phases especially because we are the original expression of love in their lives. If we cut off affection, somewhere inside they will wonder if they are no longer as lovable as they were when they were young, and we never want to let them think that. In spite of their body language, we must find creative but respectful ways to communicate our deep love for them. I have heard sons say that bedtime is a great time for mothers to be affectionate. Some have told me that a quick hug, a peck on the cheek, and an "I love you" right before bed feels comforting and comfortable. Most boys object to displays of affection in front of friends, so we must remember that and look for such private moments when our affection won't embarrass them.

Emily did this with her son Timmy. She told me that from the time he was about five years old, she and Timmy played a game every night. When bedtime came and he needed to go upstairs and get ready, one of them would look at the other and give "the signal." Then, wherever they were in the house, they would bolt for the stairs and race to his bedroom. The first to get to his door and tap on it won. This game went on for years. If she forgot, Timmy would feel hurt. Even when he was almost six feet tall at the young age of twelve, the two of them always raced to his bedroom door.

When Timmy was a college student, I asked him about their tradition. As soon as I mentioned it, he smiled. I could tell that he missed their game. "I miss my mom," he told me. "I miss the looks we gave each other and I really miss hearing her voice—particularly when school gets tough. I call her once a week and we talk about what's going on. She loves hearing about everything that I do."

I was curious about what the funny game meant to him. When I asked, he paused for a few seconds, and then told me. "I know that this sounds corny, but it made me feel that life was okay. When we had fun at night, I felt that everything in my life was secure. It's hard to describe. Plus, I felt loved by my mother. This was our thing. No one else played. My mother was very affectionate and even when I was going through my teen years, we played the game and it made me feel really loved. She knew that I felt awkward sometimes when she hugged me, but this game let me know that she loved and enjoyed me as much as ever. That meant a lot to me."

Affection can be expressed in many different ways. And even though we may feel uncomfortable as our boys grow, we must never forget that from our sons' perspective, affection reassures them that while they might change, our love for them won't. But we must always remember that the love we share will need to find different expressions, even if at its core it remains unalterable, in order to accommodate our son's needs and ensure that our love gives him strength without smothering him.

Once we understand that their teen years usher in so many confusing changes that they sometimes will lash out at us in order to cope, we won't panic in the belief that they no longer like us or need us. Because it isn't true; they need us more than ever at that time of great transition. They need affirmation that they are strong, capable, and worth loving. And they need their mothers to communicate that affirmation.

When boys are stressed by relationships, schoolwork, sports, etc., many times they emotionally retreat from their mothers. And when they retreat, sons often snarl or make snide remarks to their mothers. It's hard to not feel hurt when a son makes a brusque comment, but we need to develop a thick skin in order to keep our wits about us. As we think of ways to express affection, it is helpful to remember that while women bond through verbal communication, boys bond to others by doing things with them. If we recognize that, we will find that we can bond by playing games, riding bikes, walking to a park, or going to a football game. Playing with sons (and we don't need to talk much during such games) also gives us an opportunity to show physical affection—we can pat them on the back, tousle their hair, and give them a hug without fear of rejection.

Don't Be Afraid to Let Him Go (a Little)

If we approach our sons' teen years with the fear that we are losing them, we may respond in such ways that actually cause us to lose them. Sometimes, when we feel they are drawing away, we can become more possessive, pushing our way into their lives by forcing affection on them at the wrong times. I have known mothers who become jealous when their sons have their first girlfriend and thus subconsciously sabotage the relationship. They may call their son's phone when they are at the movies with a girl, or they may even say things like "I've worked all these years to make your life nice and this is how you repay me? By ignoring me?"

When a boy goes to preschool, he makes new friends, and most mothers are happy about that. We want our son's world to expand and we know that adding healthy relationships to his life helps that happen. As he moves into elementary school and then middle school, we realize that we are spending less and less time with him. Then, when he begins puberty, another level of separation occurs because he suddenly feels an internal pull to distance himself from his mother. This is a painful juncture for many of us, but the separation is extremely important to our son's healthy development.

As our sons mature, a large part of the separation process involves them forming healthy relationships with friends, teachers, coaches, girlfriends, etc. This can be really hard for mothers who feel dependent on their sons. Single mothers, mothers with only one child, mothers who have no other family or few friends might feel resentful toward their sons when they form new relationships. I have seen mild-mannered mothers become manipulative with their sons when they sense that friends or girlfriends are replacing them. Other times mothers simply feel insecure in their relationship with their sons and thus they become jealous.

Whether we are single, married, have eight children or one, the truth is that watching our children grow up and "away" from us is tough. But we must learn to gently let go of our sons in healthy ways as they mature. If we keep our eyes open to the process, we can handle it much more carefully and stand a better chance of having it go smoothly. To do this, remember a few things.

First, we needn't be afraid. The love that we share with our sons is unlike any other love and we must feel confident about this. No one can replace us in our sons' lives. When we really wrap our minds around this truth, we will feel much less afraid of losing them.

Second, jealousy never leads anywhere good. If we feel jealous over friends, our son's father, his girlfriend, or his wife, no one wins. In fact, we stand to lose a lot if our jealousy takes control of our actions. But we can't oust it if we don't recognize it, so identifying jealousy for what it is is extremely important.

Third, we need to realize that letting our sons grow up is our job. As they mature, they aren't supposed to stay too emotionally or physically attached to us. Good mothers want their sons to grow up and be independent. We can let our sons go and we can be strong enough to embrace the changes that happen in their lives, confident that we are no less valuable to them than we were before; in fact, many times we become closer to our sons when they mature. Ask a mother whose son serves overseas in the military if she is close to him. She will tell you that she feels a stronger connection to him in many ways, much more so than she did when he was three. Hardships and physical distance bring challenges, but when we handle them in a healthy way, when we embrace every stage, every change, and all the friendships and romantic opportunities that our sons have without fear, we can have better, more meaningful and lasting relationships with them.

Teach Him How to Love

As I have said earlier in this chapter, mothers teach their sons how to love. We show our sons that loving others makes for a richer, more valuable life: We teach them how to feel safe with love. And the more successful we are at this, the greater their life experiences will be. If we are jealous of others and never let other women—or men—close to our sons, we teach them that others cannot be trusted. This is a common, but cruel, mistake that mothers make. If we teach our sons that they are safe and loved only when they are with us, we cross the line into unhealthy territory, moving from nurture into overprotectiveness.

Bringing other women and men into our sons' lives has many different developmental and emotional benefits. Loving mothers gladly open up their sons' world to include grandparents, aunts, uncles, teachers, and other trustworthy adults. When Ed's mother did this for him, he told me, it completely changed him.

Even at forty-five, Ed told me that he was a self-proclaimed "mama's boy." "I admit it," he told me. "With a fabulous wife and four kids, I still adore my mother. No one will ever replace her in my life and she knows it. I talk to her on the phone several times a week."

I wondered how Ed came to be so close to his mother. When I asked, he began offering many stories of his experience growing up with his mother. "Well," he said, "if I have to point to one thing, I suppose that it would be how well my mother loved other people."

This surprised me. "Didn't that make you feel . . . envious?" I wondered.

"No," he said. "It really expanded my life. My mother loved so many people. She felt comfortable doing it with complete abandon, and it seemed to open her life and mine. She never showed any fear of being hurt or rejected. My mother was a teacher. We lived in a modest ranch home and many young teachers lived in our neighborhood. She was constantly inviting them over for dinner. I'll bet that four days a week, someone other than a family member was over at our house."

I asked Ed a question that seemed obvious: "Did you ever feel that you were being ignored or pushed aside by your mother?"

"Just the opposite," he replied. "Whenever other adults were at our house, my mother never told me to leave the room. She included me in conversations. She told me people's stories. She told me if they were having a hard time and asked me to be kind to them. I learned to love having others around because I could see that they loved being around my mother. She cooked for them. She helped them with their students and I was always right in the middle of everything. In fact, I learned to enjoy being around adults more than being with my peers. They had so much to teach me. I watched them over the years and they would often give me nuggets of advice on what I should do and not do. In many ways, I had a houseful of mentors who took an interest in me. That made me feel very important."

As Ed spoke, I reflected on how much I had exposed my own children to the other people in my life as they were growing up. I hadn't actually done it very often, aside from time with aunts, uncles, and grandparents. Why was that? When I pressed myself for an answer, I realized that in order to have done that, I would have had to surrender some of my time with my kids to other adults, embracing the love and support that those adults could have given my kids. At the time, I hadn't been willing to do that. Now that I recognize how helpful it could have been, I wish I had.

What we show to our sons teaches them more about how to love and be loved than what we tell them. Not only did Ed's mother show him how to love well; she allowed him to be loved by the young teachers that came to his home so frequently. Their words and interest in his life changed who he became. "I learned to enjoy being with adults, I felt important and I gained a lot of self-confidence."

Before we finished our conversation, Ed made certain to tell me one more story about his mother. He couldn't stop talking about her. "One day," he said, "I got the surprise of my life. I came home from school and my mother told me to sit down. She had something that she wanted to tell me. I was the only boy in the family. She said that she met a student who was visiting from Thailand. He didn't speak English well and needed a place to live. She told me that he would be moving in with us. Rather, me. He was moving into my bedroom with me. It wasn't a big room, but we were going to cram in together because she felt that having him in our home was the right thing to do. Sometimes I felt that I was living in the middle of a circus—there was so much activity going on."

Did having another boy share his room for the year upset him—particularly since no one had asked beforehand how he felt about it? I wondered. I couldn't have imagined saying that to my own son in high school without asking him! After all, wasn't my son's room his own, personal place?

"Not really," Ed said. "It didn't bother me at all because I had come to the point where I liked having others around. My mother was so giving, so loving, that it all seemed to work. He moved in and now, after thirty years, he is still a big part of our family. He became as close to me as a brother. I really love him."

I am embarrassed to admit that even after he said this, I still felt incredulous. Wasn't that mean of his mother to disrupt his routine that way? How could she do that without asking?

"I am so grateful that my mother showed me how to love others. She showed me that opening yourself to others really can be good. Was I mad at her for this? I suppose I might have been at the time. But not for long, because he melded into our family. I believe that the key to my mother's success at making this work was the fact that she never told me that I had to like him. She didn't put things on me; she took them on herself. And she gave me enough attention so that I never felt slighted. I wouldn't have traded having the extended family in our home for anything."

Sometimes teaching our sons to love can be done in ways that counter our maternal instincts. When we feel compelled to pull our sons close and keep them to ourselves, sometimes the best thing that we can do for them—particularly when it comes to teaching them what really matters in life—is to allow others into our private space to love them, too. In this way, strong mothers provide to their sons a road map for enriching relationships and connecting deeply with others. We are the ones who give the clues. We are the ones whose behavior instructs them to either be comfortable or uncomfortable with intimacy. Fathers have much to teach their sons, but for most boys, it is their mothers who show them how fulfilling it can be to forge connections with others built on love, affection, admiration, and respect.

It's Never Too Late

Many mothers who have been estranged from their sons worry that they can never repair their relationships. The truth is, when it comes to mending a mother-son relationship, it is never too late. Every man wants more from his mother. He either wants more great memories or he wants to heal past hurts because there is only one person who can occupy that particular space in his heart. (A stepmother, aunt, or grandmother can come occupy this place if she bonded with the boy early in his childhood when his biological mother was absent.) The dynamics of the mother-son love are intense precisely because the love is need based. While the intensity may shift over the years, the significance and impact of a mother's love never change. Even if she doesn't remain his primary female relationship, a boy always needs to know that he is loved and accepted by his mother, just as he needs his father's approval and support. When a child suspects that a mother's love has shifted or lessened, even at an older, adult age, the ground beneath him feels less solid.

Many single mothers who struggle to try to be both mother and father to their sons become discouraged because their emotional energy runs dry. But the truth is, no one can be both Mom and Dad. A woman can only be Mom, and believe me, this is good enough. So many single mothers exhaust themselves with worry and trying to be something that they can't be. Yes, a boy needs male influence, so rather than attempting to be a substitute yourself, recruit a good man or two to help you. Ask an uncle or grandfather, a pastor, or a coach to spend a little time with your son. Other men can have a profound influence on sons, so it is important to admit that you can't do it all, and to learn to ask for help.

One friend of mine, Claire, lost her husband to pancreatic cancer when their three children were five, ten, and twelve. She was despondent and felt overwhelmed by the task of raising three young children on her own. For the first few years, she tried to be both mother and father to her kids. She got a job outside the home, continued to be room mother to her middle son's class, drove them to sports games, and made lovely dinners every night. As her oldest, Sean, approached puberty, she talked with him about life changes in a way she thought her husband would have.

After two years Claire became exhausted. Sean began acting out. His grades dropped and he began drinking. When she confronted him about what was going on, he refused to talk to her. She believed that his changed behavior was due to his grief over the loss of her husband but she didn't know what to do. Then Claire had an idea. She went to the youth pastor of her church and told him what was going on at home. The two became friends and she asked the pastor if he had any chores that he needed done at his home. He did and agreed to ask her son to help him around the yard. Over the next few months, the pastor and her son developed a friendship, and Claire got to know the pastor's wife well.

The pastor decided to take his family hiking for a week. He called Claire and asked if not only Sean, but all three of her children could accompany him, his wife, and their children on the trip. She was thrilled, and all the kids were, too.

When the trip was over, Sean came home with a renewed sense of joy. Claire could hear it in his voice and see it on his face. He stopped drinking (Claire later found out that her friend had confronted Sean about it earlier) and eventually his grades improved.

Claire admitted to me that she wished she had reached out for help right after her husband died rather than waiting two years. I reminded her that she was doing the best she could and besides, she might not have been ready for help at the time. Trying to be both mother and father might have been her way of coping with her grief at the beginning of her life as a single mom. What advice would she give other mothers, I asked her one day. "That's easy," she replied. "Single mothers need to realize two things. First, help is around you, and second, boys need men. It's hard to admit that we single mothers can't be everything to our sons, as much as we'd like to be. So we need to swallow hard and ask a good man in our lives to help with our sons—even if it just means spending an hour or so a week with them. It changed Sean's life and I know it would help other boys, too."

So if you've hit an abnormally difficult time with your son, particularly during puberty and his teenage years, just remember the things we have discussed. First, your son—who appears to hate you now—needs to know that you love him, even in the middle of horrific fights. Second, hang on. If you take the high road with your son and stick to your guns in doing what is good and right, he will come around. I have known mothers whose sons have run away and lived on the streets. I have watched mothers with these "prodigal sons" stay on their knees in prayer year after year. Those whose sons return are the ones who consistently reached out (even when the sons were homeless) just to tell them that they love them. As hard as it is, it is important to continue to express love, however you can, regardless of the hardship you and your son face. Remember that in a son's eyes, a mother is always the one who will continue to love him, even when everyone in the rest of his world gives up. Sons long to return to the love of their mothers, I believe, because in their formative years, they bond to us with a love that is based on need that never leaves. It changes, but it never leaves. I believe that this connection between love and need is the very force that pulls our children back to us when disaster strikes.

———

While Tess never endured the pain of Alex running away, she and her son had experienced years of turmoil. As a child, Alex was used to spending a lot of time with his father, but when he became a teenager, his father took a job driving a truck and spent weeks away from home. That was the point when Alex rebelled; his acting out was motivated by his deep worry that his dad didn't love him as much as before. He thought that his father spent extended periods of time away from the house because of something that he, Alex, had done. He thought his father took the job to get away from him, and he believed that if he changed, if he did something different, his father would give up this job and come back. In the meantime, Alex took his anger and fear out on his mother. She was the safe person. She couldn't leave, he subconsciously felt, so he could pick fights with her, criticize her, and act as belligerent with her as he wanted. Of course, Tess had no idea where all this was coming from. All she knew was that her son seemed to resent her, even hate her. He made her feel as if everything she did and said was wrong. She didn't know what to do. She endured his teen years as well as she could, until eventually he took a job away from home and lived on his own for a period of time after high school ended.

Now that he is twenty-six, Alex and Tess have a wonderful relationship. Studies have taught us that boys don't come to full mental maturity until they are in their early twenties and Alex clearly benefited from the passage of time. The time they spent apart helped him gain a new perspective on his life.

I spoke with Tess recently about Alex and she told me a story so remarkable that, knowing the difficulty they had been through many years ago, I would have never believed that she and her son could have shared such an intimate time together. Two weeks before our conversation, she and Alex had been away from home at a family wedding. She was feeling particularly sad because her daughter was moving across the country for a new job and her husband was still traveling a lot. The distance and time apart had started causing arguments, and they had trouble resolving the disputes before he went back on the road. Money was tight and both had taken pay cuts, which intensified the arguments. She never spoke to Alex about her troubles, feeling that it would be inappropriate and cross mother-son boundaries that shouldn't be crossed. I agreed with her.

Tess said that after the wedding, she was getting ready to drive five hours back home, alone. Alex was a professional pilot and had flown to the wedding with a friend instead of driving. He knew that his mother was particularly sad, so he asked his friend if he would drive her car home and let Tess fly with him in the airplane. The friend agreed, and Tess and Alex went to the airport together.

"It was a beautiful night," she told me. "The sky was dark and clear and the stars illuminated the entire sky. Alex was flying a plane with an open cockpit, so we couldn't fly particularly high. The air was warm. We each had headphones on and I was glad that we did because I cried during the entire trip and I didn't want Alex to know. I was sad to see my daughter for what I knew would be the last time in a long time. Once I started to cry about her leaving, the floodgates opened. I cried about fighting with my husband. I cried about money. I felt as though I cried years' worth of tears.

"When we landed, Alex taxied the plane and found his car. I had stopped crying by then and he didn't say a word to me. He drove me to my house and came in with me. I asked if he wanted anything to drink and he said no. Then he said to me, 'Mom sit down for a minute. Something's terribly wrong with you and Dad, isn't it?' I was flabbergasted. How did he know? I wasn't sure if I should say yes or no. But I just started to cry again. 'Yes, we're going through a tough time,' I said. He told me that he thought so and then he said something remarkable. Without asking questions or prodding, he said, 'Mom, Dad's a broken man. You need to know that. Whatever it is you're going through, he's also going through things that you can't understand as a woman.'"

Yes, Alex bumped along for several years as a teenager, but now, as a man, he was able to give his mother the perspective that only a man can give to a woman and a son can give to his mother. He loved his father and he loved his mother, and so he was able to shed a light on a difficult situation, offering a perspective that she would have never seen on her own.

"He's an amazing young man and I admire him so much. He showed me that I need to be more compassionate, patient, and understanding with my husband. And the most amazing thing is, he helped me realize that right now, I just needed to hold on."

Every one of our sons leaves home at some point. They become men who can return to help us mothers in ways that no other human can. They can teach us how to live our lives better. If we hold on long enough, and love them always, they come back to us.

CHAPTER 2

Give Him an Emotional Vocabulary

There is a truth I have come to believe about boys: I think they are far more sensitive than girls. I have listened to teenage boys break down over failed relationships with their girlfriends, watched seven-year-old boys fall apart over the death of a pet, and seen adult men emotionally shut down over the loss of a parent. I also believe that the reason that we are seeing many young men today end up unemployed, or worse, in prison, has nothing to do with delinquency and everything to do with the kind of emotional pain that they simply have no clue how to handle. Consider the hundreds of boys who drop out of school or turn to selling drugs or joining gangs. Data shows that the rate of incarceration for men is fourteen times higher than that for women and most of these men are young (in their twenties).[1] Other young men father children only to abandon them, and many of them end up dead before their time. Yes, they've committed crimes, failed to be good fathers, and become victims of the kind of violence they themselves perpetrate, but my take on the situation is that these are young men so riddled with pain and fear that they have resorted to depending on the most basic of human survival skills: defend yourself at all costs, strike if someone comes near because you don't know if they'll hurt you, and don't open yourself up to love or be loved because you will ultimately be disappointed. They have experienced so much rejection and loss that raw, repressed grief dominates their lives and they have lost the capacity to function (or live) well.

For many young boys and teens, life feels overwhelming. When a young boy loses his grandmother, it will hurt for months. When a fourth grader is called fat and lazy, the scars never heal. When a teenage boy is forced to choose between living with his mother or his father, he may never emotionally recover from the guilt and stress the choice causes. Too many boys have no one to help them navigate their more tender feelings. Sensitivity is a wonderfully protective, inspiring, and fulfilling quality to have, but for many boys, it can feel like a curse. Unless he has a great mom.

Every boy needs his mother to give him an "emotional vocabulary" to help him identify and articulate his feelings. So many boys live with what Dr. William Pollack describes in his book *Real Boys* as "the boy code."[2] This "code" dictates that boys repress many of their feelings in order to appear masculine. This of course is extremely unhealthy for boys; if a mother teaches her son from his early childhood forward to identify his feelings and discuss them, he is able to combat the "boy code" and be psychologically healthier and generally happier.

Mothers are the ones who first identify a boy's sensitivity. They are witness to his sadness, anger, frustration, or hurt feelings. Mothers are just naturally more in tune with their son's emotional world. When he is an infant, it is mom who awakens earliest to his cry. What does he need? Is he happy or hurting? Mom is the one who sees him hold back the tears on the soccer field when he is frustrated with himself. Fathers might notice these feelings but they are also less likely to address them, because the aforementioned boy code tells dads that their sons should "man up" when they are sad. Mom, on the other hand, will scour her son's face for clues as to how he is feeling when he meets his new teacher or before he takes his first girlfriend on a date. As the natural communicators we are, we are positioned to pick up on feelings more quickly than dad.

Having an emotional vocabulary is more than simply having the words to express feelings. It requires building three crucial components: First, a boy needs to be able to identify his emotions. Then he needs to be able to express that emotion (either internally or externally). And finally, he needs to learn what to do with the emotion. If a boy can learn these important skills, he will be on his way to an emotionally healthy life.

Can a father offer these three components to him? Maybe. But mothers are in a much better position to teach these skills because of the way women are wired. Women bond to loved ones through communication (usually verbal), and teaching children to have an emotional vocabulary relies heavily on verbal communication. Men, on the other hand, bond with loved ones through actions. Add to that a son's greater comfort level in discussing feelings with his mother rather than with his father, and we are primed for the task. And our children do seem to instinctively know to turn to us; as toddlers, they look to their mother for comfort, not just because they know that she is compassionate and understanding, but because they know that she will be accepting of their feelings. A son may feel embarrassed to cry in front of his father, fearing that he might be judged or ridiculed. So mothers need to be there to let sons know that stifling their feelings is a harmful thing to do. As he grows older, a boy will receive cues from his peers, teachers, or coaches that feeling sadness and grief may not be acceptable; without an emotional vocabulary, he will succumb to swallowing his feelings and set himself up for eventual outbursts of anger and despair. Without an emotional vocabulary he may never learn to understand and discuss his feelings, which can have a negative effect on his relationships with friends, significant others, and children.

WHY HAVING AN EMOTIONAL VOCABULARY IS SO IMPORTANT FOR A SON

As boys mature, they respond to people and situations around them with as much sensitivity as girls. But as they reach the early and middle elementary school years, they learn that they are not expected to react to things the same way girls do. Boys are taught according to the "boy code" that they aren't supposed to cry in front of others or even display sadness, even in situations that call for it, or else they will be chided for acting "like a girl." The lesson our boys take from this is not that they should hide their emotions; rather, boys may learn that they aren't supposed to even feel emotions. Adults may tell a third grader to buck up and not make a scene in front of his classmates, but the message gets garbled. That third grader may be hearing that he is not supposed to be sad (or cry), not only in class, but ever. He learns that crying is a bad thing and that it is unmanly to experience certain emotions at all.

It's been my experience that by the time boys are in the fourth grade, they very well might believe they are never supposed to feel angry, sad, lonely, or grief-stricken. This becomes confusing and painful for them. When these feelings come over them, boys start to believe there's something wrong with them. A dangerous cycle ensues whereby boys feel certain emotions, refuse to show anyone those emotions, and then get angry with themselves for having those feelings in the first place. If this cycle persists over time, the boy is primed to feel both depression and anxiety.

If his mother can teach him early on what feelings are legitimate and normal, what to do with those feelings when he has them, and finally, the fact that having feelings is a good thing, he is far less likely to fall into the trap of hating himself for being weak. Tens of thousands (if not hundreds of thousands) of adult men have suppressed their feelings of pain and hurt, causing them to live with rage and/or depression. Alcoholism, drug abuse, sexual addiction, panic attacks, and suicidal thoughts more often than not stem from some form of depression whereby healthy, appropriate feelings in response to life situations get stifled and ignored and then build up to something destructive.[3] This isn't to say that all mental illness, depression, anxiety, and substance abuse stem from the lack of an emotional vocabulary, but a very high percentage of these maladies do.

That's exactly why every mother has to start the process of building an emotional vocabulary when her son is young and do her best to help him acknowledge and express appropriate feelings in the healthiest manner possible. A mother who teaches her son how to move forward with those feelings sets the course for her son's life in a more profound way than any other living person. I am convinced that, second only to giving him life, this is the greatest gift we can give our sons. Later in the chapter, we will look specifically at how mothers can help their sons identify their feelings and then express them in a healthy way.

THE FATHERLESS EPIDEMIC

We have a crisis of fatherlessness in our country: men who create children but then disappear and neglect to play the very important role of parent.[4] Too many men live with a desperate lack of meaning in their lives and therefore cannot confer meaning onto another's life. Men who live without purpose have nothing to give others. And so they don't, not even to their sons. How do men get to this point? And what does this have to do with mothers giving them an emotional language?

Viktor Frankl, in his book *Man's Search for Meaning,* writes that for men to feel that their lives have significance, first they must believe that they are worthy of contributing something to another's life. Second, they must have a sense that they are worthy of receiving something (primarily love) from another human. Third, they must believe that they have a future over which they have some choice. In other words, that they are capable of doing something for themselves that will make life better. Then they can have hope to hold on to.

Because men receive very contradictory cues regarding what feelings they should or shouldn't experience, what they should do with those feelings, and how those feelings should affect them, they are vulnerable to terrible mismanagement of their emotions. When their feelings are mismanaged, those chaotic feelings have the potential to control men's lives, and this can be very dangerous. For instance, consider a man whose father walked out on him and his mother when he was ten years old. As a result of the abandonment, he felt tremendous sadness, guilt, and anger. If he didn't have proper emotional support available to him, he would have reactively pushed many of his feelings deep into his heart and decided to move on with his life. Perhaps he wouldn't want his friends or mother to know how badly hurt he was. So instead of working out his feelings in a healthy fashion, he buried them and pretends that he really doesn't care that much about his father's departure.

But since he never dealt with those feelings, they become even more complicated. I often tell kids that pushing feelings away and not confronting them makes the feelings grow in power. Once they let those feelings out, the power of the feelings is lost. This young man would feel his anger swell over the years. It would be further complicated because he would do what any boy aged ten and older would do: He would blame himself for his father's departure. Because his father isn't around to get mad at, he gets mad at himself. He rationalizes that if he were a "better son" his father would have stayed. He finds things to blame himself for; perhaps he said the wrong thing to his father at the wrong time, perhaps his grades weren't good enough, or maybe he thinks that he wasn't turning out to be the son that his father wanted. No matter his reasoning, it stems from his inability to get mad at his father. Sadly, as he internalizes these negative feelings, he continues to feel worse about himself over time. Ultimately he may feel that he was unworthy of his father's love, and not important enough to make him stay.

As he grows into adulthood, those emotions he experienced as a ten-year-old boy still reside within his heart, but since he has made a conscious effort to avoid them, rather than allowing them to bubble to the surface, they subconsciously impact many decisions he makes in his personal and professional life. For instance, he may be overly protective of his mother and refuse to go to college too far from home; often boys who live with mothers after their father has left feel responsible for taking care of them. Or, he may suffer from acute panic attacks when he starts a new job, where his boss is the age his father would be. The decisions he makes could be varied, but the point is, most of them are driven by the pain and anger he is holding on to. His gnarled emotions may thus render him unable to make healthy decisions, which are essential to his happiness. Using Viktor Frankl's definition of what brings meaning to a man's life, this young man cannot feel worthy of giving something to others (because he believes he wasn't worth his father's love and therefore he has nothing to give others), he does not feel worthy of being loved by another (his father's departure proved that), and he certainly cannot know what it feels like to rise above a pain he never fully acknowledges.

When we recognize the connection between dealing with our feelings in a healthy manner and living with a sense of meaning and purpose, we can see how critically important it is for boys to have an emotional vocabulary. It is clear that having a healthy respect for his own feelings paves the way in large part for a man to live a satisfying life where he knows his value, enjoys strong relationships with loved ones, and lives with a sense that he has a future. And who is the one responsible for helping him on this journey? His mom.

When a mother helps her son feel comfortable with his feelings, she can help him talk those feelings out. Remember, when they stay stuck inside the boy's heart, they gain power. By diffusing that power through talk, she can help him find that yes, he is capable of helping others and making a difference in their lives. She teaches him that most certainly he is worthy of receiving the love of friends and family and finally, that he is able to do for himself what needs to be done so that he can overcome obstacles in his future. Sadly, the fatherless epidemic in our country contributes to many feelings of unworthiness, grief, and depression in boys. That is why it is so incumbent upon mothers to help boys who have no father in the home deal with their deep feelings. I fear that if they don't, they can become emotionally stuck—even crippled for years.

Nancy gave her "fatherless" son an emotional vocabulary in his early years and in doing so, I believe, she changed the course of his life. When Brandon was six, his father developed a drinking problem. Nancy tried to protect Brandon from his father's drunken episodes, but when his dad finally lost his job, Brandon and his younger sister often saw him at home, drunk, during the day. Nancy tried hard to help her husband stop drinking, but to no avail. Alcohol sucked the lifeblood out of him and even now, the man is living homeless, moving from shelter to shelter in a large western city.

After years of trying to keep the family intact, Nancy realized that her power was limited. Brandon's father became dangerous to the children and so Nancy left him. When Brandon was ten, the three of them moved out and found a new home to live in. Brandon was crushed. He feared for his father's life and began having nightmares about his dad dying. At school, his teacher noticed that he couldn't concentrate on his schoolwork and that he was sullen and withdrawn. His teacher phoned Nancy and the two of them talked about what they needed to do for the boy.

Nancy told me several years later that that period of adjustment was devastating to all of them. "I do believe that Brandon took the divorce particularly hard. He looked up to his dad (though many times that confounded me) and I know that he missed him terribly. One of the worst parts was that after we moved out, his dad never called, wrote a letter, or even acted remotely interested in Brandon's life. How do you explain that to a ten-year-old boy?" Even though she was describing something that happened years earlier, she began to weep.

Nancy proceeded to tell me that she couldn't afford counseling for her son, so she did the best that she could. She was a schoolteacher and even though she had to leave her life as a full-time mom and go back to work, she always took pains to stay connected to her kids. I wondered how, exactly, this busy, grieving mom had managed that.

"Well," she said, "I decided that the kids were probably experiencing at least the same amount of pain that I was. And I knew that the best way for me to get past the pain was to hit it head-on, so I figured that I would try to help the kids do the same. I decided that, when it came to discussing our new life, about the move, and their dad, all conversations were legitimate. We spent hours talking about it. Sometimes we would sit together and talk into the evening. Brandon knew that he could say anything that he wanted about life, his dad, or me. The only rule was that he couldn't be mean to his sister or me. Sometimes he just cried. Sometimes we didn't talk about hurt at all. Whenever he did talk about his feelings, though, I asked him to describe what exactly the feelings were so that I could understand. At first, it was tough for him. I couldn't believe what a hard time he had discerning anger from sadness from frustration. He would just say, he felt horrible. When I told him to dig deeper, at first he would get angry and stomp out of the room. But after a while, he began describing his feelings in very simple terms."

I marveled at Nancy's attitude and calm. She was in terrible pain at the time and yet she put aside her own feelings and guided her son through some very tricky territory. It's hard for mothers to see their kids hurting, and when a son grieves out loud there is nothing you can do about it except listen and encourage him to express his feelings. But that's hard, because as a mother, it makes you feel helpless. Nancy's ability to not only tolerate her son's hurt, but also draw it out of him, was crucial for his healthy emotional development.

"Over the next few years, we made a pact that when he (or his sister) wanted to talk about tough stuff, I was always free to listen. If I was busy, we set aside a specific time to talk. I had never realized before that experience how really hard listening is. For one thing, it's hard to concentrate and for another, it's hard to see someone you love so much, hurt. But maybe the toughest part was not being able to fix the problem for him. I so desperately wanted to make his father call him. How healing it would have been for Brandon for his dad to call and simply tell him that he loved him but that he was very sick. I said those words repeatedly to Brandon but it never meant the same thing it would have if his father had just called him."

Brandon is now in the eighth grade and is doing very, very well. He is no longer sullen in class, his grades have improved dramatically, and most significant, he is not getting into trouble. He still carries tremendous sadness and in the years ahead, he will have to sort through his feelings of abandonment, but for now, he is well on his way to a healthy life because Nancy intervened at a critical time. She created a time and space for him to feel what he felt. She set the ground rules and held fast to them. She made him believe he would never be judged or criticized for any feelings that he had and she pushed on him to identify specific emotions. She walked him through the process of obtaining an emotional language. And then she helped Brandon use that language to confront his deep hurts and make decisions about what he was going to do with his feelings. Was he going to allow them to rule his behavior in the future? She helped him to decide that no, he wasn't.

We can see how significant this process was for Brandon. But he was one of the lucky ones who had a mother who refused to shy away from his hurt. Boys who don't have mothers who help them confront their feelings about themselves and their fathers after the father has left the family can end up with depression, suicidal thoughts, or living a life filled with a controlling, unresolved rage. They may turn to alcohol or drugs to numb the pain of rejection and feelings of unworthiness, and doing so never helps them resolve the hurt.

The good news for our boys is that we can help. We can't bring their fathers home, but we can help them deal with the very real trauma of losing their fathers by teaching them early in life to open up about their feelings. And as they open up, we must be available to help them untangle their emotions. If we can't, then we must find someone (perhaps a professional) who can. They deserve all the help we can give them.

WHY YOU ARE THE PERSON FOR THE TASK

The fact is, most sons feel safer with their moms than with anyone else. Perhaps it's our sensitivity, or our willingness to reveal our sensitivity. Perhaps it stems from the fact that sons believe that we can handle the feelings that they show us. Boys look up to their dads, desperately wanting approval, and often they will do whatever it takes to get that approval. If a son senses that his dad is less expressive emotionally, he will in turn be reticent to let his father see his feelings, for fear that he won't like what he sees, or that his father will think his feelings make him unmasculine. Sons want the approval of both parents but sense that they don't have to work as hard to get mom's approval. In a son's eyes, moms are wired to accept them. When it comes to helping our sons develop their emotional skill set, this is a great thing. In order for a boy to become comfortable with his psychological self, he needs a place where he feels comfortable digging, poking, and chipping away at his deep feelings. You are that place.

Although that responsibility presents a difficult task, it is a privilege because we are the ones who benefit most. We are the ones who get to share our boys' deep thoughts, insecurities, and dreams. We are the lucky ones who get to probe and wonder with them. We sense the changes in their demeanor as they mature because we know them unlike anyone else in the world. As we teach them about their feelings, they learn about ours and what makes us tick, thereby learning not only how to deal with their own feelings, but also how to deal with the feelings of others. As mothers, our skill in this area helps our sons become better future fathers.

We must be careful and respect them as developing men because the pieces of their hearts that they allow us to see are tender and breakable. We must learn to handle them gently but firmly. Consider how you acted when you first held your newborn: We see the tiny legs and frail arms and we are very careful. But over time and with repeated touch, we see that they aren't going to break as long as we handle them with firm and loving hands. We must handle our sons' feelings the same way, and over time, we will become more comfortable talking with our sons about them.

Where to Start

Be confident in your abilities

The most important truth to embrace at the very start is this: You are already wired with everything you need to be a great mom to your son. If I could take an X-ray of you as a mom, I would see a picture of bones and tissue laced with an intricate set of muscles and nerves. At various times, some of those nerves and muscles are dormant, and some are ignited and on fire. You have a complete set of worry neurons that ignite when your son gets in someone's car. There are others that ignite when you watch him play football or when he brings you his report card. These are your very own, unique wires, reserved only for you and your son. Along with those that fire on a regular basis are thousands of others that are cool and quiet. They are waiting for your brain to send them signals to kick into gear. If someone hurts your son, your protective wiring ignites. If someone praises your son, your set of encouragement wires flare. If your son fails in school, your empathy wires fire up. In every situation in which your son needs your help, you must trust that you have all the equipment that you need to help him. The problem is, you aren't always aware of this. But you can train yourself to be more encouraging.

Show him you're committed

It is very important to remember to use your maternal instincts in this process. There are times when your son will open up without prompting, but there will also be many when he will roll his eyes and tell you to get lost. Boys need to talk about their feelings, but they're not always ready to do so. Since you know him, watch his body language. If you are broaching a subject that he's not ready to talk about, back off temporarily; wait a day or two and reopen the topic. Be persistent with him but gentle and patient, remembering that often boys won't respond until you have prodded several times, because they want to know if you genuinely want to listen and if you are going to take their feelings seriously. If a boy is sensitive about his feelings, he needs his mother to be willing to talk with him and show him that she is not embarrassed. Boys will talk much more openly when they sense that their mothers are comfortable. So we must convey to them that we will talk to them about anything, anytime. (Even if you are uncomfortable discussing certain subjects—like sex—with your son, don't let your discomfort show. Your son needs you to appear confident and willing to listen.) Sometimes sons will feel their mothers out by opening certain topics and watching how their mothers respond. They do this as a test to see whether or not it is "safe" to delve deeper into the topic with their mother. If you respond in a calm way, they will keep talking but if you appear disgusted or upset, boys will back away and close the conversation.

Start when he is young

Research shows that forming strong relationships and good behavior patterns with sons when they are young has a profound effect on their behavior when they are teens.[5] I recommend that mothers start as soon as their boys can talk. Use very simple language so you won't frustrate your son. When he is two and is having a temper tantrum, don't ask him how he feels; tell him. At that stage, asking a young boy to identify feelings is too hard for him, so you need to do the work for him. When you tell him "No" and he screams, tell him that you know he's feeling angry but that he needs to do as you ask. Don't discuss his feelings; simply name them so he knows you understand and so he begins to understand them himself.

Don't wait until he's angry or sad to discuss his feelings. When he is happy, tell him that you are glad that he feels happy. Take the opportunities when his emotions are particularly strong or seem important to him to mention that you recognize what he is feeling and more important, that you are comfortable with what he is feeling. This doesn't mean sharing your own feelings with your son. Some popular parenting books recommend doing this when your son does something that hurts you, but in my opinion, this only creates guilt in him about what he's done. Most young kids don't have the cognitive capacity to empathize well with another person. They simply can't put themselves in another person's shoes. Also, psychologically, boys (and girls) are profoundly egocentric from early childhood through their teen years.[6] Until they are well into their twenties, boys and girls believe that the world revolves around them. They aren't concerned as much with your feelings as they are with their own. That means, when a parent shares his or her heart with a child, that child takes the information and tries to see how it relates to him. In other words, he personalizes most things that his mother says. Adults don't do this. We hear what a loved one says and then choose whether or not to take it personally. This is a crucial difference that we must realize exists between us mothers and our sons.

Many of us make this mistake honestly and out of the best intentions. For instance, I recently heard a mother tell her four-year-old son that when he slapped her arm in frustration, she felt sad. She asked him not to hit her again because she didn't like being sad. Unfortunately, a few minutes later, her little boy hit her again. The reason I believe that he hit her again was that he just didn't know how to be concerned with his mother's feelings; he was only thinking about what he wanted at the time. Some children can empathize a little when they are young, but even if they can, guilt over hurting a loved one doesn't necessarily motivate them to change their behavior.

Other times, mothers can confuse children by revealing their own feelings. I have seen mothers of teen boys cause undue worry in this way. For instance, a single mother I saw relied on her son more as a companion than as a child. She had no other children, and when her boy was around, she talked openly about her problems with her girl-friends, men she was dating, and how discouraged she felt. She told her son that because her life was difficult, she needed him to help around the house. In other words, she used her feelings to motivate her son to do things for her. She didn't intentionally manipulate her son; she just didn't have enough female friends to talk to and she con-fided in him instead. The problem was, her son didn't like hearing about his mother's struggles. He didn't understand the complexities of her relationships and he felt that he couldn't do anything about her problems anyway. In time, he came to resent his mother for talking too freely about them. Just like the four-year-old who hit his moth-er's arm, this young man was developmentally egocentric. When his mother talked about her issues, he felt that his issues were being ig-nored and became angry with her.

Usually, the best tactic is to keep things simple with kids, because they are not tiny adults. They don't process information the way we do because they are cognitively and emotionally very different from us. I believe that it is best to help boys focus on their feelings, not ours, so as to avoid unnecessary confusion. Our job as good moms is to help our sons identify their emotions. Boys of all ages do better with simple rather than complicated instruction, so be clear and con-cise when helping him name his feelings. Once you have done this, you are on your way—but keep in mind a few pretty hefty hurdles are left to be jumped, particularly as he gets older.

A LIFETIME OF LEARNING

Some boys learn quickly how to understand their own feelings, and how to tell their mom when they are sad or mad. Others resist identifying feelings, particularly if they have been reprimanded for having them. Very often fathers will scold boys for having feelings when the fathers really mean to reprimand the way they handle the feelings. For instance, if a son gets mad and runs after his sister and hits her on the head with her Barbie doll, his father may yell at him to go to his room because he is out of line. Of course he is out of line, but unless his father lets him cool down and then tells him that it's okay to be angry, but that he is never allowed to hit his sister, the boy will leave the experience thinking that his feelings of anger are not legitimate, and that he should not have them if he wants the approval of others.

It's very difficult for most boys to separate their feelings from their behaviors. When boys are young (and even when they're not so young!), many simply react without thinking when they feel strongly about something. Just as kindergarten teachers tell their students that they can't hit, even when they are angry, we moms need to teach our sons that they can feel strongly about something, but then must choose how—and how not—to respond to those feelings. In other words, teach them they must always be in charge of their behavior. This is hard for adults to learn, let alone young boys, but it is crucial that we teach our sons early. Many of us have known grown men and women who have little control over their behavior because they act on their feelings impulsively; so, the first step in helping our sons avoid that pattern is to help them understand the difference between feelings and actions.

It is quite appropriate when boys are in the first and second grades to begin asking them how they feel. Again, you don't want to be the psychology police; you want to be a good mom who lets her son know that she's always watching from the wings, ready to help. The best way to teach him how to articulate his feelings is to keep the conversation natural and spontaneous. If he tells you that he saw Sally looking at another girl's paper when they were taking a quiz, rather than jumping immediately into his feelings about it, you might begin by asking what he thought when he saw her do it. If he seems interested in talking, keep going; follow up by asking him how he felt, or how he would feel if someone did the same to him.

Or, for instance, let's say he saw a pet hamster get stepped on and die (this happened to my son and it was a terrible day). It is perfectly natural to ask how he felt when he saw the incident. If he is uncomfortable describing his feelings, it can be very helpful for him if you ask what he thought the other kids felt when they saw it. Very often describing someone else's feelings is a safe way for your son to understand his own. Many young boys project their feelings onto other kids when they are too uncomfortable to face their own emotions.

Train Yourself to Listen Well (and Then Train Some More)

How you listen determines whether your son keeps talking or stops the conversation. If you start talking about feelings with your son at an early age, this type of conversation will become second nature to him as he matures. The threat of being socially unacceptable is perhaps the largest hurdle for boys to manage when it comes to openly sharing their feelings. But fear runs a close second. As boys mature into the teen years, testosterone levels rise, and when this happens, it can impact the intensity of a boy's feelings. Anger can feel fiercer, sadness can seem paralyzing, and worry can cause acute anxiety. When feelings become intensified, they can be frightening for boys. Couple that with the increase in physical strength and a boy may fear that if he expresses his feelings, they will make him do something terrible. For example, if he allows himself to express his anger, subconsciously he may be scared that he will physically hurt someone. Also, many boys who have experienced trauma as youngsters and never expressed their hurt sense their hidden feelings percolating close to the surface during their young adult years. When this happens, they will work even harder to repress them further because they fear that the feelings themselves will cause too much pain. I have actually heard young men say that they were afraid to face past trauma because they felt facing the old emotions associated with the trauma would kill them.

Listening to your son makes him feel worthy, important, and loved. Think about how you feel when someone stops what they are doing, asks you to sit down and talk, and then listens to what you have to say.

There is little else in the world that can make you feel so important. This is how your son feels when you stop and listen to him.

Because a premium is placed on multitasking in today's society, our minds are constantly being trained to do the very opposite of listening. We are all about work, productivity, getting meals on the table, kids to appointments, squeezing in gym time or play time, and still meeting our quota at the office. Today's moms are very busy and very tired. So how in the world are you supposed to have time to listen? Listening requires that you shut down distracting thoughts, turn off the phone, make eye contact (for more than one second), act interested, and be able to repeat back to your son what he just told you. That, friends, is work.

Listening. Hearing. Watching his body language and his eyes. All that tells you volumes about your son's day. Noticing whether he's gotten rid of that nasty nail-biting habit when he says something that makes him uncomfortable or if he can make eye contact when he talks about something that really matters to him—that is what being a really good mom is all about. It really isn't about making sure that he has new basketball shoes, gets into the college of his dreams, or whether you earn enough money to buy him expensive toys or video games. These are nice, but they don't really shape who he'll become when he is an adult. What makes him a great man is spending more face-to-face time with you. So often we mothers are convinced that our sons need the stuff we give them more than they need anything else, and this isn't true. What our sons need and want is simply more of us. I frequently tell mothers that our sons don't care if we bake brownies from scratch or from a box, or if we buy them at the store already made—all they really want to do is sit at the kitchen table and eat them with us.

He waits to see if you will listen because first, he needs to find out if you believe that he has something important to say. If he learns that you do want to listen, then he figures out that he is smart—and that his words are worth hearing. Then he needs to find out if you really want to listen to him or if you're doing it because you have to—because you're the mom. In order to show him this, stop what you are doing and set it aside. If you're cooking dinner, turn the stove on low. If you're getting ready to make a phone call, don't. Turn your phone off. Then make eye contact with him. All of these small gestures tell him that you really want to hear what he has to say. And when he sees your interest, he feels valuable to you. And once he feels valuable to you, then—and only then—will he be ready to trust you with his feelings.

As a boy matures, he protects his feelings fastidiously because they represent a large part of who he is as a man. If he allows someone he loves to see his true feelings, and that loved one fails to receive them with kindness and respect, he learns that his feelings aren't worth respecting. And if they aren't, then, he reasons, neither is he. That's why it is terribly important that you work hard on your listening skills, starting when he is small. So much is at stake. When he talks, he's not just saying words; he's telling you about himself—what he thinks about himself, what he hopes for, and what he fears. It's all there, tucked between the sighs and the shoulder shrugs, and you will miss it all if you aren't truly listening.

THE DIFFERENCE BETWEEN SONS AND DAUGHTERS

We know that boys use fewer words during the day than girls do.[7] Rather than say what is on their minds, boys tend to keep their thoughts to themselves and share them only with friends they know they can trust. If a son has strong feelings about something, he may ponder those thoughts for a time and wait until he finds a friend he knows will appreciate those feelings and not make fun of him.

Girls, on the other hand, express themselves more freely. If a thought comes to mind, they will share it more quickly than a boy will. Girls are more natural communicators, in part because, as I have mentioned, talking is the means by which girls bond with others, whereas boys bond by participating in activities with others. Whether they speak during those activities or not, just throwing a baseball, biking, canoeing, or playing in a sandbox with a friend makes a boy feel closer to that friend.

This is a very important difference for mothers to understand. If a mother has a daughter and then has a son, she will be surprised by how differently they react to the same situation. Her son may say fewer words and his language may develop later than her daughter's, and as he gets older, he may not talk about his feelings as readily as his sister does. A mother may thus start to feel that her son doesn't like being with her as much as her daughter does, simply because he speaks less. This isn't true. Boys feel the range and depth of emotions that girls do; they just don't express them. So we mothers need to watch our sons more carefully to pick up on cues that alert us when something is wrong with them. We need to pay attention to our sons' moods, their body language, shift in friendships and grades. These changes are often the first clue we have that something is wrong, because sons are just far less likely to talk about their troubles than daughters are.

Brody's mother, Elayne, was a terrific listener. She would tell you that it came easily to her; after all, she declared to her many friends, she was introverted and quiet. Even as a child, she preferred listening to talking. Elayne adored her firstborn daughter, Savannah, but when Savannah turned three, Elayne was stunned by the amount of talking the little girl did. Sometimes, she said, she would be driving down the highway completely distracted by the chatter and questions that were fired at her from the backseat. She said that until Savannah was born, she didn't realize that children could talk so much.

When Brody was born, however, life was very different. Honestly, though she never said this out loud, I think that Elayne was relieved to have a child who wasn't so verbally intense. She seemed comfortable parenting Brody right from the start. As he matured, Elayne admitted that she felt closer to Brody than to Savannah, because she felt that she and her son shared similar personalities. And Brody was always a happy boy and did well in school—at least until the sixth grade. That's when everything changed and Elayne came to talk to me. She was deeply worried that something had happened to Brody.

Elayne confided in me that until the fall of his sixth-grade year, though Brody had been quiet he had always seemed content with life. He practiced his cello without being asked, because he loved playing.

He always seemed to enjoy going to school and never got into trouble. During the fall of his sixth-grade year, however, his teacher called Elayne and asked if she could talk to her. Brody had been caught cheating on a math test, she said. When the teacher had confronted him about cheating, he lied to her about it.

"When she first told me that she found him cheating, I was taken off guard. He'd never done anything like that before. I was embarrassed, but more than that, I was worried. I asked him about it and at first he denied it. After months of talking about it, he finally admitted that he had cheated. He's so stubborn," Elayne said.

I didn't know her son well, so I asked questions about his character and what had been going on in his life. Apparently, his grades had always been excellent, but after the cheating episode, everything seemed to fall apart for him. His father spent two months at a time working overseas and then two months home, a pattern that had been established several years earlier. I asked about Brody's friendships and Elayne told me that he had several close friends, and that those relationships hadn't changed. He hadn't suffered anything traumatic; hadn't changed schools, gotten sick, or gone through any difficulties that she could identify. She felt helpless and confused.

Winter came and then spring. Brody's grades continued to plummet through the entire sixth-grade year. Elayne said that Brody often came home from school and went straight to the study to practice his cello or play video games—and even those had changed. He used to play soccer and golf games; then he started to play more violent war games. She hated them, she said, but Brody had slipped them in the house somehow.

I asked to speak with Brody and my time with him confirmed everything that Elayne said. He was quiet and well spoken but seemed profoundly sad to me. When I gently probed for trauma, drug use, girlfriends, anything, I came up empty. There wasn't an obvious reason for his depression. But I take depression in kids very seriously and I told Brody that. I told him that there was help available for him and that I wanted him to see a male counselor that I recommended. Neither Elayne nor Brody came back for a visit until months later. Then one morning, I got a phone call.

"We need to talk immediately," Elayne said. She sounded frantic. When I saw her, she burst into tears. After months of silence, Brody told her something that changed her life. While he was walking home from school one day (shortly before the changes in his behavior had started), a young man had cornered him. At first, the man spoke to him in a friendly manner. Brody had seen him around town before so he didn't feel threatened. Suddenly, he said, the man pushed him behind someone's garage and pulled his own pants down. Then he made Brody touch him. He also asked Brody to perform oral sex on him. Luckily, he didn't have any weapons and Brody managed to get away before he was forced to do so.

"How did all of this come out?" I asked Elayne. She looked at me as though she was surprised by my question. Her answer was so simple and profound, it has stuck with me.

"I waited," she said. "I just knew something terrible was wrong. I know my son. My friends, my mom—even my husband said that he was just going through a tough adolescent period and that his behavior was par for the course. Every single one of them told me not to worry. They said it would pass, but in my gut, I never believed them. I decided that I wouldn't give up trying to get Brody to talk to me."

And how, exactly, did this worried mom get her adolescent twelve-year-old to confide such a terribly painful experience to her?

"Every night after he got ready for bed, I went to his room. I pretended to pick up dirty clothes, stack homework papers—anything to give me an excuse to be in there. Then I would sit on the edge of his bed and ask how his day was. Sometimes he would answer; sometimes he wouldn't. At first, he told me he didn't want to talk and, quite honestly, he could be pretty unpleasant. But every night, I did the same thing. Pick up clothes, go over to the bed, sit, and wait. I did this for months. Eventually he started telling me that he didn't like school. He didn't know why, he said. Then he complained about his friends, and having his dad gone all the time. You name it, he complained about it

"After months of sitting on the edge of his bed, I went in one night and he seemed to be asleep. I knew he was faking it and he just didn't want me to be in there. When I leaned over him to kiss him good night, he started to cry." And telling me this in my office, she began to cry too.

"He started sobbing. For the longest time, I didn't say anything. I just held him and let him cry. During that night, he unloaded everything. He was terrified, humiliated, and I felt like I was holding a three-year-old in my arms."

I am happy to report that Brody is doing very well now. And I believe that in large part, he is doing so well because of what his mother did. Elayne handled the situation beautifully. Let's look at what she did so well.

First, when she felt that something was wrong with her son, she didn't listen to the well-meaning friends and family who said that she was overreacting, that it was just normal growing pains. She acted on her instincts. Second, she was determined to find out what was wrong and she made a great plan. Rather than badger Brody for answers (as many of us so often do), she realized that he would talk if, and only if, she gave him space and convinced him that she would listen whenever he was ready. It took several months, but she got through to him. Every night that she went to his room and sat on his bed, she was communicating one thing loud and clear: "I'm here to listen to whatever it is you have to say and I want to hear it." Sometimes she talked, but most of the time she just sat and listened.

As a mother, I think about all the moments I had with my own son and I wonder if there were things that he really needed to say but didn't because he didn't have confidence in my listening. Or maybe I communicated that I didn't have time or the interest. I think about how much time I spent on my laptop, in front of the TV, or chatting with friends, so preoccupied with what I thought was important at the time that my son never really saw me ready to give him attention. Remember: Boys won't talk unless they know that we are ready to listen as a mother.

How wonderful for Brody that his mother took communicating with him seriously. Her instincts told her that something was wrong but that he just wasn't saying anything. With patience and resolve, she decided to work at helping him open up and she succeeded. She didn't let her evenings slide away by checking emails, talking on the phone, or finishing up her work. If she had, Brody might have lost out. But he didn't, because she waited and listened.

I often imagine being in Elayne's shoes. I would love to think that I would have done the same, but I doubt it. I imagine that you, like me, might have fallen into one of the following familiar traps, the most common ways we fail at getting our sons to talk about their feelings. We do all of these things with our daughters, too, but in my experience, we do them more frequently with our sons, because boys are so much harder to engage in conversation than girls.

1. We become impatient

Many well-meaning mothers try to draw sons out by talking to them. We ask questions and follow them around the house. When this doesn't work, we ask more questions and begin using a more insistent tone. We get demanding because we want to let them know that we are serious and really want to hear what they have to say. But the more we talk and the more serious our tone becomes, the more our sons clam up. It may take months of conversation to learn what is going on in your son's mind or heart. Don't demand his attention. The only way to get it is to be extraordinarily patient.

2. We interrupt when we mean to teach

In my experience, daughters handle being interrupted better than sons do. Daughters, like us, are communicators and they like using lots of words. If we interrupt while they are speaking, many of them simply interrupt back. Not so with sons. If they are interrupted, their feelings get hurt because they think we don't value what they have to say, and they stop talking.

Usually, we interrupt because we have something to say back to them about what they just told us, and that "something" is a lesson. How many times have you asked your son a question and started formulating a response even as he's giving you his answer? We all do this. As mothers, we may feel that we need to constantly correct or teach a lesson to our boys while we have their ear. But oftentimes boys aren't ready to hear what we have to "teach," so they just shut down. Many times as we try to tell them something that we feel is very important, they tune us out because all they hear is that we want to tell them something, not that we want to hear what they have to say.

3. We can't put the cellphone down

Maybe your primary distraction isn't your phone—maybe it's your computer, your work, your other kids, exercising, or even knitting. We all have our private lists of obsessions that occupy far too much space in our heads. The things that we just can't let go of.

It's important that you identify your obsession. Perhaps you don't want to call it an obsession; maybe it's just your "very important, pressing work" that needs to be done. If you aren't quite sure what yours is, ask your son. He knows exactly what takes your attention away from him. And the problem is, he feels that whatever repeatedly takes your attention from him is more important to you than he is.

Once you have recognized it, then it's time to work toward disciplining yourself to break from it. If it's your phone, turn it off from 6 to 8 P.M. If it's the computer, same thing. Cancel meetings, keep your work contained, do whatever you need to do to make time for your son. We think that we are great at multitasking, and while this may be true, one thing that you cannot do while multitasking is listen.

When it comes to changing our relationships with our sons, it is the small moments during the day that matter. One conversation can change your son's mood; fifteen minutes of your ear may prompt him to see a problem in a new light. The scheduled vacations or special one-on-one times that we carve out to be with our sons are very important, but they don't always influence who he becomes as a man as much as we'd like to believe. Rather, it's a few words of encouragement during the day, exercising patience with him when he really needs it, or giving him a smile of affirmation when he feels like a failure that can change how he feels about himself and his life.

Stay Intentional

Being bold enough to look at ourselves, our behaviors, and our priorities is one of the first steps we need to take in order to provide our sons with an emotional language. So I encourage you to take the steps just outlined and begin to give your son a healthy emotional repertoire from his early days. It will serve him well when he is grown and has left your home. You don't need a psychology degree and you don't need to be even-tempered or have a certain personality type to do this. If you feel nervous about starting the conversation with your son, don't worry, most mothers do. When it comes to trying to help them with their feelings, most of us feel ill-equipped and even a bit scared. It's hard enough for us to face our own feelings and talk about them, let alone help another person do the same. Know that you are in good company and never let your fears stop you. Remember, your son wants you to do this. He wants (and needs) a good emotional vocabulary and the only way he will get it is if you do the work.

In order to complete the task, there are a few fundamental principles to follow that will make the job easier for you. As you work through them, remember to stay positive and keep things simple. If you get discouraged and feel as though you aren't making progress, don't worry. Shelve it for a time and then try again. Being intentional doesn't always mean doing the same thing repeatedly. Sometimes it means staying on course but simply taking a break. Be encouraged by our friend Elayne's patience. If she could get her son to tell her about such an awful incident, one that felt shameful and shocking to him, you can get your son to talk about how he feels about the lunch lady, an ex-girlfriend, or even his father, who did something to disappoint him.

BE TOUGH ENOUGH TO HANDLE HIS FEELINGS

Sons want three things when they talk to someone. They want someone who isn't shocked by what they hear; someone who won't ignore them; and someone who won't feel sorry for them. It is very important that you communicate to your son that no matter what he says (as long as he does so in a respectful tone), you can handle it. You won't gasp, you'll let him talk, and you will be calm and understanding.

If he gets in trouble at school, he is far more likely to tell you if you don't yell about what a rotten kid he is. On the other hand, if his trouble stems from something he did wrong, you don't want him to think there will be no consequences for his actions. There must be, but that's different than becoming enraged at the situation.

Older boys may fear talking to their mothers because they are afraid to lose their respect. Shame is a powerful motivator to stay silent. Your son needs to know that you will never shame him or feel ashamed of him—no matter what he does. He needs to know that you may get mad, but you won't scream. He also needs to know that you won't turn the focus onto yourself, asking how in the world does he think that makes you feel. It's tough, but you need to appear as open, accepting, and neutral in your reactions as possible. Again, this does not mean that you won't be upset, disagree with him, or be disappointed; this is about how you handle your initial reaction so that you pave the way for him to open up to you.

Many moms inadvertently shame their sons. Usually this happens when a mother criticizes her son rather than his behavior. When a son disappoints his mother, she feels hurt. Her natural response is to lash out at him in anger and point out his faults or attack his character. Another way moms tend to shame their sons is by telling them that they are embarrassed by their behavior. For instance, a sixteen-year-old boy who is caught drinking might phone his mother from a police station and hear his mother say to him, "How could you do this to me?" Rather than think about her son, the mother focuses on her own hurt. All of us mothers have done this at some point, because the truth is, we take our son's behaviors personally. On some level, we feel responsible, too.

Shame Is a Conversation Stopper

Shaming sons also frequently happens when boys have a sexual encounter—especially one related to seeing pornography on the Internet. Again, because many mothers feel uncomfortable discussing sexuality and sex with their sons, they react with disgust and criticize the boy. Studies show that on average, boys see their first pornography around age eleven.[8] Even twenty years ago, the age of first exposure was fourteen, but with the swell in electronic gadgetry, boys have far more access to pornography than ever before.[9] I remember when my own son was young. He was in my study looking up some musicians on their website and up popped a pornographic picture that shocked him. He made a loud sound, a mix between a groan and a scream. I ran into my study and he quickly closed the picture. "What's the matter?" I asked.

I could tell by his face that he was not only embarrassed by the picture but also by the fact that I knew he saw the picture. I could tell that he was upset and I, too, was upset—not at him, but at the fact that he had been "assaulted" by the image, caught unaware. Since I had encountered situations like this before (he is my fourth child, and I had spent hours talking to my daughters about healthy versus nonhealthy sexual situations), I sat down near him.

"I'm sorry that you had to see this," I started. "You must have felt shocked."

"Mom!" he said. "That's disgusting!" I could tell that he wanted to keep talking but that he was still embarrassed. I decided to keep the chat short and to the point.

"There's a lot of bad stuff on the Internet," I told him. "Unfortunately, you will probably come across pictures like that again. When you do, part of you will feel gross and part of you will want to stare. That's totally normal. They will make you feel embarrassed. I strongly encourage you to shut them down as quickly as they pop up because looking at them repeatedly can take you down a really dark path. And I'm sorry for you that we live in a time when pictures like this find you and you don't have to go looking for them."

The tone of voice we use with our sons and the words we choose speak volumes to them about what we think of them. I felt that it was important for me to use a tone of voice that communicated to my son that he wasn't a bad kid for seeing porn, but that the world around him was harsh. Blaming boys for a situation that isn't their fault is an easy mistake to make, and we must be careful to discern what is truly their fault and what isn't. This can be tough.

Sometimes we inadvertently shame our sons by calling them names that hurt them. We may be trying to joke around by teasing them, but since many boys are very sensitive, this is usually a bad idea. And when mothers are mad, it is important for us not to let our anger get the best of us and demean our sons by telling them they are disgusting, worthless, or stupid. Whenever a mother attacks the character of the son, he will feel shame because deep inside, he wants his mother to be pleased with him. He wants to know that no matter what he does, she will always love him. When she criticizes his character, he feels that he may be unlovable to her and this compounds the shame. So whenever a son does something that is disappointing, it is very important that his mother separate his behavior from his character, and criticize the behavior, not his person, even when she is very upset.

A boy may also feel ashamed when he experiences emotional turmoil. If he struggles with anxiety, depression, or outbursts of anger, he may feel that he is mentally "off." I have heard many teen boys tell me that they won't see a counselor for very treatable illnesses like depression because they don't want to feel like a "nut case" or a "psycho." When a son experiences any of these psychological problems, he needs his mother to be loving and supportive, even though she may feel embarrassed, guilty, or ashamed by his problems, reactions that can easily be communicated to her son. So we must be very careful and make sure that our sons know at all times that there is nothing they can do to shake our love for them. Sometimes we need to say this out loud. I have encouraged parents to tell their boy that even if he said he was going to live on the street for the rest of his life, they would love him just as much as they do today. Saying things like this helps dispel any shame that he feels about his struggles. And this is critical, because once his shame is relieved, he is much more likely to open up about what he is feeling and experiencing.

Mothers whose sons struggle with depression feel extreme stress. The pain of watching a child feel helpless and hopeless can seem unbearable. One mother described it as feeling as though her son were locked inside a wrecked automobile and she was unable to get him out. All she could do was watch and hope and pray that he would find his way out of the depression.

A struggling boy needs a mother who can handle whatever he feels, whatever he has to say. This is challenging: Too often we succumb to feeling sorry for them, telling them that we are worried about them or are afraid they will do something to harm themselves. In other words, oftentimes we make things worse by projecting our fears onto them. It is natural to be scared for your son, but those fears should be discussed with adults—professionals or a spouse—not your child. What he needs is for his mother to handle the pain he feels and say to him, "There is hope. You won't always feel this way and I love you no matter what." Many times when a son is depressed, his mother must repeat this often until the depression begins to resolve.

Velma was quite good at handling her son's feelings. She had been married for twenty years to a husband with a terrible temper. He had a problem with rage, and while he never physically hurt her, he screamed at her viciously and often. She told me, "He'd push me into the bedroom and close the door—as if a door was going to silence his voice. Then he would yell obscenities, accusations; on several occasions he accused me of having affairs. All of the accusations were false, but he was paranoid. Afterward, he would speak to the kids as though nothing had happened. I think it made them feel crazy."

After her son Rod left for college, she decided that she had had enough. She moved out and got an apartment of her own. When Rod came home for a visit during his freshman year and discovered what she had done, he got furious with his mother. How could she do this to Dad? He yelled at her just like his father used to. For several months, he refused to talk to her, siding completely with his dad. But over the next two years, he slowly warmed back up to his mother and began to spend the summers with her. Sometimes during the night she would wake up to hear him crying, but when she asked him about it, he would only say that he'd had a nightmare.

She suspected she knew what the nightmares were about; after all, he'd grown up watching his father emotionally abuse his mother. But she was afraid to talk to him about his dad's behavior; she didn't want to turn her son against his own father. She also knew that she needed to do something to keep Rod from following in his father's footsteps and repeating his abusive patterns with women in his own life. She had begun to see her husband's bad behavior already coming from her son. She knew that the first place to start was to help her son heal from the hurt that his father's rage had inflicted on him. But trying to open the conversation with Rod was proving to be difficult.

When Rod began his junior year in college she decided to come see me. She asked me for advice, but the truth is, she really didn't need it. She had tremendous insight and courage and all she needed was some encouragement to do what she believed she had to do.

"I've been terribly worried about Rod," she said. "He's been agitated and edgy. He doesn't want to go over to his dad's anymore when he comes home and he's never felt that way before. You know how I feel about his dad, but I want to do whatever I can to help them have their own relationship. I don't want my feelings about his father to interfere with that."

As she talked, I marveled at her maturity in wanting to keep Rod from knowing how much she disliked her ex-husband. Little did she realize, but that was the most powerful thing she could do to help Rod sort out his own feelings about his dad. When mothers spill their anger about a boy's father onto their son, boys immediately go on the defensive, feeling that they need to stand up for their dads. They automatically hide their true feelings from their mothers because they feel torn. The best thing that a mother can do for her son's emotional health when a divorce occurs is to make sure she never insults the boy's father to the boy.

"I tried hard not to criticize his father. I didn't want Rod to see how ugly life had gotten between his father and me. I so desperately wanted to free him to form his own feelings, to have his own relationship with his dad. But now, something else is going on. His father has a girlfriend, and Rod has alluded to the fact that his dad screams at her, too. It frightens him. That must be so awful for a twenty-year-old son, to be frightened of his father."

Her words struck me as brilliant. To see how unnerving it was for her son to fear his dad was extremely insightful. "I know that he doesn't want to go to his dad's because it brings back all the memories he has of his dad yelling at me," she continued. And she was exactly right. Sons who stand in the wings and watch their fathers abuse their mothers, and then watch the parents act as though nothing is wrong, become confused and conflicted. If the abuse occurs during a boy's teen years, they are especially confused because remember, during the teen years, sons (and daughters) are still developmentally extremely egocentric. They feel that they have an unusual power to change people and situations around them. For Rod, he might have felt that he could have stopped his father's yelling, and deep down, he might have felt guilty for not being able to change his father's behavior. This is a common reaction for teen boys who watch their mothers be abused. They want to stop it and when they can't, they feel enormous guilt, especially because they are usually afraid to stand up to their fathers. Many sons feel that they shouldn't correct or argue with their dads because then their fathers will be angry with them. Add to this the fact that both of Rod's parents pretended the abuse never happened, and you can see how confused this young man was. Since they never admitted what had happened, Rod believed that he was kind of crazy—that the abuse was no big deal. If it was a big deal, he reasoned, they would have addressed it. Of course, he wasn't crazy and deep inside he knew it. He knew the truth and he wanted help untangling the mess created by his father's behavior. Velma very wisely recognized this. She could see intense feelings of sadness and anger erupting in her son.

"I needed to go to Rod and talk to him about everything that happened," she told me. "I figured that we needed to bring everything that made him feel so crazy out into the open. I began by asking him what he saw happening at his dad's. At first he didn't want to tell me, so I made guesses about what I thought was happening, based on my own experience. At first Rod was defensive so I stayed as quiet and nonjudgmental as I could. Pretty soon, I told him that I knew that he had heard everything his father had said to me throughout the years. I told him that I was sorry that I didn't do anything about it then. I should have handled the whole situation differently at the time, but I didn't. I needed to face what I had allowed him to endure. I guess that I was so absorbed with myself and trying to hide things that I completely overlooked his feelings."

She went on: "I told him specifics. I asked him if he remembered the time when his dad called me a whore. I told him that I knew he was outside the door all the time. Instead of telling him how much it hurt me, I asked how much it hurt him. Suddenly he jumped up from the couch and screamed at me. He called me names, told me that I was a horrible mother and he wished that he had never been born. He told me that over the past several years, he wished that he were dead."

Velma choked back tears but continued. "I let him yell. He needed to. He was furious with me and with his dad. He said that he didn't know whom he was angrier with. I don't blame him."

Velma told me that Rod's anger had dissipated after this conversation. It took months, but she continued to encourage him to tell her how mad he was at her and at his father. She said that she tried not to give excuses for her behavior or for his father's. Most important, she never talked about her feelings or said anything negative about his dad. She let Rod's feelings be the focus of the conversations. Helping him talk brought enormous healing to Rod. Over time, he sorted out his anger and came to understand that his father was a deeply troubled man. This level of objective reasoning is unusual for a boy his age (most sons come to see their parents as broken people only when they are much older) but I believe this happened because of Velma's strength. She allowed Rod his due feelings. She never panicked, never felt guilty (at least openly to him), and never superimposed his feelings onto herself. She had the guts to simply sit, listen, and then help him figure his feelings out.

Let's go back and revisit the beginning of Velma's story and see what could have happened if she had reacted differently to Rod. When he came home for a visit from college and she saw his anger toward her, she could have gotten angry back at him. She could have called him disrespectful, unappreciative, or spoiled. In other words, she could have taken her own hurt and thrown it back at him, attacking his character. Many mothers would have done exactly this. When our sons act out, we become defensive and strike back, rather than taking a deep breath and attempting to figure out where the anger is coming from. But remember that when we strike out at them, we end up compounding the shame that they feel. If Velma had gotten upset with Rod in the beginning and refused to speak to him unless he got rid of his ugly anger, she would have compounded his shame and shut down any further conversation between them. Instead, she put herself in his shoes and empathized. She tried to understand that he wasn't a bad man or bad son; he was a sad and angry one.

———

Every mother feels guilty for the mistakes that she makes with her kids. When it comes to parenting sons, we often feel responsible for all of their bad behaviors, bouts of depression, acting out, drug use, you name it. The truth is, sometimes we are to blame. In those instances, we need to "woman up" and deal with it. But many times we aren't at fault. Yet we still carry excessive and unnecessary guilt for every bad choice our sons make. We need to learn to differentiate false guilt from true guilt and get on with our lives. Carrying around false guilt does no one any good—least of all our sons. The truth is, Velma made the best decisions that she could while she was married but later she realized that what was really hurting Rod was his father's behavior, not just hers. She got herself out of the situation, and understood that when Rod was ready, he would work through it. And when the time came, she was ready and waiting to help him.

TEACH HIM TO EXTERNALIZE HIS FEELINGS

As I have said earlier in the chapter, helping sons to recognize and name feelings is very important, and it's best to start that process when they are young. But this is only the beginning of teaching an emotional vocabulary. The tough part starts as he matures and his feelings become more complex. But don't be intimidated by more complex feelings, because the principles that you need to follow in order to help him identify them and then deal with them are fairly simple.

Once you help him say what his feelings are, then you need to teach him what to do with them. Many boys (and men) know exactly how they feel; they just don't know how to express their feelings in a productive, or at least harmless, way. The most important thing you can do is to tell your son that he doesn't need to keep his emotions hidden inside. If he is frustrated, he must talk about it. If he is agitated, he needs to go to a place where he can let his agitation out without bringing others into it. The same holds true with anger. If your son struggles with frequent anger, buy him some Nerf toys and let him loose in the woods. Boys need physical release more than girls do and this is particularly true during adolescence, when testosterone levels are rising. Make sure that he has a plan to physically release his anger and frustration. Talk to him and brainstorm together about healthy things that he can do when he is mad (rather than hitting his sister, screaming at you, or punching kids in his classroom).

In addition to this, make sure that he is getting regular exercise regardless of his mood. Keep him outside and busy. The worst thing that boys can do for their emotional well-being is to sit in front of a PlayStation, television, or computer screen and play video games (especially violent ones) for hours. All of their pent-up frustrations, agitation, anger, and sadness rest dormant in their muscles, waiting like time bombs to go off. Even if your son doesn't have anger issues to begin with, he will develop them if he sits still too long. His body simply isn't made to be inactive. He literally has a physical need for exercise in order to release his built-up energy and emotions.

If your son is going through a tumultuous time, be intentional about instructing him how to confront and then release his emotions. Don't drive him crazy, going overboard asking him how he's feeling, but watch him carefully. If anger starts to build, acknowledge it out loud to him and then ask him how you can help him get it out. For instance, you could ask him, "You don't seem to be yourself today; everything okay?" or "I can tell that anger's getting to you; anything I can do to help?" Sometimes simply asking your son if he wants to go for a bike ride or a brisk walk shows him that you want to be with him even when he's mad. Also, it might afford you time to have a helpful conversation.

Let him know that you are available anytime if he needs to talk and that you are comfortable talking about whatever is on his mind—even if he's angry with you. He may not be ready to talk, and that's fine. Give him space. You might try buying him Nerf bats and simply putting them on his bed with a note. You can unplug the video games or television and smile as you tell him that you've noticed that he needs more time outdoors. Be sensitive, be subtle, and don't chase him around, nagging at him. He doesn't need to be reminded of things over and over; I can guarantee that if you tell him things once or twice out of love, he'll hear you. He won't let you know he hears, but he will.

While physical release of intense feelings is important, many emotions can be handled simply through talk. If your son gets in an argument with his older sister, a simple "I'm sorry" on both sides may suffice. If a girlfriend breaks up with him or his grandmother calls him lazy, he can get angry and hurt but these feelings can often be externalized through dialogue. Just sitting down and talking to him about what happened and allowing him to hear himself speak can sometimes be all the healing he needs.

Humans are wired to feel emotions and not to keep them stuffed inside, ignored and forgotten. Some feelings are superficial and can be dismissed more easily than others. But there are deeper ones, like the hurt that Rod felt toward his father, that need processing. A large part of that process is having the feelings identified, externalized, and examined because only after this happens can they be resolved—otherwise, the pent-up hurt, anger, sadness, or hopelessness (as we've seen earlier) can rule a son's behavior well into his adult years without him ever realizing it.

HELP HIM SEPARATE HIS FEELINGS FROM HIS ACTIONS

Kindergarten teachers inevitably struggle with children unaccustomed to sharing. One boy yanks a toy from another's hand and the victim lashes out and hits the yanker on top of the head. Even though it was his toy that was stolen, the teacher tells him he cannot hit other students, no matter how angry he is or what the circumstances are. The missing component here is teaching the child how to get his anger out in a healthy way and let it go. That doesn't mean stifling the boy's anger or ignoring the kids who are mean; it means finding ways for your son to express his feelings without harming others.

There are overly protective mothers who tell their sons that they have every right to be angry and that they deserve justice when they are wronged. Sometimes we teach them to compete with the one who hurt their feelings or to drop that person as a friend. We tell them to get even and even encourage them to stay mad. Instead of helping our sons find a resolution, we continue igniting their anger, which then becomes paralyzing. The anger suddenly has power over them and they are no longer in charge of their lives. Their anger is.

Men have become CEOs of companies, excelled as physicians, and become outstanding policemen because anger runs their lives. (Of course, many who don't have anger issues have excelled at these professions, too.) The reason for this is that anger provides energy and can act as a driving force in a man's life. For instance, if a son thinks that his father has never respected him, he feels unworthy and angry at himself for being a "loser." As he matures into adulthood, however, that same anger and hurt may drive him to excel at his career so that he can "prove" to his father—and himself—that he isn't. Conversely, a boy may carry hurts from being yelled at repeatedly by his mother and his buried anger can drive him to misery. He may become depressed, anxious, or very aggressive. Some men rage at women, for instance, because of hurts they experienced as children at the hands of a mother or grandmother. In short, if a son's deep wounds from childhood are not resolved, he can become a man driven by those wounds in his careers and relationships.

We mothers never want our sons to be a slave to their feelings, so while they are still maturing, it is critical that we help them face their feelings and then make smart, healthy choices. And yes, even though we may not be ready to deal with our sons' feelings (especially negative ones like anger and hurt), we need to acknowledge what is best for them, and do what is right.

Sandy did just this with her two sons. When her youngest, Ethan, was seventeen, he was dating a girl whom he loved deeply. He had been close with his nineteen-year-old brother, Ted, since they were young. Over the course of one year, Ted took a liking to Ethan's girlfriend. He knew how much his younger brother loved her but his feelings for her trumped his loyalty to his brother, and Ted asked the girl out. And then—you guessed it: Over the next year, she fell hard for Ted and dumped Ethan. The young man was crushed—both from losing the young woman he loved and by the fact that his older brother had betrayed him.

Over the next few years, the two brothers finished college and the relationship between Ted and Ethan's ex-girlfriend fizzled. Perhaps Ted had just liked the chase, Sandy thought. For five years the brothers did not speak to each other. First, Ethan refused when Ted tried to mend their relationship. Then Ted became hurt by the insults that Ethan threw at him and before long, the anger between the two escalated to the point where neither knew what they were really mad about.

Sandy sought counseling because their rift broke her heart. She tried talking to each boy separately, but to no avail. Counselors recommended that if the two disliked each other, so be it. After all, they had the right to be angry. She received a lot of lectures on boundaries between brothers and then on those between her and her sons. Ethan married and Ted refused to go to the wedding. Ted married and Ethan did the same. When Ethan had his first child, he was told that his baby girl would live for only a couple of years; she had an incurable heart condition. Still, Ted refused to reach out to his brother.

Ethan's daughter died when she was eighteen months old and he was devastated. His marriage began crumbling and he started drinking heavily. He desperately missed his brother and in fact could barely remember what had caused the rift between them in the first place. What had they said to each other? Whatever it was, he didn't care anymore—he needed his older brother. He was going down fast and feared that in addition to losing his daughter and perhaps his marriage, he might lose his job as well. He felt that his life was getting out of control.

Sandy communicated all of this to Ted, but he wouldn't budge toward making amends with Ethan. Finally, in a moment of desperation, Sandy visited Ethan. She later told me about their conversation.

"Ethan, you're dying a slow death. I need to be frank and tell you that unless you get over moping, you'll hit a point where you will die. Maybe not literally, but at least figuratively."

Ethan lost his temper. He screamed at her, "Mother, you're out of line and I'm sick of your meddling. Leave my house!"

"All right, I will," she began, "but not without telling you that you have chosen a life of misery. It is no one's fault at this point but yours. You have never let go of your anger at your brother and you have decided to let it kill you."

"Shut up and leave!" he demanded.

"You still have a decision to make. You can either decide to ask your brother to forgive you for all of the hurtful words and pain between you, or you can continue to give power to this awful anger and let it destroy you. You're a man. The choice is yours."

Sandy didn't hear from Ethan for weeks. And she didn't hear from Ted. She worried, but she had also taken her own advice to heart: She decided to acknowledge her own hurt, do what she could with it, and then let it go. No longer would she allow her pain over her sons' relationship to rule her life. She had finally said what she needed to say.

About a month later, Sandy learned that Ethan had also followed her advice. He went to his brother's home and told him that he was miserable because of the hurt in their relationship. Even though he believed that his brother had "started" the war between them, he decided to apologize for his part in all of it, and asked Ted to forgive him. Then he left.

Since that time, Sandy learned that Ethan had cut back on his drinking and his marriage was improving. She learned that after she confronted him, Ethan got a more clear and honest view of his emotions and his behavior. His mother helped him drill down to the core of many of his old hurts, and when she encouraged her sons to forgive each other, both men felt great freedom. Now the brothers get along well—in fact better than they ever did before the initial falling-out, according to Sandy.

As we teach our sons to handle their feelings, we can't drop the ball halfway through. We must finish the job and communicate clearly that feelings are only that; they aren't relationships, they aren't people, and that we always have a choice as to how to respond to them. Stephen Covey described this same principle in a different way in his bestseller *The 7 Habits of Highly Effective People.* Covey articulated the importance of being proactive with our thoughts, perspective, and behaviors. Many times it is our feelings, rather than actual circumstances, that cause us to be overwhelmed, discouraged, or hopeless. Covey went on to state that we need to adopt "proactive language" rather than "reactive language." For instance, reactive language is when we say to ourselves, "There's nothing I can do," "That's just the way I am," or "He makes me so mad." This is an unhealthy perspective and leaves us feeling trapped. Changing our perspective and restating our thoughts in proactive language would sound something like this: "Let's look at our alternatives," "I can choose a different approach," and "I can control my own feelings."

This is exactly what mothers can do for their sons as we teach them that their feelings may be intense but they needn't rule their behavior. It means taking our sons from feeling angry, sad, impatient, frustrated, or guilty and challenging them with, What are you going to do with those feelings? Are you going to allow them to dominate your decisions or are you going to take charge of them?

In a culture that prides itself on self-expression and being transparent with feelings, this notion may seem heretical. We are taught that our feelings matter more than our behaviors. Is this true? In fact, no. Behaviors are what determine our long-term happiness and success.

Unfortunately many entertainment art forms like television, video games, and movies, encourage boys to allow their feelings to dominate. Video games and movies, for instance, can be "hyper-real," where sounds are louder than in real life and where violence occurs far more frequently than it does in reality. These things encourage boys to feel angry and to act out violently in response to anger. In fact, studies show that boys who are exposed to repeated violence on the screens act out more aggressively when they are in their twenties than boys who aren't. Much of the music that boys listen to focuses on negative feelings and attempts to draw them into those feelings. In other words, most art forms in some way encourage boys to express more anger. This may appear therapeutic on the surface—especially for boys who have real, deep-seated anger—but in fact it does just the opposite. It works to focus on superficial feelings, rather than helping boys deal with the root cause of their emotions. Clearly we must help our sons dial down on contrived violence and work at resolving real anger in healthy ways.

Some men vent emotions so freely, they destroy the lives of loved ones. Others withhold feelings and destroy themselves. The problem we face lies not in the feelings or in the men, but in the distorted handling and placement of those feelings in the human heart. We must help our sons grow up in an environment where feelings take their proper place. If done well, this can be one of the most significant gifts we give our sons to ensure sound psychological health. And every son deserves that much.

CHAPTER 3

He's Got a Bow and Arrow
(And the Target's on Your Back)

At some point in his development, you can bet that every son will wage war against his mother. Some boys wage war at age four, some at fourteen. Some do it once, others ten times. No matter what age this happens at, or how often it happens, these wars are lonely and confusing, and every mother who goes through them—as every mother will—is convinced that she is losing her son, and often blames herself for it. If this is happening to you, if you have recently been declared the enemy, or feel that it's only a matter of time (it is), hold on. There is hope ahead.

There are a few key rules to surviving the mother-son wars. The first is that you need to have a thorough understanding of what's going on. The second is to recognize that the war your son is waging has very little to do with you, and everything to do with male development. Finally, since you are the grown-up and he is the child (yup—even at eighteen) you can get the upper hand pretty quickly—as long as you keep your wits about you. And we moms are good at that. Let's tease apart the reasons for and stages of war so that we can equip ourselves to survive a bit better.

YOU JUST DON'T UNDERSTAND ME

Several months ago Carrie came to my office with Jaden, a bubbly, towheaded five-year-old with most of his front teeth missing. He had just entered kindergarten and was in for a checkup. Carrie seemed close to tears during the exam and at one point, she announced to me that Jaden was for sale, if I was interested. When she said this, I glanced down at her son and saw an impish smile. He seemed to enjoy the fact that his mother was upset by his behavior.

When I asked Carrie what was wrong, she blurted out, "Everything! He opposes absolutely everything I tell him to do. Six months ago, he was a dream. We would go to the park together and play with other kids in his class. He would get to bed on time, even help me around the house when I asked him. Then, it seemed as if overnight, he turned into"—she put her hands over his ears and whispered—"a monster!"

Jaden kept pretending to read the *Highlights* magazine in the exam room while Carrie was talking. He sat quietly next to her, listening to everything that she was saying. Once she started, she kept going, seemingly relieved to be saying out loud what she had been struggling with for several months.

"I tell my husband that I'm worried. I mean, maybe something's wrong. Maybe he has a b-r-a-i-n t-u-m-o-r or something." Carrie spelled it out so that Jaden couldn't understand what she was saying. "I've never seen such a sudden change in the personality of a child. And another thing—he used to play easily with other boys in the neighborhood, but now he's even gotten mean with them. I see him boss them around. He doesn't hit them, but he's come awfully close. When I pull him aside and tell him that his behavior is unacceptable, he just smiles. Of course, he's never like this around his father; I don't know what I've done, but for some reason, my son has begun to hate me."

Carrie spoke irrationally because she was so upset. Of course, she didn't really think that her son had a brain tumor and I believe that Jaden realized that. Her words were harsh for a young boy to hear but her near-hysterical tone let Jaden and me know she wasn't serious;

she was simply bloviating. Still, Carrie should have spoken these words to me privately, and I knew that. Before she could continue, I turned my attention to Jaden.

No, I thought to myself, not this freckled, quiet-mannered boy sitting in front of me—he didn't seem capable of the behavior Carrie was describing. I decided to bring him into the conversation.

"What do you have to say about what your mom just told me about your behavior?" I asked.

Without looking at me, he shrugged his shoulders a couple of times.

"Jaden," I said again. He wouldn't look up, so I squatted down to get on his level and tried to make eye contact. "She says that you're different than you used to be. Do you feel different?"

"I dunno," he answered politely.

"Your mom says that you yell at her. Do you yell?"

"I guess so." He still wouldn't look at me.

I waited, and then asked him, "What does it feel like when you yell at her?" I thought that would hit a nerve but he was silent.

I waited longer and it was clear he just didn't want to answer my questions.

"Being in kindergarten can be very hard," I said. "It's tiring and the teacher wants you to pay attention for a long time and the other kids can be bossy. Do you think so?"

Suddenly I saw Jaden's bottom lip quiver. He looked away from me and over to his mother with a glance that said, Please tell her to go away. That was my cue to press on. "Jaden, this is important," I said. "It's important because your mother is concerned that you aren't acting as nice as you used to. Is something wrong at school?" I knew that there probably wasn't because I had seen so many boys his age go through similar mood changes, but I wanted to give him an out.

"No, school's fine. I like it. My mom just won't let me do what I want to do. She doesn't understand."

After prodding both Jaden and his mother about life at school and at home, I realized that there were no major problems. Jaden was experiencing the normal exhaustion that kindergartners get after the first few months of transition, and he was having a psychological growth spurt, if you will. He was feeling strong, independent, and quite capable. When his mother told him what to wear to school, he argued. When she told him what to eat for breakfast, even if he liked it he ate something else. When she reminded him how to talk to the other kids in his class, he snarled and said he knew how he was supposed to talk. And when she made him stop playing too aggressively with his friends, he became frustrated, believing that "moms just don't get it." And the truth is, Jaden's right.

I explained to Carrie that Jaden was primarily struggling with two things: exhaustion and pressure to behave. I tried to help her see life through his eyes. First, Jaden got up early every morning while he was still tired, went to school, and mustered all the energy he could to concentrate and behave. He came home each day tired and then let all of the emotions he kept under control at school spill onto his mother each afternoon. Second, he was transitioning from feeling dependent on his mother to trying to be more independent. This was a struggle as well. For a five-year-old, experiencing both of these at once felt overwhelming and each day, he was having mini "meltdowns," if you will. I simply told Carrie to be patient. I advised her to help him relax on weekends and give him ample time to play. He couldn't handle one more venue like piano lessons or soccer where he had to focus and behave. With a few more months of maturity, he might be able to, but at this point Jaden needed time to be home and just play, nap, or choose whatever it was he wanted to do.

With regard to his bad behavior, I told her that I expected much of it would disappear when his fatigue left. In the meantime, however, she couldn't ignore it. So I coached her how to set clear rules and state them during a time when he was calm. Carrie told me that there were so many things that he did that she didn't like, she wondered where to start. I told her to pick two behaviors that she found most offensive and work only on those.

"That's easy," she said. "He yells at me and it hurts terribly." I said that she should start there. I encouraged her to find a time when he wasn't upset to sit down and tell him that he wasn't going to yell at her anymore. If he did, he was to go to his room and stay there alone until he was ready to tell her that he was sorry. Only then could he come out. I warned her that training him to stop might take time. Most important, when she said something, she had to mean it. If she told him that he couldn't yell at her and then he did, she was committed to following through with consequences. At first, he would test her to see if she was serious. He might yell and then run away and hide. I told her that strong-willed boys often intentionally do what they've been told they can't just to see what will happen. In a sense, they "declare war." I told her that when Jaden did that in the future, she had to take as long as it took to win. Really stubborn boys will refuse to comply for hours. So mothers like Carrie need to be ready to make consequences stick even if it takes up their whole afternoon, a day, or even a week. Strong-willed boys need stronger-willed mothers.

BOYS ARE DIFFERENT FROM US

Boys realize very quickly that they aren't like us. We are female and they are male. Even at age two, sons seem to have a sense that we function on different planes—not simply because we are older, but because of our gender. And the truth is, many of us mothers feel this way as well. We understand where our daughters are coming from— why they cry suddenly, how they color so neatly in their coloring books, and why they are afraid of snakes. But when our sons tackle their friends in the living room, our discomfort communicates to our boys that yes, indeed, we are a very different species. And that's a good thing.

As boys mature through different developmental stages, the fact that we are different becomes intensified and, often, misunderstood. When they first feel the urge to strike out and do something on their own, they can't imagine we ever felt such inklings. We are the adult, but since we are also female, we experience our yearnings differently from them, and they intuit that. When our three-year-old decides to dress himself or our sixteen-year-old insists that he buy a car with his own money, they genuinely don't believe that these desires could resonate with us because we are female. They want independence and control and they believe that these are strictly male feelings. Here's the good news: They don't need to know that we understand and we don't have to exhaust ourselves convincing them that in fact we do have the same desires; we just have to negotiate well during the battle.

———

When sons wage war against their mothers, much of it stems from a need to exert some independence. While we want our boys to be independent, we can only trust them to make decisions they're ready to handle. Our job is to figure out how much latitude to give them and how much to hold back. This can be very tricky.

Life became easier for Carrie after we talked about two things. First, we discussed the fatigue issue. All kindergartners are overtired, I said, and when they are, all bets are off. When your child enters school, it's the first step into their adult life. It comes with a new sense of adventure, but also with a more structured day, and those two things can both be exhausting. Tired kids fall apart easily and much of Jaden's irritability stemmed from that. Beyond fatigue, however, we talked about the war that he was waging—and waging only against her. Jaden needed a way to feel independent. He needed to make some decisions on his own, while still recognizing that mom was the boss. So I encouraged her to pick her battles. Don't fight over clothes or games in the backyard. This is "boy stuff" and not a battle you are likely to win. Make sure that he behaves well at school and that when he is with other kids he is kind. Focus on the big picture and let the little stuff go. If she worked on just a few issues at a time, the stress level in the home would dramatically diminish. She did, and it worked.

I Love You, Get Away from Me

Sooner or later—and sometimes sooner and later—every son will feel threatened by his mother. We can do nothing to avoid this. It is simply something that they, and we, must bear. When a boy begins to feel cramped by his mother, he strikes out, telling her that he wants to be able to make more of his own decisions.

But there's another element that underlies much of the mental and emotional turbulence brewing in the maturing boy; every boy reaches a time when he needs to make an emotional break from his mother. As painful as this feels at the time, it's one of the many steps a son must make on his journey to becoming a man. Bruno Bettelheim used to say that sons "kill off" their mothers during adolescence in order to survive. As they mature, boys who love their mothers feel a conflict emerge because on the one hand, they want their mothers to love and care for them, but on the other hand, they hate that they still want this. They want to be men—independent and capable of standing on their own—all the while yearning for the comfort their mothers offer. Daughters don't go through this. They don't feel that their independence is challenged if they remain emotionally tied to their mothers. But boys do. We need to understand this and respect it. And we need to go one step further—we need to help them make the break that they are so conflicted about. It's painful for both parties, but necessary, if they are going to mature into men and not stay trapped in adolescence. Plenty of us have seen (and maybe lived with) men who never quite wiggled out from a mother's control, and the results are disastrous. A boy who can't leave his mother at the appropriate time and in the appropriate way will never become the type of man who will find a sustaining and happy marriage. He may find a woman who wants to experience a deep connection with him, but he will be unable to because he remains in emotional conflict with his mom. He is attached in unhealthy ways and he is stuck with those attachments. A good mother cannot let this happen. So it may turn out that the war our sons wage is actually a good thing. But it is nonetheless painful for us mothers.

Trying to Right the Wrongs

Typically, the battle between a boy and his mother begins at the onset of adolescence, but it may rear its head a bit earlier, as it did in Jaden's case. For Sonya, her son Tyler was seventeen before the war they'd been waging quietly broke out into the open. Most of their difficulties had their roots in issues that Sonya had experienced as a young girl.

Sonya had grown up in a large, middle-income neighborhood. Her father was a truck driver who traveled a fair amount and her mother was a nurse at a doctor's office. She was close to her parents but shielded them from her difficulties because she knew that they worked hard and she didn't want to burden them with her own worries. She struggled with academics and being bullied in junior high because she was a bit chubby. In high school, when her boyfriend broke off their relationship, she cried alone in her room because she didn't want to bother her parents. When her father was home, she never wanted to do anything that would make their time unpleasant, because she didn't want him to go back on the road upset.

She was a nice girl and had lots of friends in their neighborhood. One night, during a sleepover at a friend's house, her friend's father snuck into the bedroom after everyone went to sleep. He went to Sonya, covered her mouth so that his daughter, asleep in the same room, wouldn't hear her, then proceeded to fondle and kiss her. When he was finished he told her that if she spoke about it to anyone—including his daughter—he would hurt her family. In an effort to spare her parents worry about her, Sonya suffered in silence. Little did she know the man was doing the same thing to many of his daughter's other friends.

After this attack, Sonya had trouble sleeping. When she did fall asleep, she was plagued by nightmares. She left her overhead light on at night and when her mother turned it off, she would turn it back on as soon as her mother fell asleep. She couldn't concentrate during school. Her friendship with the daughter of her attacker was strained and she began to feel enormous guilt over what had happened; she wondered if she had done something to attract the man into her friend's room during the sleepover. Should she have screamed when he first came into the bedroom? Her mind reeled with scenarios of what she should have or could have done. She emotionally berated herself because of the things that she didn't do that night. But she never said a word to her friend, or to anyone.

Sonya eventually married a kind, hardworking man. He did not learn about the abuse until they had been married ten years. When Sonya finally divulged her traumatic secret, he simply looked at her and said, "Well, honey, that was a long time ago." Sonya told me that when he said that, she wanted to jump across the room and choke him. That statement shut down any further conversation about her abuse and she began to feel that she couldn't trust her own husband to offer the sympathy and caring she deserved.

Tyler, the oldest of Sonya's three children, was an outgoing, bubbly kid. His only problem, as she would come to admit to me years later, was that he was male. He didn't really do anything wrong; she just couldn't help but put him in the same pot as her husband, her father, who had never been home, and (though she didn't want to admit this) her abuser. Somehow deep in her soul, a part of her connected all four men. Too bad for Tyler. Too bad for her.

Throughout his childhood, Sonya found herself mad at Tyler for no reason, particularly as he became a teenager. This bothered her terribly. Sometimes, she told me, she didn't want to be in the same room with him, even though he hadn't done anything wrong. He smiled like his father and this bothered her. He walked liked his dad and she hated it. "He moves like a wounded duck," she told me once.

By the time Tyler was sixteen, he routinely snapped at Sonya. Then he became verbally abusive. He called her names and swore at her, but only when his father wasn't around. Sonya decided to seek help from a counselor because her son's behavior was so antagonistic. During her sessions with the counselor, she began to see patterns in how she related to men. She realized that since the time her friend's father assaulted her, she harbored deep animosity toward men. Because she never resolved her anger toward her offender, she carried it forward into all of her relationships with other men—her husband, her son, and even her father. But she didn't feel anger alone—she felt a complex web of emotions toward men, which stemmed from her assault. She couldn't really trust them, allow herself to get close to them, even to completely love them. Once she recognized her feelings, she was able to see how they impacted her relationships with the men she cared about, especially Tyler.

Once she realized this, she decided (probably subconsciously) to overcompensate for her animosity toward men by treating Tyler differently. Rather than discipline him when he did something wrong, she made excuses for him. She tried to treat him more like a peer than a child. Many times, she spoke to him with the tone she would use if he were one of her close girlfriends.

This made Tyler uncomfortable and angry. He wanted his mother to act like a mother, not a friend. So when he spoke to her, he acted disrespectful and defiant, which in turn made Sony feel rejected and hurt, and the anger between them spiraled out of control. That's when she brought Tyler in to see me. She wanted to know what she could do about her relationship with Tyler. We began to dig together.

"What are the themes of the arguments?" I posed.

"It seems like we fight about everything," she said.

"How about at the beginning, when you first started fighting?" I asked.

"Well, at first he told me that I treated him like a child. That I didn't trust him. Then things got worse. He told me that I did his laundry the wrong way, so I made him do his own. Then we had a knock-down, drag-out one night over his girlfriend. He was out until two A.M. with her. I waited up and when he came home, I was seeing red. He broke curfew, he had been drinking, and when I confronted him about it, he pinned me up against the wall and told me to stay out of his business. He said he didn't want my advice, he didn't respect me, and I was too controlling. And that I didn't understand him."

She took a breath and then continued. "I was scared. I'm not going to lie. He outweighs me by fifty pounds and he's a good six inches taller. For the first time since my abuse, I was physically scared of a man. I recoiled from him, ran into my bedroom, and cried for two days. I didn't speak to him. He didn't speak to me, either."

That had happened a few months before our conversation, and I could tell that she was still shaken up from the incident. I told her that I would like to speak with Tyler. She agreed and one week later, he sat with his mother across from me in my office. He didn't appear engaged at all. In fact, he looked quite annoyed.

"Your mother tells me that the two of you haven't been getting along," I said.

"Nope," he said curtly.

He clearly thought I was on his mother's side and he in turn wasn't about to give an inch. I was enemy number two. So I spoke up boldly.

"What do you think is wrong with your mother?" I knew that he would like the way I framed the question.

"She's psycho! That's what's wrong. She treats me like a kid—like I'm ten, not sixteen. She tells me what to eat. She tells me what to wear. If she doesn't like my friends, she tells me that I need to make new ones. What does she think they're going to do—stick me with needles and shoot me up with drugs?" His voice was cracking and he was getting angrier as he spoke. I was glad for that. Sonya looked embarrassed but relieved; from her point of view I was getting to see the side of Tyler she always saw.

I tried to interrupt but Tyler kept talking, so I let him. "And there's another thing. She's always bad-mouthing my dad. Poor guy. He's not even around to defend himself. I know he gets home late, what doctor doesn't? He works hard and she complains about him. I know he's not perfect—he's got problems, I mean, who doesn't? She tells me stuff about him. She tells me that she's not sure she loves him anymore. Then she tells me not to tell anyone. It's our secret. Gives me the creeps."

"Tyler and I used to be real close," Sonya blurted. "We used to do so many things together. When his dad was away on a trip, we would stay up late and watch movies. He would have friends over and I would cook for them all. He used to love it. I'd even take him shopping every once in a while and he'd tell me if something looked good on me or not. I knew that, unlike my friends, he'd be honest."

As the two of them bantered, the reason for their conflict began to surface. It was as clear as the nose on my face.

"Tyler," I interrupted. "Did you ever feel like one of your mother's girlfriends?" I asked.

"That's a strange question." He paused. "Of course not. I mean how could I be like her girlfriend if I'm not a girl?" *What a stupid question* was written all over his face.

"Here's what I mean. Do you ever feel like your mother talks to you the way she might to her girlfriends? Or do you feel as though she talks to you the way you'd expect, and want, your mom to speak?"

He looked at the floor and Sonya looked at me. I think she was even angrier at me than he was.

"Now that I think about it, maybe I did feel the stuff she talked to me about was stuff that I thought she should tell her friends instead of me. There were all kinds of things that I wish she just wouldn't have said."

Sonya jumped in at this point. "Like what, Tyler? That's not fair! I always treated you with a lot of respect. I never wanted to be a burden to you. Sure, maybe I shouldn't have criticized Dad so much. I'm sorry for that. But what else did I do? Is this 'Let's beat up on Mom time?'" She stopped, looking quite forlorn.

We talked for a while longer and I tried to get Tyler to let Sonya have a peek into his mind. He felt suffocated. He felt that his mother needed him to be there for her. He saw her as fragile. He said that sometimes he felt that his mother leaned on him too much. She called him whenever he was out with his friends. Sometimes he felt that she was even jealous when he brought a girlfriend home. As he revealed his feelings, guilt mixed with relief swept over his face. I could sense that he didn't want to hurt his mother's feelings, but that he needed to tell the truth.

Sonya was a good mother. She adored Tyler, and once she absorbed his feelings and allowed them to percolate in her mind, she began to look back on her behavior from his perspective. She had been so worried that he would somehow pick up on her dislike and mistrust of men that she overcompensated by treating him like a friend rather than a young man. She was determined not to let her anger (even hatred) toward men spill onto her son. In order to prevent this, she went overboard with Tyler by treating him as a close confidant. This sounds ironic, but we mothers do peculiar things with our anger. It doesn't simply erupt with shouting matches, but often triggers us to compensate for it by acting too nice toward the ones we feel angry with or too sympathetic with people we feel animosity toward.

The problem for Tyler when his mother overcompensated by acting too much like a friend was that *he didn't like* being treated like her friend. He felt that something was wrong when she confided in him that way, when she leaned on him as she would have an adult. Furthermore, his mother shared things with him that weren't appropriate. Tyler knew enough to be uncomfortable when this happened, but, because he was still a child, he couldn't put his finger on what was wrong. So he went to war against his mother.

Sonya made a few important changes and the war ended fairly rapidly. She stopped confiding in him. She stepped back into an authority role. When she wanted to complain about her husband, she told a friend, not her son. She became the figure Tyler needed: a grown-up mom whom he could lean on, as opposed to one who leaned on him.

Being a mother is complicated, especially when we have sons. Sonya wanted to be a good mother; everything she did was meant to benefit her son, not harm him. But after she recognized the patterns of her behavior that were affecting her relationship with her son in a negative way, she changed them, and became a better mom for it. Not a perfect mother, but a grown-up who could begin to look at her relationship with her son through his eyes, and give him what he needed.

The Contradictions of Mothering Sons

They say boys take longer to mature than girls, and in a number of ways, that's very true. Girls, from a young age, seem to anticipate their future as a woman. When boys are young, they seem to be less fixated on their future and more able to enjoy the moments of childhood. But one of the pressing issues that all boys will face one day is that they will need to learn how to be a man. When they are young, they don't consciously pay attention to this. But as they grow older, their awareness that this transition must take place swells. And as it grows, so too does a mom's fear that the process may not go well.

When boys hit their preadolescent years, they begin to sense that manhood is around the corner. As I said, girls seem to start moving toward womanhood at a younger age, and more gradually than boys, who mature in spurts. But while, as women, our transition into becoming adults was probably smoother, we can still understand what

our boys are going through. What is more difficult for us to understand is a boy's concern that we are going to impede the process.
Here is the real rub: A son needs a man to help him navigate the
transition. Boys are visual creatures. They need to see what a man
looks like, speaks like, and behaves like in order to mimic that behavior and internalize it.

This is very important for mothers to understand—especially single mothers. Often sons who live with only their mothers don't have
the opportunity to spend time with men they look up to and therefore don't observe healthy masculine traits to mimic and internalize.
So it is especially important for single moms to ask a grandfather,
uncle, coach, pastor, or friend to spend a little time with their sons.
Hard as they try, single mothers can't be both mom and dad. This is
both good news and bad news. The good news is that mothers should
relieve themselves of the pressure that they put on themselves to be
everything to their sons and just focus on being really terrific moms.
The challenge for single moms is to recruit a good man or two to
spend time with their sons in order to show them how great men
behave.

So where, we mothers wonder, do we fit into this process? Or do
we? That is the question that every son grapples with as well. An
eleven-year-old boy comes home from school and tells his mother
about his day. How gym went, what he got on his science test. Maybe
he cries or complains because his teacher is terrible or someone in his
class made fun of him. He has a problem, and so he unloads his troubles on his mother. This is a more natural occurrence with mothers
than it is with fathers, in general, because women tend to display their
empathy more easily than men. And, many of us coddle our sons.
This isn't all bad. As a matter of fact, this can be good—up to a certain age—because there comes a point in every boy's development
where he needs to emotionally pull away from his mother and stand
on his own two feet. In other words, we mothers need to learn when
it is appropriate to coddle and when it isn't.

Since mothers tend to allow sons to express a broader range of
feelings than fathers do, sons develop a deep level of comfort with
their mothers. They don't have the sense that they need to automat-

ically "man up" when they are with them. In fact, until he is about ten or eleven, life for a boy is often all about his mother. And then the tide changes. When he enters preadolescence, he suddenly—dramatically—gets a glimpse of his future as a man. And he may start to wonder how his emotional comfort with his mother fits into his emerging manhood. He begins to question whether it's manly to be so close to his mother. The answer can be elusive, and sons can find their confusion disturbing.

From a son's perspective, his feelings for his mother can be fairly messy stuff—even if we've tried to do everything right. We mothers must understand that every son feels this internal conflict as he enters the teen years. In addition to physically maturing, trying to figure out who he is becoming, and enduring emotional shifts that hormonal changes bring, he struggles with his feelings toward his mother. He wants to stay close, but something inside him is pulling away from her. These changes are all part of the process of becoming a man. Once we understand this, life becomes easier for us because we won't take their changing behavior so personally.

He Needs His Independence but He Needs You, Too

At five, a son may see your affection as comforting and wonderful. He can curl up into your lap and burrow his head into your chest while you read his favorite story. If he is tired, he can even pop his thumb into his mouth for a bit, though he's technically long since stopped sucking his thumb. He knows you won't tell. You are his safe harbor.

At thirteen, he wants you to give him some freedom, but when you do, it doesn't make him feel good, because he lacks confidence in himself. Just like a two-year-old, he wants to do everything for himself, but he can't. He yearns to be able to function like a seventeen-year-old but his mind and body won't allow him to. He feels confused and conflicted. And he feels disappointed in himself because he can't make his body and mind do what he wants them to.

At this juncture mothers tend to become confused, too. When a young son asks for independence and then a mother gives it, it is mystifying when he still seems dissatisfied. This happens because he really doesn't know what he wants. So no matter what you do, it seems you can't win. Our instinct as mothers is to draw our sons close and talk to them. But he does not like this, either, because *he* wants to figure things out. He doesn't want you to explain and he certainly doesn't want you to draw closer. He feels that since you are a mother, you can't understand him. You are female. He is not. You are not supposed to think like him because if you do, then the two of you are alike and this idea makes him shudder.

As he hits his teenage years, a boy begins to feel an increasing sense of power. Testosterone levels are rising, he becomes more aggressive, and his muscles are changing their architecture. He is growing hair in many places and his voice is cracking. He is no longer the person that he was. Some boys are perfectly comfortable with this fact; others aren't. Some sons are dying to surge ahead into manhood and embrace the changes, while others are insecure in the transition, frightened by the prospect of being a different person. It is at this point that boys start to feel that they are leaving their mothers behind.

Adolescence for boys is about transitioning from a posture of dependence to one of independence. If a boy feels secure in his relationship with his mother, he will try separating himself from her. Because even if he turns into a complete monster during the separation, he knows deep in his psyche that mom will never leave him. He can be as bullheaded as he wants and his mother will always be there for him. He feels that he can try on new faces, thoughts, attitudes, and behaviors in front of her because she is safe. She can handle his changes when others (including dad) might not be able to. This reasoning can be extremely tough on mothers, because we are forced to weather all of the experimenting our sons do.

So what, specifically, does he want that he feels you can't give? First, he wants male approval. He wants to know that since he is becoming a man, he is accepted by men. For boys, the teen years are all about male attention. Your lovely, once-affectionate little boy seeks out attention from coaches, teachers, and especially, his father. He needs reassurance from them that he "fits" into the male order.

Teenage boys try on manhood and then show it off. Have you noticed your son walking around the house acting like a tough guy?

Are you terrified to watch boys who seek thrills through dangerous activities like driving too fast, skateboarding, racing a dirt bike, or bungee jumping? Your son will try on for size whatever he identifies as "male." Boys watch their fathers make many decisions—about their jobs, hobbies, sports, or how they treat women. Boys observe them intently to try to figure out what being a man is all about. Then they mimic their behaviors—not just to see how it feels, but also to see if it garners them approval. In my book *Boys Should Be Boys,* I discuss the importance of a son receiving a "blessing" from his father. This occurs when a father communicates to his son that who he is as a man is acceptable and pleasing to him. Some fathers give this blessing to their sons and some don't. If a son receives it, he feels strong and self-confident. He learns to like himself because he knows that his father respects him. If a son doesn't feel that he gets this approval from his father, he will drive himself crazy trying to prove to himself (and subconsciously, to his father) that the man he is and the work he produces are worthy of his approval. (It is important to note that when sons don't receive this blessing from their fathers, it is necessary for us mothers to help find other men in our sons' lives to affirm them.)

Mothers want so much to provide everything for our sons and so it is hard to accept the reality that the one thing we are not capable of providing—male approval—is the one thing that at some point our sons desperately need. But it is important to recognize that fact, because if we live with the illusion that we can be all things to our sons, we put too much of a burden on our own shoulders, and, more important, we deny our sons something that is crucial to their successful development. And we must not only recognize their need for male approval; we must help our sons recognize it as well. Once we help them realize that receiving such a blessing is an important part of feeling complete as a man, then, if they fail to receive it from their fathers (for whatever reason), we can help them recognize a few things. First, we must help them see that they had a need to receive approval from their fathers, validating the desire in the first place. Then we can help them see that the reason they didn't receive it was the fault of their father, not the result of something they did. Often young people subconsciously feel that if they failed to receive something important that they needed, it is because of some mistake they made. They become angry with themselves. Helping sons see that they needed approval and that they didn't receive it because their father failed to give it (for whatever reason) allows them to feel sadness and resolve it. Once it is resolved, then they can let the sadness go.

Single mothers have an added burden, because if their son's father isn't involved in their lives, finding healthy male role models can be tough. But it's not impossible. There are good men all around us. There are teachers, neighbors, coaches, rabbis, youth pastors, uncles, and grandfathers who are available to model good behavior to our sons. Many single mothers ask how much time a son needs to spend with a man in order for it to make a difference, and the truth is, time is less important than the authority a man has in a boy's eyes. If a boy looks up to a man, he will adopt his behaviors and attitudes very quickly. If he doesn't respect the man, then he will not mimic him. And if a mother can't find healthy male role models, she can talk to her son about men she admires, bringing such a man to life simply by telling stories about him. She could choose a president, a biblical figure, or a wonderful grandfather who has passed away. She can talk about what the man looked like, what he would have said or thought about subjects her son finds interesting, and what he did for a living. She can tell her son about his character and why he made the decisions that he did. In other words, she can create a strong visual image of a good man for her son to imitate. Sometimes, for many single mothers, a healthy image is the best she can do.

Mothers who are married or who have sons whose fathers are involved in their lives should ask themselves, "What can I do to help my husband, or son's father, be a good role model for my son?" It is important to do everything we can to help a father have a more positive impact on our sons. And there is a lot that we mothers can do to help our husbands (even ex-husbands) be good fathers to our sons.

The most important thing we can do is to recognize those moments when our advice can feel like criticism. As mothers, we all tend to feel that we always know what is best for our sons, but the truth is, sometimes we do and sometimes we don't. Sometimes fathers just know how to handle boys better than we do, and we must always be open to this, particularly as our boys mature through adolescence. It's a difficult thing to accept, especially because when our sons are young, they depend on us almost exclusively. But when they hit adolescence, our sons may gain much more from their father's influence than from ours. But because we are the Mom, we often can't help feeling that it is our job to interject our feelings, opinions, and corrections, even when we're not exactly sure we're right. Many times, we need to simply hold back and wait to see how the male in our son's life handles things. He may innately have a better understanding of something our son is experiencing by token of the fact that he has lived it and we haven't.

If, through our need to constantly be a mother, we end up criticizing the job being done by the male in our boy's life, the message that gets sent to our sons is that men just don't know how to do anything right; that we women need to be there to correct them. When sons hear such criticism repeatedly, they begin to believe that their fathers (and by association, themselves) aren't very valuable people. There is so much anti-male sentiment circulating in our culture these days that it is very easy for us to reinforce this idea at home without even meaning to. Consider popular movies and sitcoms; fathers are portrayed as weak or goofy. Ray Romano's character in *Everybody Loves Raymond* is funny, but he is depicted as a doofus. When is the last time you saw a movie where a dad was depicted as smart? And even advertisers even chime in. I remember an ad that shows a father trying to throw a baseball (a skill that most fathers are expected to have); he is so bad at it that ultimately he reassures his son that while he can't provide him any athletic skill, he can at least give him a nice car.

But anti-male sentiment is prevalent in real life, too. Often in a divorce situation, fathers receive less parenting time than mothers so sons don't see them as often. And if there is animosity between the divorced parents, sons often hear their mothers rail against their ex-husbands. I see this all the time, even in marriages where the couples aren't separated or divorced. When a mother allows her anger toward her son's father to surface in front of her son, the person who loses the most is the son. It is terribly painful for him because it muddies his relationship with his father. He feels torn between his mom and his dad.

Many angry mothers don't intentionally hurt their sons this way, so it is important to understand that we must always keep our anger toward our son's father to ourselves. Because unless the father is abusive or otherwise unfit, every son deserves to have his own relationship with his father, and this relationship should never be lived through the filter of another person's point of view.

The most important thing that we mothers can do for our sons who are maturing into manhood is to offer them support and encouragement and allow them to break free emotionally for a time. We must teach them that they can stand on their own two feet in every way. We must guard against doting on our sons too long or coddling them too much. Yes, many mothers have strong emotional connections to their sons, but as I've discussed, there comes a time in every mother-son relationship when we need to pull back. For some boys this happens during the latter years of high school but for others it comes when they go off to college. Every boy develops differently. But the most important thing to remember is that since we are the adults, the burden is on our shoulders to see what's coming and give our sons permission to be men who don't need us. Often sons will give us clues that they want independence. They will ask to make decisions on their own regarding which classes to take or what time their curfew should be. So when our sons display such signs, we must work with them to find age-appropriate ways to offer that independence. Yes, they can love us and we can love them back, but the intense bond that stems from need must be broken, painful as it may be for both of you.

WHAT WE DO TO TRIGGER WAR

Once we wrap our minds around the fact that a boy wages war against his mother, not because she is doing anything wrong, but because he is experiencing certain stages of his own development, then war is easier to bear. And once we recognize what's really going on, we can change our own behavior and take a step back, in response to the knowledge that it's not about us. Such behaviors that we sometimes impose on our sons, without being conscious of the fact, include:

- Being too dependent on our sons for emotional comfort
- Expecting our boys to act as men when they are still boys, and on the flip side,
- Refusing to let go when our sons try to separate from us emotionally
- Talking to our sons as if they are confidants and protectors, much as we'd treat an adult partner
- Being overly critical of all male figures, especially the boy's father
- Being overly protective and overly possessive in our efforts to be good mothers

We need to keep a check on our feelings, expectations, and emotions when it comes to our sons because when they are inappropriate, they not only trigger the war that is inevitable, they make it much worse. Sometimes, the mother-son war is a painful but useful way for us to see that we need to make some adjustments, but our ability to make those adjustments depends on our willingness, as mothers, to see clearly where our behavior needs changing.

There are those sad cases where sons never feel that early, deep emotional connection to their mother at all. This can happen with a mother who's addicted to drugs, abused by her husband, or depressed. Some mothers love their sons deeply, but simply don't have the emotional capacity to show them. That mother can seem distant and disengaged. So, in those cases, will the son still wage war? Yes, and that war can be even more disturbing. When that son, who has wanted but not received his mother's attention and support, hits adolescence, he goes to war more ferociously because not only does he yearn to break away from any dependence on a woman, he is emotionally charged by the fact that he never had the intimacy in the first place. He wages war with an underlying anger at the fact that mom was never there.

How to Survive the Wars

One of the real delights in raising boys is that they are, in general, less complicated than daughters. They aren't less emotional than daughters but they are more pragmatic in general. When a problem arises, they try to identify the problem and then find a solution. Girls might experience the same problem but overanalyze it to the point of missing the solution. Many women experience this with their husbands as well: Men see a problem and immediately try to find a way to fix it. And if it's a quick or "easy" solution, we get doubly irritated! Women are not as cut-and-dried. We look at the complexities of situations—where they originated, why they continue—and we try to find our part in the problem. In short, we mothers approach problems that arise for our sons very differently than they do. So we must be careful to listen to our sons, because when such problems arise, sometimes the solutions are simpler than we think.

For instance, a boy may struggle at school and find his grades dropping. Rather than simply asking her son what's going on, a mother may overanalyze it; she might speak to the teacher about how her son is being treated in class, or if his mood has changed, or if he has learning issues. But perhaps the child just needs glasses! Or he isn't getting enough sleep. I've seen cases where the answers to a son's problems were as simple as that.

Sometimes we need to talk with our sons directly and ask them what is bothering them. I have found that very often, boys from middle grade school on will tell you what's wrong if you simply ask. No matter the case, once you learn what the issue is, the first step is to believe him, and to make sure he knows that you do. Then you can both work toward a solution.

If your son won't or can't reveal what is bothering him, you may have to dig a bit. Take the time and ask your son to go for a bike ride or do some other fun activity. Often when boys are relaxed, they are more likely to open up and tell you what is bothering them. Boys hide their feelings because they fear that they might look "stupid" or "weak." If a boy feels hurt by a comment a friend made or if he feels badly about a poor grade, he will be quicker to hide his feelings than a daughter will. This can be difficult for mothers to understand because we are more verbally oriented than men, and because daughters are quicker to communicate feelings than sons are (in general). The larger problem for us mothers is that when we fail to understand what is going on with our sons, we react poorly. We take their lack of communication personally and we become defensive and then angry. This only fuels the wars.

Many times, however, boys strike out against their mothers because they want more independence. They may not really be angry; rather, they simply need to show us that they want to pull away and act more like a man. Because they don't come out and say this, we misread their behaviors. We get hurt or feel that they don't like us or want us anymore. So we must remember that they do want us and they do need us, but the way they want and need us is constantly evolving.

We must also always remember that usually there is more going on with our sons than meets our eyes. Because we think differently than they do and because they mature through developmental levels that we are not experiencing, we must be careful to stand back and not jump to conclusions too quickly when a war is brewing. We must exercise patience and realize that very often, we aren't the cause of the war. Sometimes sons just feel very conflicted. And other times, if we are contributing to the wars (by exhibiting one of the behaviors listed previously), then we must own up to our part and correct our mistakes. We can get through the mother-son wars and come out the other end with a stronger bond, but we must stay loving and calm and, most important, never let them forget that we are the adult.

Find Some Grit

Has your son ever had a remote-control race car? If so, you've seen the thing race around the driveway or your kitchen floor, screeching before it suddenly slams into a curb or your kitchen cupboard. BAM! It flips over onto its back with all four wheels spinning in the air.

Your preadolescent or adolescent son is like that race car. He too charges from one mood to another, from one activity to another, from one stage of his life to another. He, like the race car, so full of high-octane fuel and fervor, bangs into things repeatedly. What does he run into? Sometimes his father, sometimes a teacher, and many times you. He runs into things because that's what boys do. They need to hit boundaries head-on because they need to find out exactly what those boundaries are. When they find them, they begin to understand their own limitations and the limitations that life imposes on them. We all live with those limitations, but boys need them to be clearly defined.

It feels awful to have our sons slam into us. It makes us feel guilty, and bruised, and it pushes our buttons. We don't like our authority challenged and we most certainly don't like telling our sons that they can't do something only to have them turn around and do the exact thing that we just told them not to do. When our sons bang into us in this way ("No, you can't stay out past your curfew," "No, you can't go to a party of a friend whose parents we don't know") it's exhausting and dispiriting. We want to fight back, or throw up our hands, because we don't know which way to turn. Sometimes it makes us second-guess ourselves. Often we give in to their demands thinking that will make life easier. That's a mistake. Don't let up. Remember, when our boys were toddlers, they needed literal fences placed around them to keep them safe. Teen boys are the same, though the fences are figurative. They need us to implement rules for them to keep them safe. They need a safety zone because they can do serious damage to themselves. And they need to know where the boundaries to that safety zone are. Of course, they hate boundaries and feel that they should be able to create their own, but you have to remember that they can't. They aren't cognitively mature enough—sometimes even at seventeen or eighteen. One of the biggest mistakes that well-intentioned, good mothers make is to take down the figurative fence too early. Boys naturally need to run into things, and if they aren't hitting fences erected by their parents, then they will have run-ins with teachers, coaches, or even the law. And if a teenage boy doesn't learn how to respect boundaries and rules at home, you can bet he won't pay attention to them anywhere outside of his home. With testosterone flowing in their veins, they test boundaries because they want to see how strong they are. So if a son sees that the boundaries you impose really aren't enforced, he will plow right through them and get into trouble.

I see this fairly routinely with sons of really easygoing mothers. When a boy tests his mother by staying out too late at night, going to a party he was told not to go to, or sneaking out at night with friends, he waits to see how his mother will react. In fact, he is sometimes more interested in seeing how his mother will react than he is in actually going to the party or breaking curfew. What he really wants to find out is whether or not his mother cares enough to see what he's done wrong and then give him consequences. Rules actually make teenage boys feel loved, as odd as that sounds. Without them, they feel lost and uncared for. And that's when they really get into trouble.

Make rules he—and you—can live with. Determine what you think is reasonable and stick to your guns. This can be really hard because many sons know exactly how to get their mothers to change their minds and renege on rules. My son, for example, knew he could get me to change my mind on rules more easily than he could get his dad to, so, naturally, when he wanted to do something he knew he wasn't allowed to do, he came to me. Sons use language they know will pierce our armor. Typically, boys will say something like "You just don't trust me," or the old "If you really thought I was a good kid, then you'd let me . . ." Boys are smart when it comes to getting mothers to bend, so we need to be on guard. They don't manipulate intentionally or maliciously. They do so because being crafty increases the odds they'll get their way. So, if your son ever draws you in with arguments like these, don't take the bait. Rules have nothing to do with trust. Everyone—including us—lives with rules, and good mothers help their sons learn how. You can always show him that you trust him in a variety of other ways (trust him to do his chores on time or get his homework done!).

Love is gritty. Saying no and keeping clear boundaries and solid rules makes sons feel loved. A deep voice or a thick beard should never fool us. Boys can't reason like men until they are in their early twenties, so until then, we need to be strong mothers to keep them safe from themselves.

Never Take Him Personally

I had a young, teenage patient whose mother taught me a trick she used when her son was in a horrible mood and she didn't know how to communicate with him. "I pretend that he is someone else's son," she told me. Her approach makes sense. When you're in the midst of battle with your son, it's important to separate yourself from the situation emotionally by reminding yourself that this is not about you. This emotional distance cuts down on the guilt and anger we feel and enables us to approach our son's behavior in a much more rational, patient, and matter-of-fact way. Think back to when your son was two. When he threw his skinny body on the floor, flailed his arms violently in protest, and screamed, "You are such a bad mom!" did you believe him? Did you call up a psychologist and make an appointment to come in and talk about how you were ruining your child's life and needed training on how to be a better mother? Of course not. You knew that he was two and that part of being a healthy two-year-old was to have temper tantrums. The same is true with older sons who wage war: They strike out at you for no good reason except to see how you'll react. And, as it was when they were toddlers, their temper tantrums (yes, teenage boys have them) still aren't about you—they are about them.

Colleen was superb at staying self-assured when parenting her kids. As a single mother of three, she determined early on in her children's lives that she would do everything that she could do in order to be a good mother and that would have to be enough. Her confidence in her parenting was a breath of fresh air. She didn't beat up on herself, and if her kids acted out she wasn't always examining her own behavior to see what she had done to make them upset; she looked at them and held them responsible for their part. She was Mom. She wasn't Dad, teacher, psychiatrist, or coach. She was Mom and it was a role she loved.

Colleen had her work cut out for her because she knew her two strong-willed boys were going to need a male influence more than her daughter. Her ex–husband had moved out of the state and saw the kids only a few times during the school year and during the summer. As the teen years approached, her younger son began challenging her. She had a curfew for all of the kids, but Craig, who was fifteen at the time, decided to ignore it. He decided to sneak out at night and go to parties where kids were drinking heavily. Colleen found out what he was doing and devised a plan.

She confided in her brother what her son Craig was doing. She told her brother that a party was being held at a certain boy's house on a Saturday night and that she anticipated Craig would lie in order to find a way to go. She was right. When she called Craig's cellphone at 11 P.M. to see what was happening at the friend's home where he was supposedly staying, she could hear a raucous party going on in the background. She called her brother and the two of them drove to the party, walked in, and found Craig in a corner smoking pot and drinking vodka from a paper cup. They went up to him and demanded that he leave. When he refused, his uncle grabbed him and literally manhandled him out of the house. Craig didn't speak to his mother for a week.

When I asked Colleen if she regretted embarrassing Craig, she looked at me quizzically. "Of course not. That's what we need to do with our kids sometimes to save their lives. He was headed down a terrible path."

Had Craig returned to lying and partying after the incident, I wondered? "He tried it once about a month later. My brother and I did the same thing. Being embarrassed once is tough but twice is unbearable," she told me.

This occurred about four years ago and I can say that Craig is doing quite well now. He finished high school and went on to play basketball in college. During his senior year of college, at a basketball ceremony, he made a point of telling his entire team that he would have never made it through college had it not been for his mother. He thanked her for her encouragement and her strength during all of the "tough times" in his life. What he was thanking her for was her grit and her ability to do what was right for him, even when it felt *really* uncomfortable for her. When I asked her years later what helped her most in getting through those tough times, she said it was her ability to not take Craig's actions personally. Bingo.

Be Patient Once and Then a Thousand Times

It's difficult for mothers to stay patient with our sons, and with ourselves. We want our boys to behave and we want to be better parents, too. But the rules are changing all the time, because as our sons grow older, the circumstances change. It's hard to be the first-time parent of a toddler. It's equally hard to be the first-time parent of a teenager. Just when we've figured out how to best handle a certain situation, our son shifts gears and enters a different stage. He becomes whiny when before he was always compliant; he becomes moody when he never was before. It feels as though we can't get a firm hold on how to be a good parent.

Every stage of development, every battle, every temper tantrum, and every breakup with a girlfriend requires a new batch of patience from us. And patience requires mental and emotional energy. It's tough to handle. When our son craves male attention and begins taking his frustration out on us because we can't give him what he needs, we need to be patient and let him vent. And when he challenges us by trying to break down rules and boundaries we set for him, we must dig deep within ourselves and find the resolve to keep the boundaries well built and the rules clear and fast.

The great rewards in parenting boys usually come later in life. Sure, there are wonderful moments of tenderness and laughter when he says something that tickles us. There are days when all we want to do is keep him home in his footed pajamas and read stories together. The moments when we want the world to go away and leave the two of us alone. In those moments we believe that we can manage just fine, the two of us together as a team. But life progresses and one day turns into another and the alarm clock tells us that it is time for school. Then it's time for soccer practice, campouts, homework, you name it.

The moments of joy far outweigh the anguish in raising boys and the best way to ensure this is to remember a few things. First, tension and misunderstanding are part and parcel of raising them because they are male and we are female. So expect it and prepare for it. Second, realize that at some point in your son's life, you will make mistakes and he will get mad. Every good mother misunderstands her son and makes mistakes, so learn to accept them and move forward. We all go into parenting with issues and scars, and sometimes these work their way into our relationships with our children. But the important task each mother has is to recognize what those issues are and then to separate them (the best we can) from our relationships with our boys. Third, we must face that at different points along the way, our sons will begin to pull away from us. We can't keep them close forever, because every son needs to separate from his mother in order to find out who he is as a man. When we embrace this, we survive better.

Because of all this, wars will ensue. Sons will get mad and the anger will come out sideways. Sometimes they will be mad at us; other times they will be mad at someone else. Either way, the anger will come out onto us because we are his safety net, and therefore his target. We are the ones who will never leave. We are the ones who can take the arrows because we love our sons when no one else will, and they know it. And we will always be there when they return, regardless of how volatile the wars have been. How blessed we are to be the mothers of sons.

CHAPTER 4

You Are His Home

Have a meaningful conversation with an older man and ten to one, he will talk about his childhood. And the subject he will return to the most often is his mother. Maybe his memories have been overlaid with a few coats of shiny polish but they are there—the rules she made, the fun they had, the struggles they shared, and the meals his mother cooked best. So many men will tell you that no one cooked like their mothers. The funny thing is, many of the meals that they ate as children might have been nothing special, but that isn't what matters. What makes them so cherished is that they came from their mother's hands. Several weeks ago, my eighty-three-year-old neighbor, a single man who never married and cared for his mother until she died fifteen years ago, proudly brought me his mother's handwritten recipes. He is anything but a sentimentalist, but he was excited when he marched through the patch of woods separating our driveway from his with a cardboard recipe box in his hands. He knew I liked to cook, but that's not what motivated him. He believed that his mother's ginger cake was unmatched. Even with the Food Network and thousands upon thousands of cookbooks to access, he thought that nothing could ever taste anything as delicious as his mother's cake. He brought me her cookbook because he wanted to show his mother off.

As I interviewed men for this book, I came across this nostalgia for their childhoods and their mothers in many conversations with both the elderly and the middle-aged. I always asked, "What do you think were your mother's best qualities?" Sometimes they could pinpoint specific attributes and sometimes they couldn't. This frustrated me because as the mother of a twenty-one-year-old man, I wanted to know what in particular might make my son love me even more. I wanted to be able to fill him with warm memories. I wanted to know what I should do or how to be in order to help him continue to mature into a happy, well-adjusted, and great man. But none of the men I interviewed could really tell me exactly what it was about their mothers that made them love them so much.

Then one day, a young man in his thirties named Bill summed it up perfectly. He said, "My mother is Home. She represents everything good and right, comforting and safe. She is where I want to go when I hurt and the first person I want to call if something good happens. My wife loves me, but my mom is my biggest fan."

I intuitively understood what he meant but I asked him to clarify further. "My mom being home for me? What does that mean? Well, she's where I go in order to feel better about myself and about life. She's where I started but she's also what I had to leave. She's where I want to go when I'm lost and she's where I first figured out who I was. Sometimes she's my plumb line and my moral compass. She's the one person who accepts me for who I am because she *knows* who I really am. I don't need to hide anything from her. She's the one who can hurt me the most but comfort me the most. Does that make sense?"

It did make sense to me. But I also wondered, is our role in our sons' lives really that broad? When I interviewed adult women about their fathers for my book *Strong Fathers, Strong Daughters: Ten Secrets Every Father Should Know,* I routinely found one of two very clear responses: Women either boasted about their dads and couldn't tell me enough wonderful about them, or they burst into tears. When it comes to our relationships with our dads, it seems there is no middle ground—at least for women. But sons talk differently about their mothers. I believe this is because men have difficulty wrapping their minds around what we mean to them and what we do for them, because we do so much. As Bill said, to our sons we are home. And think about describing home—you simply can't do it in a sentence or two. Home represents so much on so many levels that we don't even try to articulate exactly what it is. When our sons talk about us, they can't unravel the intertwined emotions and memories stemming from their relationships with us because they blend together in a miraculous way to create powerful experiences that defy precise analysis.

We may have difficulty articulating the meaning of home because everyone knows exactly how home is supposed to feel. It is important, however, to tease apart a few of the most important aspects of home so that we can understand what we as mothers mean to our sons.

HOME IS WHERE HE FINDS HIS ROOTS

If you have ever spent any time gardening, you know that even the strongest species of any plant doesn't stand a chance of survival unless it establishes a root system. If you start with a seed, you need to make sure that enough earth covers the shell so that it will sprout. If you transfer an established potted plant into the ground, it stands a poor a chance of surviving if the roots don't take. Whether you have a hearty or delicate type doesn't matter; neither will fare well if they don't quickly set a few primary roots into the earth.

You are the place where your son's first roots develop. This phenomenon has been highly studied in research highlighting the maternal–infant bond. In the 1950s and 1960s, American psychologist Dr. Harry Harlow used monkeys to study infant bonding. He found that monkeys who were isolated from other monkeys instead attached to material in the bottom of their cages. In other words, the need to find attachment is so primary in animals that without a mother, monkeys would latch on to a piece of cloth. In the same way, human babies are born with a primary need to attach to their mothers. Other researchers have gone on to study the attachment of infants to their mothers and found that those with the most secure maternal-infant attachments tend to enjoy better emotional health and suffer less psychopathology later in life. Mothers are first and foremost social beings, and when our sons are young, they are as well. Their need for human affection, touch, care, and bonding from their earliest days on is of utmost importance.

In the first months of his life, your son literally clings to you. He needs nourishment and warmth and all of his physical needs met. Equally fundamental is his need for emotional attachment, which acts as the nutrient-rich soil into which his roots are set down. He turns to you, his mom, to see if you will give him what he asks. If you do, he will return the same. This is how your son plants his roots and begins to shape his identity—by looking to you to meet his needs and watching how you respond. If you succeed, he feels secure enough to "stick" himself to you. Through the first months and then through the early years of his life, he will ask for more from you to see if you will come through for him. The more he trusts you, the more love he receives from you, the deeper his roots sink. This is extremely important because while many others can care for him—babysitters, a nanny, a grandparent, or the like—his roots originate in mom's love. So if he can trust you, to love him, protect him, comfort him, and feed him, he can begin to trust others to do the same. You are the one he wants more than anyone else. We see this concept fleshed out in studies of children under the age of five who spent various amounts of time in day care. These studies show that kids who spend fewer than thirty hours per week in day care (away from their mothers) fare better as they get older.[1] Boys who spend more time with their mothers when they are young exhibit fewer behavioral problems as they get older.[2] Your son needs one primary source to which he can turn for love and sustenance, for trust and affection, and when he finds that one source, he sets his roots there. For most sons, that source is mom.

If a boy's roots are strong and he feels deeply connected to his mother he will feel safer when it comes time to move out into the world. For example, as your son starts middle school he can spend more energy figuring out what he likes to study, what sports he likes to play, and what friends he likes to do things with, because he doesn't need to use all of his energy safeguarding his relationship with you. That is, of course, if his roots are firmly established. Boys who don't bond well with their mothers and haven't grown deep roots are easily swayed by every gust that comes along. Just as a young plant with shallow roots is easily torn from the soil, so too is a boy made vulnerable to the pressures of his immediate world if he doesn't have a solid relationship with his mom. He is easily thrown off balance because he doesn't have a solid sense of himself.

In order to provide the good soil our sons need, we need to be there for them at all times. We need to be steady, constant, and at times unshakable. We need to act as the anchor in our sons' lives, and when they look as though they are ready to pull away from their roots, we need to be tough enough to handle it, letting them know that the place they call "home" will always be there for them. If we don't provide the connection that our sons need during those early years, they literally never learn to attach themselves to anyone, and this can lead to very serious psychological trouble such as severe attachment disorders. Many children who live the first three or four years of life in homes or orphanages where no mother or father figure provides the basic love, trust, affection, and care that every infant and toddler needs end up never being able to bond to another human in a meaningful way. When this happens, they go through life devoid of many feelings intrinsically normal to human relationships: joy, happiness, love, acceptance, affection, and trust. For instance, children can emerge from situations where there was severe emotional abandonment and be comfortable with only negative feelings like hate and anger. They lack the ability to have empathy for another because they never experienced emotional bonding.

Children with severe attachment disorders are likely to grow into adults who are so emotionally detached from other humans that they pose a serious risk to themselves and others. They can hurt others without a feeling of sadness, remorse, or guilt. A boy who never sets roots in anyone during his early years, who spends hours upon hours viewing violent movies or playing violent video games, receives no psychological help and is isolated from any healthy interaction with adults, lives with a perfect storm brewing inside him. When all of these factors come together, he can become the kind of boy who can go into public places and shoot people without batting an eye.

So often we think of serious psychological illness as something that boys are born with. To some degree this is true, but in many instances, serious psychological illness isn't a genetic disorder—it can stem from simply never bonding with a mom. That's a pretty powerful truth to know as a mother.

Does that mean that every mother who doesn't bond well with her son ends up with a son who is prone to violence? Absolutely not. I use this extreme example of attachment disorders to make a point: When it comes to healthy emotional development, mothers play a critical role in boys' lives, and we need to understand just how serious it is. We are the ones in whom our boys put down roots. We need to accept the precious responsibility of knowing how much our sons not only love, but *need* us during those early years of their lives.

HOME IS WHERE HE BEGINS TO LEARN THE MEANING OF LIFE

Since fathers bond with their sons by doing activities with them, it is more natural for fathers to invest more energy in helping sons develop their athletic and physical abilities. Of course, fathers don't ignore the intellectual, mental, or emotional growth of their sons; they simply tend to focus more on a boy's physical development. They throw baseballs, work on cars, take sons fishing or hunting, or do woodwork with them.

Fathers and sons tend to do these kinds of activities together, and because dads too are male, they can become competitive with their sons. Often this competitiveness is subconscious; other times it is overt. Interestingly, mothers can pick up on this dynamic more easily than dads can because the moms are on the outside looking in.

Mothers, on the other hand, tend to focus on a boy's physical *and* emotional development. This isn't to say that fathers don't care about their son's happiness; of course they do. A mother's focus is simply different. Since we are female and our sons are male, we are naturally less competitive with them and we are more comfortable verbalizing our feelings than many fathers are. This makes it easier for us to focus on our son's physical and emotional development.

One of the most important aspects of good mothering is making sure that before our son leaves home, he has a deep sense of what his purpose in life is. Every boy needs to know that his life was intentional and that he was born with unique talents that he can use to find his place in the world. This is extremely important, because we see many boys today living without a sense of understanding about why they exist. They wonder, Do I have anything to contribute to the world? Do I matter to anyone? If a boy's family is broken, he doesn't know what his role in that family is. If no one helps guide him through life, he never comes to recognize what he's good at and what he isn't good at. More important, he never learns how to take the gifts that he has been given and use them for the good of those around him. When he learns to combine his gifts with the utilization of them for the good of others, then he begins to understand what his purpose in life really is.

Having talents is great for any boy, and of course as parents, we want to help our sons recognize those talents and develop them. This can help a boy's self-esteem, but it doesn't raise it completely. In fact, if we focus too much on developing a son's abilities, we can turn him into a monster by making him self-centered and too prideful. We've all known men who are full of themselves because they feel that they are better than everyone else. So having talents and developing them is good, but parents must find the right balance. Also, having talents doesn't necessarily help a boy understand the reason that he was born or help him discover his role in life. This lesson he learns by taking what he's gifted in (and it isn't always athletic, academic, or musical) and then using it to help others. Combining these two steps is what teaches a boy his deeper sense of purpose in life.

Today we see high school boys with rising levels of depression and anxiety,[3] twenty-somethings living at home, middle-aged men walking out on their wives, and all ages of men addicted to pornography, drugs, or other unhealthy habits. In many cases, this happens because these young men don't find real meaning in their lives. Our culture doesn't encourage young men to find purpose—it teaches them how to compete with one another, but not how to challenge themselves. From the time a boy is in preschool, he learns that he needs to get out among friends and find his spot. Is he better than they are at football, piano, or science? We push until we locate a place where he can find his footing and then we plant him there so that he can learn self-confidence. There is nothing wrong with helping our sons this way, but the truth is, it isn't the best way to teach boys self-confidence. What really helps them feel good about themselves is something that we frequently overlook: discovering what they were born to do. That may change from day to day or year to year, but every son needs to know that there is a purpose for his existence. Finding meaning in life acts as a primary driving force for men, and even for young boys.

This is more of an existential question than getting on the soccer team or picking the right college. Many parents aren't comfortable with it, but it is too important to ignore. Whether it is to understand his role as his father's son, to seek a spiritual vocation, or to discipline himself to fulfill a career aspiration, every boy needs to know that life is bigger than he is and that somewhere in that large life, he fits in. He was born to carry out a work beyond himself. If finding this meaning begins at home, the question then is, what can a mother do to help? Isn't this something that a boy naturally discovers on his own? One might think so, but in fact, in today's culture, neither school nor society focuses on the meaning or purpose of our children's lives. That is left to his mother and father. While fathers are busy teaching boys the perfect curveball, or how to drive, our task is to nurture a strong sense of self in our sons. The good news is that the lessons a boy learns about the meaning of his life often come from the mundane goings-on of day-to-day living. It is by performing simple tasks, experiencing daily activities, and reacting to specific events that a boy realizes the significance of his life.

Helping a boy find purpose begins through teaching him certain general principles. First, he needs to be taught that his life is bigger than he is. Most boys are taught to figure out what their interests are and where their talents lie. Then they must learn how to develop those talents and interests. They ultimately learn to hone their skills, and usually find that, as a result, their lives feel more fulfilled. But being accomplished doesn't necessarily give them answers regarding what the purpose of their life is. Success doesn't necessarily provide the ticket to happiness. The self-contempt, loss of hope, and over-whelming sadness that sit at the heart of depression don't occur only in men who have never found anything worthwhile in which to in-vest their time and energies. It occurs even in men who are highly skilled.

For a boy to learn early in his life that what he likes, what he is good at, and what he wants are all important. But, in the end, *unless he learns how to use those things to help others around him* he will *never* recognize the true purpose of his life, nor will he live a more fulfilled life. Often parents make the mistake of encouraging sons to achieve academic, athletic, or some other type of success but then never teach them to use those abilities to help anyone but themselves. Many suc-cessful men use their talents, but they do so only for their own gain, and fail to intentionally help others. If we allow sons to focus only on what they want and what they are good at (helping them to pursue their own happiness) and fail to help them see their lives on a larger scale (that others need their help), we raise self-centered, narcissistic boys who never find happiness. Real joy comes from fulfilling a pur-pose, not in being self-focused. When a boy begins to see that he is part of a larger world and a bigger humanity, he learns to look outside himself and use the talents he has been given to make the world a better place. It is then that he begins to comprehend the deeper pur-pose of his life.

Adam had majored in English at an Ivy League college. He told me that he felt proud of his academic achievements. He made many friends in college and really didn't have many negative things to say about his time there. He felt he eventually wanted to go to law school, but he was looking to spend some time working at a law firm before he applied because he wanted to be sure of his decision. Adam said that while he was looking for a job, he had a gnawing feeling inside that something in his life was missing. He often wondered what that was, but he couldn't pinpoint it.

"While I was looking for work, a friend asked me to go on a medical trip to Ecuador. I wondered why he asked me because I was anything but science-minded. He told me that they needed general helpers to teach kids how to brush their teeth, give out vitamins, etc. Since I didn't have a job yet, I decided to go. 'Why not?' I thought. I had nothing to lose."

Adam went on his first trip beyond U.S. borders that wasn't for vacation or academic study. He went to help others, not to enhance his own intellectual, emotional, or physical development. He told me that his focus up to that point in his life had always been himself. His parents provided him a private high school education. They made certain that he skied, took piano lessons, and had nice things. He told me that he appreciated the sacrifices they made in order to provide a wonderful life for him.

"I had no idea what was about to happen to me when we first landed in Ecuador. We got off the plane and took a bus to a remote area. We passed homes with holes in the walls. I saw children running about clothed in rags and playing with sticks because that's all they had.

"I'm embarrassed to say that I was shocked. Up until that point, I had lived a very sheltered and cushy life. Since we only had one month in Ecuador, our team quickly got to work. I helped them set up makeshift medical clinics and used my broken Spanish to teach kids about the basics of nutrition and how to care for their teeth. They acted like they couldn't get enough of my time or attention.

"To make a long story short," he said, "something about the trip made me feel deeply satisfied. I had honestly never felt that way before. While I worked with children in such poverty, I felt that this was what I was born to do. Was I supposed to move there? I didn't know, but for the first time in my life, I realized that I was put on earth for a real purpose. Life wasn't just about developing my skills and building an impressive résumé. It was about something much deeper and richer, and I can't even describe it. But I do know that I felt a passion emerge in me that I hadn't known. So when I came home, I told my folks that law school was out. I was going to do whatever it took to go to medical school and help more poor people who have little to no medical care."

Each of us mothers must help our sons find whatever it is in life that triggers passion in them. Sure, we can sign them up for extracurricular activities and summer camps and find them the best schools—and these are all laudable things to do. But we can't simply stop there. We must help our sons look beyond themselves and serve others, because often it is in the serving where they begin to understand a deeper meaning to their lives.

Second, a boy must be taught to orient his life toward meaning, not just happiness. Making himself happy is a pretty simple thing to do. When a boy is young, a mother simply needs to feed him, entertain him, or find something that he enjoys doing and allow him to do it. But as a boy grows older, happiness becomes more complicated. Puberty is a prime time to really encourage him to begin to think about finding purpose rather than simply happiness. Purpose brings eternal satisfaction; happiness is temporary. So look at what your son is good at, or interested in, and help him use those qualities to help others. This is the best way to aid them in their search to find what they were put on the earth for.

Third, a mother needs to teach her son that he doesn't exist in a vacuum. Since he is born as a relational being, he cannot know the meaning of his life without knowing that it involves other human beings. He is born into a larger unit and therefore he needs something to live for other than himself. Everything he does impacts others. Girls seem to absorb this naturally as they grow older—perhaps because they mature faster and are more interested in the emotional makeup of various kinds of relationships. Boys have to be *taught* to look outside themselves, by example and by lesson. Sometimes boys get the wrong messages. Perhaps unconsciously, we teach them to outshine their friends but without also teaching them what this does to their friendships. We teach them to better themselves just for the sake of getting better at something. But it is critical that we also teach them that everything they do impacts the lives of others around them in a positive or negative way. And then of course help them impact others positively rather than negatively.

Our children are growing up in a very competitive culture in the United States. As young as three years of age, they are taught to learn the alphabet before their peers. Boys are taught to run faster or kick a soccer ball straighter. They hit elementary school and we want them in the fast reading group, not the slow one. We want our boys on the A tag football team, not the B team. When they hit middle school, we want them to be at the top of their class and we believe that it is our duty to help them get there. We need to find a tutor if they are learning too slowly because we want them to *get ahead*. Ahead of what? Their peers, of course.

By junior high school, we are thinking about college and doing what we can to procure a shining portfolio for them to send to admissions officers. The résumé must display great grades and unusual ventures, volunteer work, and stellar athletic accomplishments.

If we are truthful, we mothers can see that much of our lives centers on helping our kids get to a place where they are primed for success. There is absolutely nothing wrong with helping our sons be successful. But we must be aware that success can have negative effects on them and their loved ones if they—and we—aren't careful. For instance, they can develop an attitude of superiority that makes them obnoxious company. We have all known boys who are so self-centered, no one wants to be around them.

We would be bad mothers if we didn't help, encourage, and teach our boys to excel at many things. But, in doing so, we often end up teaching our sons to be painfully self-centered by focusing only on self-improvement. Our world is so competitive that it almost dictates that we parent this way, because in order for us to prepare our kids for college, and then for a career, they must start hoofing it from the time they are small children.

So we must pull back from this unhealthy paradigm and realize that "success"—making money, having a great job, living in a nice apartment—is great but it won't help sons feel real satisfaction, unless we remember to teach them *how* to use everything that they work hard for to help others. In other words, a mother can push her son to be a professional football player but if it doesn't give him deep satisfaction, has she really done him a favor? A mother can help her son go to an Ivy League college and encourage him to get a job commanding a high salary, but if he comes home every night lonely, has he really been successful? Have we? Unfortunately, we mothers jump on the success bandwagon with our peers and try to give our sons all the good things and great opportunities we can to ensure their success. The problem, however, is that if where we have led them doesn't ignite their passion or give them a deeper sense of purpose in life, what have we given them? If we are honest, each of us wants our sons to find real happiness, not just be "successful," but we focus more on helping them advance their careers through developing talents instead of finding out what really gets their juices flowing.

We can all understand and repeat the concept that it is better to give than to receive, but we don't always teach our kids why this is true. All of us, but especially our sons, can use the lesson that giving to others in some way gives great purpose to our lives. This is what I call teaching boys to be "other oriented" rather than self-oriented.

Consider that when men are under duress, their tendencies to help others often supersede their interests to protect themselves. We see this during wartime. For example, Viktor Frankl, a captive and physician in one of the German concentration camps during World War II, writes of a specific time when some starved inmates broke into the food storage and stole a few potatoes. The guards told the prisoners that unless they disclosed who the thief was, the whole camp would be punished. "Naturally," he writes, "the 2500 men preferred to fast" than give up names, knowing those men would be horrifically punished.

One of the most poignant illustrations of how meaning in life comes from our connection to other humans is found in another of Frankl's experiences of life in the concentration camp. Frankl had an opportunity to escape with some other prisoners. Before he left, he writes,

"I made quick last rounds of my patients, who were lying huddled on the rotten planks of wood on either side of the huts. I came to my only [Austrian] countryman, who was almost dying, and whose life it had been my ambition to save in spite of his condition. I had to keep my intention to escape to myself, but my comrade seemed to guess that something was wrong (perhaps I showed a little nervousness). In a tired voice he said, 'You, too, are getting out?' I denied it, but found it difficult to avoid his sad look. After my round I returned to him. Again a hopeless look greeted me and somehow I felt it to be an accusation. The unpleasant feeling that had gripped me [when he'd agreed with another inmate to escape] became more intense. Suddenly I decided to take fate into my own hands for once. I ran out of the hut and told my friend that I could not go with him. As soon as I told him with finality that I had made up my mind to stay with my patients, the unhappy feeling left me. I did not know what the following days would bring, but I had gained an inward peace that I had never experienced before. I returned to the hut, sat down on the board at my countryman's feet and tried to comfort him. . . ."

Frankl's story shows us that when men choose to help others, putting the needs of friends, colleagues, and even strangers above their own, they find deep peace and joy, even in the harshest and most inhuman conditions. Notice that Frankl tells us that when he decided to stay behind for his friend, his "unhappy feeling" left him. This is a crucial point that we must not miss in the story. Frankl decided to leave the camp and fend for himself, but when he decided this, he felt uneasy. Acting only to protect himself led him to feel dissatisfied. But when he consciously chose to sacrifice for a fellow captive, he says, his uneasiness left him and peace came to him.

Many of our sons never feel this type of satisfaction, because they are not called to sacrifice anything. Of course, we would never wish them to be in such a horrific situation as Frankl, but the underlying message is the same—being self-focused doesn't lead to the joy that serving others does. As mothers, we try hard to make life comfortable for our sons. We want life to be pleasant, happy, and as easy as possible. But we also need to teach them how to love and serve others, and how to put themselves in another man's shoes.

I watched Helena do this with Will when he was eight years old. Will was born with an eye disorder that required multiple surgeries throughout the early years of his life. After his fourth surgery, Will told his mother that having his stuffed elephant with him in the hospital brought him a lot of comfort. He could pretend that his elephant was a person, he told her, and that made him feel safe. And it was then that he had an idea. He told his mother that other kids on his hospital floor didn't have stuffed animals and asked if he could bring extras to the hospital the next time he had surgery. His mother said yes and brought several to the hospital to give out to other young patients having surgery. Will loved buying the animals and giving them out. The problem was, he said to his mother, that he didn't have enough for everyone. Within one year, Will and his mother collected enough stuffed animals to fill their entire garage. She didn't have room to park her car inside it.

Will himself told me about collecting the animals, and I could see from his facial expressions and tone of his voice that he was very proud of himself but also excited. He loved helping the kids in the hospital who faced similar surgeries. Collecting them and giving them out gave him a deep sense of purpose and peace.

This is how we help our sons dig more deeply into their lives and find purpose. It may be as simple as helping them collect stuffed animals. But helping them find purpose always begins with encouraging them to serve others.

Be Good Soil

Good soil is nourishing, accepting, and well balanced. These are the qualities that we need in order for our sons to attach well and find their first roots. But being well balanced, accepting, and ready to take on whatever comes our way isn't easy! And being a mother is one of the hardest challenges anyone will face. It requires us to act against our nature at times. We need to be tough when we want to give in. There are moments when we want to throw up our hands and tell everyone we're *done*—but we can't. Mentally, it requires an ability to take a lot in, process what we hear and feel, and then decide what to do. Mothering needs to be a rational act, even when sometimes we want to be irrational and make decisions based on our emotions. Physically, it requires pushing our bodies beyond what we can bear (I really didn't think I was going to be able to push my son out without splitting open from end to end). Spiritually, we are forced to our knees to find the God who will make everything right when we or our sons have screwed up.

So how, when faced with such an arduous and daunting task, can we be good soil for our sons, who look to us to set down roots? With a lot of sweat!

First, we need to realize that we must do whatever is necessary to live emotionally balanced lives. This is one of the best ways we can ensure that we will be good soil for our sons. Many moms struggle finding this balance, and for many reasons. The most common is that we try to be all things to all people, and when we do this, we become exhausted. How many times have you seen your friends burn out while attempting to juggle work, marriage, kids, and running a home? The truth is that we try too hard to carry a load that our minds and bodies just can't handle.

I routinely see young mothers become discouraged and fatigued in their thirties. By trying to be great moms, great women in their chosen careers, and good wives to their husbands (not to mention being kind to their parents, siblings, and friends), it's no wonder that so many moms suffer from anxiety and depression. We push ourselves to the breaking point, and when we do, everyone in our family suffers. Why do we do this? I am convinced that much of it comes from hidden peer pressure. It is the caterpillar principle that Dr. James Dobson writes about in his book *Bringing Up Boys*. He cites a study done by the French naturalist Jean-Henri Fabre. In the experiment, Fabre lined up many caterpillars around the edge of a flowerpot and for three days watched them march around it in a never-ending circle. At the end of the third day, Fabre placed some pine needles (which caterpillars apparently love to eat) in the center of the pot to see which of the hungry creatures would find the food. You can guess what happened. They continued to tromp in their circle for four more days, until one by one they rolled over on their backs and died of starvation. We moms, while of course smarter than the caterpillars, find ourselves involved in a similar exercise. We do what we do because that's what other moms around us are doing. Do you doubt it? Ask yourself this: Do you find yourself comparing your son's activities, grades, weight, looks, to his classmates'? If you do, do you find yourself wanting to get him into different sports, hire a tutor so that he gets better grades, or buy him nicer clothes? If so, then you are succumbing to peer pressure. I'm not pointing the finger; I've been there. I remember when my own kids were young and I was preparing dinner one night. My kids were sitting at the table doing crafts when a light flashed in my front living room window. I went to see what it was and saw my neighbor taking her kids out, after dinner. It turned out she was driving them to ski practice. It was six o'clock at night. Then I saw another neighbor taking her kids out as well. In that moment I thought, "What kind of mom am I? They're taking their kids somewhere and mine are home doing crafts at the kitchen table." I felt the twangs of guilt that I should have been doing more for my kids. Why? Not because I thought my kids needed to learn to ski, but because I wanted to jump into the caterpillar line. I'll bet you have done the same—especially with your boys.

Being really good moms for our sons means that we must constantly check ourselves and ask if we are striking a healthy balance between caring for them and caring for ourselves. We need to be emotionally and mentally available for our boys, and this will be very hard if we are exhausted all the time. Some of us are exhausted because we're trying to do too much. Others are tired because all they do is care for their children and never take time to do something healthy and fun for themselves. We don't need to spend every waking hour with our sons, but we do need to take care of ourselves so that we have the mental, emotional, and physical energy that is required to meet our son's needs. This is really hard to do and many times calls for making tough decisions. We need to decide to get out of the caterpillar line and do what *we believe* is best for ourselves and our kids. The problem for us mothers is that we can't always see clearly, because we are too focused on parenting the same way our friends and peers do. So I am telling you—for your sake and for the sake of your relationship with your son—to do it. Society needs courageous moms who are willing to make the hard choices.

So often parents ask my advice on what they need to do for their kids. How should they discipline? Should their teens have a curfew? I routinely frustrate moms by responding with advice for them—not about how to parent, but about how to take care of themselves, because I have learned a profound truth over my twenty-five years listening to mothers and kids: If you aren't happy, your kids won't be.

This isn't to advocate selfishness but to help mothers in distress. The average mother carries inappropriate and unhealthy expectations of herself when it comes to work and family. We carry guilt, fear, resentment, and self-contempt because as much as we want to, most of us just can't handle the multitude of tasks we take on and still stay healthy. Sons need mothers who feel at peace, comfortable with themselves, content with their lives, and reasonably rested. What most of us give our sons (even when they are infants) is exhaustion, irritability, and mood swings because we just won't take care of ourselves. Being good soil for your son means taking really good care of yourself so that you find balance. Some mothers do this by refusing evening meetings or obligations. Others allow their sons only one sport per semester so that they don't have to live in the car after school every day. Some mothers find jobs they can do at home; others work part-time and forgo extra income in exchange for a less stressed life. Set up boundaries. So stop trying to lose the last ten pounds, because it's making you really irritable. Go back to school if you're bored. I don't know what you need to balance your own life, but you do—so do it. Be strong for your son. However you find a way to ensure a sense of peace in your life, do not mar it by struggling with guilt over the choices you make. We have come to believe that the busier we and our kids stay, the better mothers we are. This simply isn't true.

One more word on this subject: Many mothers think that living a balanced life means doing a little bit of many things every day or week. For some, this works, but for a lot of other moms (like me), it doesn't. Many moms are intense and have trouble doing anything halfway. For women like us, the idea of exercising for ten minutes instead of thirty, of working part-time, simply doesn't resonate. There are those of us who can eat an entire pack of Oreos in a single sitting. And for us, balance seems like a four-letter word. But it doesn't have to be. It simply needs to be expressed in a different way than you are familiar with.

Here's what I suggest to those women who want to do everything, but at the same time want to live a balanced life: You'll die right on time no matter what you do. If you really need to get something done, you will have enough time to do it; it doesn't all need to be done in one day. For example, if you want to have a successful career and four kids, do them in sequence, not at the same time. Either one puts enough stress on your life; both at the same time will exhaust you. Many women forget that after the child-bearing years are done, we have decades to excel at our careers. If you want to compete in triathlons, you don't need to train when you have a four-month-old; enjoy your son, and when he is older, train your heart out. After I finished my medical training, I took a few years off to be home with my kids. My friends and colleagues told me that I was out of my mind, "wasting my training," and that I would never go back to work. They were wrong. At the time, their advice shook my confidence but not my resolve—I knew what I needed to do for my life. So I did it. And of course, I did go back, once my kids were older. Some mothers have to work and don't have the option to defer a career. For those women, I say look for ways to find time for yourself so that you are ready and able to be with your kids when they need you. Look for some chore you can postpone or task that you can put off and use that energy to spend time with your children.

Interestingly, as a side note, my colleague Dr. Will Aguila, an obesity specialist and author, said that one of the most common reasons for eating disorders (primarily obesity) in women is their "trying to be all things to all people." He told me that women simply can't handle it, and find the comfort they're missing in food. In those cases, their health—as well as their children—pays the price.

I recently had a mother in my office who birthed twins. While she was in the hospital, she was making phone calls to find a nanny in preparation to get back to work in six weeks. She was stressed to the max and at her two-week checkup was showing many of the signs of postpartum depression. When I gently told her that she needed more time off, she burst into tears. She didn't want to go back to work at all. I asked her why then was she going back and she said that she loved her job and that she respected her boss and didn't want to disappoint her. After all, she had worked many long years to get to her current position in the company.

"I'll look like a fool—a wimp," she told me. "I'm so afraid that if I quit, I'll get bored and resent my boys." I felt sad for her. She was afraid of letting go of what she had always known, afraid of feeling like a failure, afraid of being a bad mom.

I asked her what she felt she needed to do to relieve some stress, improve her depression, and make life as wonderful as possible for herself and her sons. Without skipping a beat she said, "Oh, that's easy. Quit my job." I think even she was surprised by how quickly she answered!

"There you go," I told her. She looked astonished and stared at me as if I had three heads.

"No way!" she replied.

"But you just told me that would be the best thing for your health and for your kids right now," I said.

We talked back and forth and the conversation was painful for her, I could tell. She felt sad about not being able to spend more time with her newborns, and guilty about wanting to leave her job. She thought she would be letting herself down if she gave up the career she'd worked so hard to build, that all those seventy-hour workweeks would have been a waste. She was worried that she'd lose the respect that comes with a career—that even her kids wouldn't respect her. You name it, she felt guilty or anxious about it. But mostly, I think, she felt afraid. She was afraid to change her mind, afraid to do what she felt she needed to do, deep in her heart.

I get it. I've been through many of those feelings myself and talked with countless mothers who have struggled with hard choices. And I have learned at least one thing for sure: Acting out of fear rarely works. What does work is taking the tough road. But it is really scary. Listening to our hearts as mothers and acting on those gut feelings makes life better for us and for our kids. Staying on the same path because we are afraid to change is a terrible mistake. I told her so and welcomed her to motherhood.

"Really good mothers make the tough choices," I said. "And they don't look back. Being a strong mother means having a backbone of steel and resolving to always do what is best for your kids. And there is never anything easy about that, because many folks around you, including friends and family, will tell you you're crazy."

Being good soil for our sons sometimes means having to make the hard choices, not just for ourselves, but for our boys. Many times this means having the courage to do what we need (and secretly want) to do so that we can offer them a content, happy mom when they are with us. The truth is, they need us in better moods more than they need tutors, nicer clothes, more friends, or a better coach. Remember, we are the ones in whom they grow their earliest roots.

HOME IS WHERE HE LEARNS THE GREAT LESSONS

Ask men where they learned about courage, acceptance, and forgiveness and most will quickly tell you that they learned these things from their mothers. We are the ones who haul them home after losing the championship game and witness the choked-back tears in the car. We are the ones who see the report card first and decide that next semester can be better. And we are the ones who believe that deep down, he can find the courage that he needs to ask a certain girl out for a date, take the ACT again, or reapply to his dream college. We encourage and support because we believe in our sons. That's what feels right and what comes naturally to us.

There's another reason that our sons learn the great lessons from us. We are able to see our son as a whole being, not as someone who can be compartmentalized into various attributes or roles, ones that please us or don't. That's not the way we think. The best mothers accept the qualities in our sons that are difficult to deal with as well as accepting the qualities we like. Madeline knew this.

Great Lesson #1: Courage

When Connor was a young boy he was a handful. He was a bit hyper-active and very opinionated; couple that with the fact that he had a similar personality to his mother and Madeline knew that she had her work cut out for her. Connor was strong-willed, just as she had been as a child, and they would spend years butting heads over everything from what shoes he could wear to school to what sports he would play. Nothing came easily.

As Connor grew up, he pursued his passion of videography. In fact, he was very talented. When he was fourteen, local companies hired him to help shoot events and before he was much older, he was editing and producing his own films. School was a "drag," he said, and academics just didn't interest him. So after high school, he decided to go to film school.

He stuck with film school for a couple of years, but eventually found that it was too academic. Something inside him just seemed to fizzle and his passion for the work began to fade. He wanted to do something different. This frustrated Madeline because she felt he was too old to switch gears. But Connor left film school despite her worries and decided to reveal to his mother a hidden dream he had held but never dared divulge to anyone: he longed to be a Navy SEAL. When Madeline found out, she was stunned. This dream seemed so different from anything he had ever pursued, and it wasn't exactly what a young man who doesn't like to take instructions might be well equipped to do. On top of that, Connor was afraid that he wouldn't make the cut. He hadn't finished college. He'd abandoned his pursuit of film. Madeline worried that failure was not something that he would swallow well, and the chances of failing to make the Navy SEAL team were great.

Remarkably, Madeline decided to challenge Connor. When he timidly told her of his secret dream, she never let him know that she believed fear that he wouldn't make it. She challenged him to take a risk. Put himself out there and see if he would fail or succeed. Then she swallowed hard and watched him follow her advice.

That was ten years ago. Since the day Madeline told her son to dig deep and find courage, Connor not only made the team, but has gone on to work on top-secret, elite military projects requiring the highest level of physical and mental courage imaginable. Along the way, Madeline said, she spent many nights encouraging him to not be afraid of failure. She never told him that failure was "not an option"; instead, she taught him that it very well might occur, but that failing was acceptable. He would never know if he could succeed unless he was courageous enough to try.

Mothers teach their sons courage by being strong themselves. Think about it for a moment. Trying something for which success is guaranteed doesn't take courage. Attempting a task with a high rate of failure does. And this is where mothers come in. We can teach our sons to take risks and to fail without fear, because we know that when they fail, we will still love them, accept them, and help them stand up again. And they know it, too.

Great Lesson #2: Acceptance

Boys need to learn two forms of acceptance. First, they need to learn that they are acceptable to us—their parents. Acceptance doesn't mean ignoring a failure, or pretending that it hasn't happened. It means saying "yes, that didn't work out but you tried and now you can move on." Knowing that they are loved and accepted as they are is critical to a sense of emotional well-being. Boys who never receive such acceptance look for it for the rest of their lives. And the only way they can really see that acceptance is if they go out and gain experience and watch how we respond.

The best way to demonstrate acceptance is to show your boy that you love him during a time when he feels unlovable. We can champion our sons successes, tell them that we are proud of their accomplishments, and verbalize that we will always love and accept them, but it's how we *act* during their failures that really counts. Maybe your son flunked a test or repeatedly failed to make a team that he desperately wanted to play on. During those moments, take him out for ice cream. Celebrate that he tried and let him know that while it feels like a big deal at the time, such events don't define who he is. Losing doesn't define him as a failure. Let him see that your affection and love define him as a young man who has terrific potential and a wonderful life to live.

Every time a son is disappointed in himself because he feels he has failed at something, look at it as an opportunity to teach him the lesson of acceptance. We accept his failures and still love him, so he learns that he can accept his own failures and keep taking risks.

The other aspect of acceptance that mothers teach sons is how to accept others as equals. As women, we have likely all experienced unequal treatment in different professional and social arenas; that is why it is so important we teach our sons to love and accept all humans, regardless of gender, race, religion, or disability. James told me that this was one of the greatest lessons that his mother, Darcy, taught him. When he was three, his mother gave birth to his sister, Allie, who had severe cerebral palsy. She couldn't speak or walk, and her arms were bent up toward her torso. Even as a first and second grader, he remembers his mother becoming indignant when well-meaning friends asked how she was coping with her handicapped child. "They spoke to her as though she should celebrate my sister's life less because she had a special need," James told me once. "I even remembered wondering what she was mad at them about, because I also saw my sister as being harder to raise. As I got older I asked her why she got upset with her friends and she told me that to her, my sister was every bit as wonderful as I was. When she said that to me, I understood what she meant. It wasn't that she loved me less, but that she loved my sister more than I thought she should. She accepted her just as easily as she accepted me."

While he was growing up, James helped his mother take care of Allie. He babysat her, helped feed her, and even drove her to her prom when she was a junior in high school. Over the years, James watched his mother refuse to apologize to anyone for his sister's handicaps. He watched his mother take his sister out to play, along to restaurants with him, and on vacation, and be his sister's classroom mother for several years. "I think that I learned to really accept all human beings as having equal worth because my mom did. She not only treated Allie like she was not handicapped; she taught me that the value of Allie's life and the value of anyone else's life is exactly the same. That has had a huge impact on how I live."

As James and I were winding up our conversation, he asked if he could say a few more things. "I want you to know that I learned about accepting others by watching my mother's friends and their kids, too. For instance, my mother had a friend named Cherie. She and my mother were close friends because Cherie had a son, Reid, who was born with Down's syndrome. He was about five years younger than my sister. He was very high functioning. He could go to school, had a lot of friends, and he could speak really well. He was (and still is) a great guy. My mother and Cherie became close because of their struggles, I suppose," he said. I knew that he wasn't finished, but he sat silently for a few moments.

"Anyway, like I said, I drove my sister to her junior high prom. You must wonder why because she couldn't dance, she couldn't talk, and most people would wonder why would she go to prom? She went because Reid asked her to go. He called my mom and asked if he could escort Allie to the prom. My mom started crying." I watched James choke up.

"Reid rented a tuxedo and bought Allie a corsage. My mother took Allie to a hairdresser and had her hair done. They put little ribbons in her hair. My mother bought her a lovely blue prom gown and when she was all ready, I drove her to Reid's house, picked him up, and took them to the school. When we got there, he jumped out of the car and opened Allie's door. He helped me get her wheelchair out of the car and we sat Allie in it very carefully.

"He insisted on wheeling her inside so I let him. When we got in, I stood in the background and watched him with Allie. He was so kind. He tried to give her something to drink. Then he pushed her wheelchair onto the dance floor and spun her gently around. He danced, pushed her forward, pulled her backward. I watched my sister's face and she was smiling. That made me cry."

Allie went to the prom because her mother poured her heart into taking care of her and made it possible for her to go. Reid accompanied her to the prom because his mother raised him to reach out and be kind to others. And James learned from both of these mothers that these two young people were born to be a blessing to others. Watching his mother raise Allie taught James that the greatest joys in life come when we learn how to take care of others.

Great Lesson #3: Forgiveness

We don't often think of teaching forgiveness as being high on our list of responsibilities as mothers, but we should. The reason is simple. Men who are able to forgive others their offenses are happier people. Period. Nothing frees a man like the ability to forgive a person who has deeply wounded him.

When it comes to forgiving someone, both men and women often need to talk their problems through with another person in order to come to a place where they are really ready to forgive. Certainly, someone can forgive another without talking to a friend about the problem, but in my experience, usually a third person is needed to help prompt a person to forgive someone who has offended them. The difficulty for men, however, is that they don't always talk with others about their mistakes. When they hurt or offend someone, they might not share this with others. So we need to teach them to open up about what hurts them or even what they have done to hurt others so that they can forgive.

When Caleb was thirteen, his father walked out on him, his two sisters, and his mother. "He told us that he was going on a business trip and just never came back. I'll never forget him coming into my room that morning and giving me a pat on the head. He told me that he loved me."

Caleb was thirty-seven when he told me this story and I could still hear the pain in his voice. What I didn't hear, however, was bitterness. I was sad for him but as he told me his story, he didn't seem to be terribly sad. At least the sadness hadn't held him back from living a full life. Since I wanted to know about his mother and how she handled such a tough time, I asked what she did to help him and his sisters through it.

"Those were terrible days. For my mom and for all of us," he said. "And we didn't make it any easier for my mother. She cried a lot. She told us that he left because he was having a hard time. She didn't tell us that he had a girlfriend, but we all suspected it. He had been leaving for longer and longer business trips and my folks fought a lot when he got home. Kids know so much more than parents think they know!" I nodded in agreement.

"After my father left, and I got to high school, all hell broke loose. I drank, got into drugs. It's a miracle that I didn't get a girl pregnant. My grades plummeted and I hung out with the troubled kids. My mom panicked at times and, well, I guess she had reason to. I was on a fast track to killing myself. The funny thing was, I knew it all along. You know how some people say that kids don't know what they're doing? They're wrong. At least my doctors were. I knew exactly what I was doing."

He continued. "My mom, though, she's one tough bird. She got strict with me. She tried her best to rein me in and in many ways it worked. At least temporarily. She knew that I needed a man and she wasn't one but she was going to get as close as she could. But she also knew what was going on with me. She saw through the antics—the clothes, the drugs, the girls, and the grades. I'll never forget the day I came home from somewhere and she was paying bills in the kitchen. When I came into the room, she looked up and smiled at me. Not just a 'hi, what trouble have you gotten into today' kind of smile but one that said she really loved me. She asked me if I would sit down. For some weird reason, maybe I was just sick of myself and doing what I wanted to do, I did."

Caleb paused. We were talking on the phone, so I couldn't see his face, but I sensed that he was holding back tears. Not tears of grief, but tears of gratitude and marvel for his mother. "I'll never, ever forget what she told me next. She said, 'Caleb, you're going to be eighteen pretty soon and you are a man. The problem is, you're acting like a kid. Do you suppose that has something to do with your dad?' I choked and told her, 'Absolutely not.' She waited and looked at me for a long time. Then, and I can't believe I let her, she reached over and patted my arm. 'He hurt you more than any man has the right to hurt a son. He wasn't a bad man and you weren't a bad kid. It just happened. Now, you need to forgive him.' I'll never forget how incensed I became. Forgive my dad for hurting all of us so badly? How could she say that? I felt that she was betraying me—taking away my right to be mad.

"I screamed at her and stormed out of the room. Then, I thought about what she said. I went to her a few days later and asked if she had forgiven him. She said, 'I'm working on it. And it feels really good and bad all at the same time.' Over the next few months, she got through to me somehow. She's a remarkable woman. I can honestly say that when she said that to me, something went off in my head and once I listened, it changed my life. I don't know if it would be an exaggeration to say that my mom saved my life during that period."

The power of forgiveness changes people's lives. Hopefully, your son will never experience the kind of pain that Caleb did, but you need to know that if he does, he really can be freed from being a prisoner to his anger. Fortunately for him, he can learn. Tough as it might be for you, you're the one to teach him because the great lessons all come from home.

The second lesson we must teach our sons about forgiveness is to learn to ask for it from others. This can be even tougher than teaching them to extend forgiveness because in asking for it, they must admit fault. Some boys apologize easily; if you have a sensitive boy, he may quickly recognize his mistakes. Then, what you must do is help him discern whether or not his mistakes hurt another person(s) and then if they did, you can help him tell those people that he was sorry. Other boys are tougher, though. They will do something they know they shouldn't do right in front of you—pull their younger sister's hair, steal a toy from a friend—and insist that they did nothing wrong. These are common but tricky situations. Some young boys go through periods of strong denial where they simply don't want to believe that they can do anything wrong. The best thing to do is to firmly insist that they did indeed make a mistake, and send them to time-out or to their room. If you didn't see them commit the offense, then you must make a judgment call and decide whether or not you think they are guilty.

Most boys grow out of this denial in time. But it is very important not to let them off the hook at any time because you need to teach them to live with the truth of what happened, regardless of whether they are ready to acknowledge it. You don't need to complicate the situation by insisting that they admit to their guilt; simply state what happened and then give them consequences. Over time, they will relinquish their denial and come to accept that it's okay for them to come clean when they mess up.

It is harder to get stubborn boys to apologize for their actions. But even though they are tough, you must be tougher, because admitting wrong and asking for forgiveness is crucial to happiness in adulthood. If you never press this point, you could set your son up to be miserable (or at least set up his loved ones for misery). A general rule to follow is that the younger the child, the quicker they should be encouraged to say they are sorry. This is due to their lack of attention span and their different concept of time. If your son is three and hits his sister, he should be punished immediately and made to apologize. Don't worry that the apology isn't heartfelt. If you waited for that, you might wait days. So make him apologize right away so that he gets in the habit of recognizing that he is doing wrong and that when he does, he hurts other people.

HOME IS WHERE HE RETURNS

Ask any woman who has been married more than a year or two and she will very reluctantly admit that to a large or small degree, she is mothering her husband. Some wives see this as positive; others resent it. But like it or not, it is a common phenomenon. Women are nurturers by nature and when men come into our lives, we nurture them. We feed, correct, and counsel them. We try in every way possible to make their lives better. Many of us do this quite well and any son who has a solid relationship with his mother will proudly admit that. As we raise our sons, we teach them to do things that they aren't always naturally good at. We help them communicate better; we help them learn to be disciplined. We teach them all sorts of things that they can't teach themselves. In some ways, they become dependent on us for these lessons.

There is nothing psychologically or emotionally unhealthy about this unless it prevents boys from maturing into men and separating from their mothers in a timely, healthy manner. Most mothers know when this separation is happening and can handle it without desperately trying to control their sons in order to keep them dependent. But even sons who separate from their mothers in a healthy manner have learned to enjoy maternal comforts, so they seek them out in other women. They like their girlfriends to cook like their mother did. They want their wives to comfort them the way their mother did. Sometimes they want maternal affection and the adoration that their mother gave them. So, early in their adult relationships, men commonly seek out women who will nurture them in an adult manner, but in a manner that also reflects their mother's style. Men gravitate back toward what they know because early childhood experiences powerfully shaped their behavior.

As men mature, often their desire to return to maternal roots grows stronger. I learned this as I interviewed older men about their mothers. Specifically, I spoke to a man with a strong military background. He was quite old and had served in World War II. He talked to me about the hardships of war. He recalled some of his friends who fought with him and told me that there were events that he just wouldn't speak about. He had been a prisoner of war and had seen his friends die. Decades had passed since his service, but the feelings were still raw. One thing that he said struck me more than anything else. He said that it was common to hear men on the battlefield cry out for their mothers as they felt themselves dying. Something deep inside drove them to want maternal comfort as they lay wounded and bleeding. It makes sense that a man would ache for the primal comfort that he first felt as a tender young boy, when his mother held him, kissed him, and loved him. When the male heart is young and raw, the love that he receives never leaves him. It is no wonder, then, that when a man reaches the end of his life, natural or otherwise, his heart wants to return to the love of his mother.

Teach Him to Have Hope

A mother must teach her son that he cannot find meaning in life unless he has hope. Men who live with a sense that the best is over, that life cannot get better or that nothing can be changed, fall into despair. Teaching a son to constantly look forward rather than backward is key to keeping a sense of purpose in his life. Again, this is not something that we as mothers are naturally prompted to do in our culture. We become so focused on making sure that our sons are comfortable, competitive, and happy in the moment that we forget they need to have a strong sense of future. Not only do they need to know that a future awaits them, but they need to understand that they can make decisions about the future—they can choose how to move their life forward and believe that better days lie ahead.

As mothers we know that life beats us up. When our sons are young, much as we try to keep them from being hurt, bullied, and battered, we can't always prevent bad stuff from happening to them. Many times, when we watch them get hurt, it's hard to know who suffers more—us or them. But teaching our sons how to live with a positive attitude and hold on to hope can make or break their futures. We know that living without a sense of hope feels devastating and can hold a person back from experiencing the best that life has to offer. So we must be careful to teach this extremely important skill to our sons.

When we live without hope, we believe that we have no good future in front of us, that nothing but darkness is around the next corner. Some psychologists say that when a person finds himself at this place, he has lost all meaning in his life. Men who believe that there is nothing to look forward to don't want to live; they feel that they have no purpose, and man cannot live without a sense of purpose. Even if he is suffering terribly, if a man believes that his life has meaning, then his suffering has meaning and he can bear it.

The task before good mothers is to teach our sons to have hope when life seems bleak. Giving them hope when life is good is pretty easy. When your son makes it onto the best soccer team at school, hope is a given. Chances are his team will do well, that he has victories to look forward to and life will seem grand. If your son gets strong grades and gets into the college of his choice, it appears that he feels hopeful because he is secure in his immediate future. A young man can look forward to success but this is different from living with a sense of hope. Success doesn't always deliver in the end. By the time he wraps up soccer season, graduates from college, or lands his first great job, he might find that even amid the success, he feels empty. How can he feel down, he will wonder, when he has it made?

Having hope really isn't about outward success: It is an inward decision. Hope tells a man that life will be better, that good things lie ahead regardless of his outward state. Hope is something that he feels deeply whether he is successful or not, and therefore it gives him deep satisfaction. Hope brings life to his soul.

The best way a mother can teach her son to have hope is to lead by example. When you are down and feel that the future looks dark, you can articulate to your son, regardless of his age, that you have faith that things will ultimately work out well. This is far easier if you have a religious faith. If you do, you can hold on to a belief that God is real, that He is good and that He can be trusted with your life. Faith allows you to keep hope more concrete because it helps you put your trust for your future into the hands of a more powerful being than yourself.

When your son is young, he will put his faith in you because you are the one who provides everything for him. But as he grows older, he will begin to see that you can't do everything and that you aren't perfect. You will make mistakes and let him down because you are human and have limitations. The great news is that you don't have to always be the only one in whom he puts his faith and trust. You can teach him about God. This is extremely important because, during these times when you let him down, you can tell him that God never will. This will be an enormous relief for you because it takes pressure off you to be perfect. And it helps your son because knowing that God cares for him allows him to begin to put his hope in God to provide for him.

Hope is a decision that must be made. It isn't a feeling that we have (though we can feel hopeful); rather it is a *choice* that we make when life hits the skids. When your son faces hardship, doesn't understand why certain things are happening to him, or feels that his life doesn't have any purpose, talk to him. Choose a time and place when you know he can really listen. Then explain that believing that life will get better, that good will come even though things look bleak now, is a choice he can make.

You can try baby steps in teaching your son hope. If he flunks a test, you can assure him that he can do better and tell him that you will help him the next time around. If he gets fired from a job or doesn't get into the college he wants, or the girlfriend he thinks he loves breaks up with him, he becomes really vulnerable. During these times, you have opportunities to tell him to have faith that he will find another job, fulfill his academic dreams at another college, or go out and meet new girls; teach him that there is always the possibility of happiness waiting around the corner. That the loss of one job, one college, one girlfriend, can't ruin what is the rest of his life.

When you teach him to look forward rather than backward, you will be giving him one of the most important lessons that he'll ever learn.

Accept Him—Always

Earlier in this chapter I wrote about the importance of teaching your son acceptance. Now I want to discuss acceptance of a different sort: your *own* acceptance of your son. In a culture abuzz with the popularized notion of loving our children unconditionally, the truth is, most of us moms aren't terribly good at it. We try, but loving and accepting someone just as they are is really, really hard. Sometimes we tell our sons that we love them but hate what they do. What the child hears is "I have to love you, but I don't think very much of you or your behavior." But kids want our acceptance as much as they want our love. Statements like those tell them the opposite.

We all have hopes and expectations for our sons. When they are born, we create an image in our minds of what they will be like. Usually, this image comes from what we want them to be like. It is the ideal version of our son at different ages. He will be the smartest

in his class at math. He will read earlier than his peers. He will be
kind, compassionate, the best skater on the hockey rink, or the best
pitcher on the baseball team. Then they begin to grow up. They
don't get math. They can't skate or throw a ball with power. They
have a big nose or horrific acne or don't even want to finish high
school. We feel deeply disappointed but don't want to admit it even
to ourselves. And then we turn our disappointment onto ourselves
and feel that we have failed somehow. If they have a low IQ, then we
are to blame. What did we eat while we were pregnant? If a son suffers from panic attacks or depression, we agonize over what we did
wrong. Now our feelings for our son become more complicated because we "messed up," and watching them reminds us of that constantly.

In my experience, there are a few things that we can do to love and
accept our sons better.

Look him in the eye frequently. Nothing communicates acceptance to a son like looking him in the eye and smiling. It's a small
but extremely effective way to communicate love.

Don't be shocked by him. Boys try to get attention from their
mothers by shocking them. Let your son know that you can handle whatever comes your way. This way, he won't feel the need
to do stupid things to test your approval. He'll know you accept
him and he won't have to test you.

Try not to get rattled. If a son knows that his mother is tough, then
he knows she can take whatever he goes through.

Skip the blame game. When boys make mistakes they hurt. After
your son has made a mistake, talk it through, put consequences in
place, and at some point, discuss what he did. He will need to
learn to ask forgiveness from those he has hurt and you must help
him to do this. (Some sons have trouble forgiving themselves, but
you must teach them to because it's just as important as forgiving
others.)

Don't bring up past mistakes. Moms can hold grudges and let their
sons know by reminding them (usually during an argument)
what they did wrong in the past. This never helps anyone.

Forgive him. Many times sons hurt us directly or indirectly. They may do something mean. Or, they may hurt us simply by failing at something. Whether we admit it or not, we may be angry at them because they disappointed us, and although it might not seem to make sense, we need to forgive them in our hearts. If we don't, we won't be able to fully accept them.

Teach Him to Find His Purpose

When life feels overwhelming and complicated for boys (and us), it helps to pare it down to a few fundamental principles and remind them of these principles. Doing this helps boys find clarity when they feel they have lost it. These principles: *You are not here by accident, you are deeply loved, and your life has a purpose.* If a boy doesn't have these, he will have difficulty all of his adult life trying to find his footing. Finally, he needs to know that he is no accident. He has a unique, cherished, and needed purpose to his life. That purpose extends beyond him and may feel like a mystery, but it is there and you are the appointed one to help him begin to find that purpose. All boys find their purpose in life by doing the following things.

First, they must understand that they possess certain gifts and talents. Those talents may be athletic or intellectual or simply be an element of his character (he may be especially compassionate or patient). Your job as his mother is to help him identify these gifts and then help him develop them. Luckily, your strengths as a woman serve you well here. Your son learns that he lives in a family and community through you. You are the communicator, the one who knows how to have friendships, how to give to others, and how to receive from them. Mothers typically set the tone in a family for how the members should reach out to others, extend a helping hand, or be a good friend. We are usually the ones to do this because in most families (though this is changing) mothers spend more time at home with kids than fathers do. Even when we have jobs outside the home, we handle a heavier load of the social schedule and the goings-on of the family.

As I mentioned earlier in this chapter, the best way to teach our sons to find the meaning in their lives is to avoid focusing solely on self-improvement. It's great to help them be better students, athletes, etc., but it is far more important to help them be good men. We need to help them develop character skills and we need to challenge them to live more deeply. They can be A-students, but they can't be jerks. They can be on varsity football, but they need to have compassion and respect for other people.

Ask your son questions and listen to his answers. Start early, when he is young: two to three years old. Stimulate him to wonder about the world around him. Ask him questions about his thoughts and feelings, about what he's learning and what his friends are like. Kids love to be questioned, particularly when we pay attention to their answers and aren't quick to interrupt.

As your son grows older, tell him that he was born for a reason. He was born to be your son, a member of his family, and to be loved and accepted. He belongs with you. He is an integral part of something larger—the family unit—and that unit depends on him for many things. Even if you are a single mother and he is an only child, you are a unit. You provide things for him and he provides things for you. Even very young children need to know that they are needed and that they belong. Ask him to participate in the family—through sharing ideas, chores, and whatever else he can.

When your son reaches middle school, begin to question him about what gets his juices flowing. He may like to read, play the trombone, listen to his friends' problems, care for animals, or fix cars. There are thousands of things that excite boys and your job is to help him find what he loves to do. You need to be open because chances are that what he wants to throw his energies into may not even be on our radar.

As he hits junior high and high school, begin to really challenge him. Ask him about the meaning of life. Ask him what he thinks he was put on earth for. But be ready to keep the conversation going because he probably won't know the answers right away. And he may not recognize yet that his life has an impact on others, especially those people who love him. He may perceive that his life is all about him, and this is healthy and normal as a teen, but push him to look at it another way. Keep prodding him and ask him what he means to others. Ask him what he can give to others. If he is open, begin to take him on community projects so he can see what service is like. He may hate it; he may not. You might be surprised by how he responds.

You will stumble along for years, perhaps, helping your son with this very important quest, and he may not find the answer while he is living under your roof. But that's okay. If you wire him to keep searching, to keep asking himself those same questions as he matures, he will find it. When you plant deep and important questions in his mind, those that cause him to search his own soul, they stick. They will haunt him until he finds a purpose for his life, because your teaching resonates deeply with him. Your questions, your love and acceptance, stir up a deep truth that resides in him, and he will feel that stirring until it is quieted by fulfillment.

For good or bad, you were his beginning; you were the soil in which his roots were planted and you shared a connection that no one else will ever have. There will always be a portion of his heart with your name on it and it will stay with him beyond your death. It will stay with him until his.

CHAPTER 5

If God Wore Lipstick, He'd Wear Your Shade

Hold on to your hats. When it comes to your son's understanding of God, the first glimpse of God he gets is from your face. As a baby, his world is concrete. What he sees exists and what he doesn't see doesn't exist. As he grows older, though, he starts to have a sense that there is more to life than he can see. Many young boys hit age four or five and begin to comprehend that there is a spiritual element to the universe. But since their young minds are still unable to completely grasp abstract concepts, they blend the abstract with the visible. That means that your son will look at your face and through it, figure out some things about God.

He doesn't believe that you are God, but he will form his opinions about God from being in your presence. If you smile frequently, then he may decide that God is friendly. If you are trustworthy, patient, and kind, then he thinks that God probably is, too. The impressions that he forms about God can be both positive and negative, fluctuating with your mood, from day to day. So, if you have a particularly sharp temper, he may believe that God can be mean. If your son hears you say "Stop that right now!" a lot, he thinks God is a disciplinarian. The good news is that these impressions will change as your son matures and develops more sophisticated thinking. If we have misrepresented God (which we of course all do), it is likely that as your son matures, he will come to understand that God does things a whole lot better than we do. In the meantime, there is much we can do to shape our sons' lifelong appreciation of God.

Even though your son's image of God is shaped by your behavior, most boys will say that God is not a woman. Many boys picture him as a huge man with a flowing gray beard who floats in the sky, because they have seen drawings like this in a book. But boys also know that God is more than that. They understand that if He is real, then He must have a personality that they can relate to. That's where you come in. Because your son trusts you, receives love from you, and feels close to you, he finds God trustworthy, loving, and kind, and feels that he can be close to Him as well. In short, your son sees God through the prism of his relationship with you. He spots many of your character qualities in God when he thinks about Him. This is a good thing because in many ways, you are the first one to help him understand the concept of a kind and loving God.

According to the Old Testament, Yahweh is neither male nor female, and over time, your son will come to realize that God isn't a really big guy with a long white beard floating in the sky, nor is he a woman who wears jeans like you. He is a Spirit, with both female and male attributes; so your son's vision of God, with you reflecting God's personality, matches that melding of male and female.

The renowned psychiatrist Robert Coles wrote a wonderful book called *The Spiritual Life of Children*. In it he describes the delightful approach that many children take toward God, their openness toward—a simple trust in—the spiritual dimension of life. He writes about their curiosity and the depth of thought that even very young children have about God. Young children, Coles writes, form opinions about God's personality and create images of what He looks like. They wonder about his kindness, why He allows bad things to happen to people, and what heaven looks like. Having cared for thousands of children in his psychiatric practice, Coles makes the important observation that all children have questions about God and want those questions answered.

HOW TO TALK TO HIM ABOUT GOD

Approaching the subject of God from a strictly theological standpoint isn't a great idea with sons, because boys want more than just ideas about religion. They want to know in concrete terms about faith and how it can help them. So you need to be bold enough to start talking with your son about your faith. God, heaven, spirits, and souls are all part of your little boy's (or big boy's) world at some point. As a very young boy, he will begin to ask some difficult questions: Is heaven real? Is God real, and if so, does he like kids? Does he have teeth and does he smile? We don't place those thoughts in our boys' minds; they simply appear. It is human nature to wonder about the nature of God, and to explore the spiritual side of ourselves. Regardless of your adult beliefs about faith and spirituality, your son has an inner burning to have those deeper questions answered. And here's a big secret: At a certain age, your son wants to hear what you have to say about these things, more than he wants to hear from your pastor or rabbi. When it comes to faith, in my experience, mom is the one who has the ability to transform her son's spiritual life.

I find this phenomenon utterly fascinating. We read in psychology texts that sons look to male role models for identity formation, and this is true. We have long been taught that because boys are visual people, they need to see adult men in motion in order to figure out what life as a man is like. Boys see behaviors and they try them on. If a son sees his father speak with a kind tone in his voice, chances are excellent that he too will speak kindly. But when it comes to God, our sons watch us—their mothers—to form their opinions about God because we are the wellspring of nurture and emotion. If boys look to men to secure their identities in big matters, why would it be that those same boys look to their mothers to figure some things out about God? Based on interviews with hundreds of men regarding their experiences as children, I think that there are several reasons for this.

First, mothers, in general, are more comfortable talking about God with our boys. In fact, most mothers are more comfortable than fathers talking to kids about all the tough topics—sex, drugs, and faith. As I have noted, it comes down to the fact that where the man in our son's life may be more action-oriented, mothers are driven by a desire to communicate. That's how we bond. Even if we think we're not ready, or comfortable, talking about spiritual issues with our sons, we're there, available and easier to talk to. We have no choice but to come up with an answer that will satisfy them. When we're at the wheel of our car, driving them to school or coming home from a baseball game, and a small voice from the backseat pipes up, "Mom— did Tabby go to heaven when we buried her in the backyard?" we can't avoid an answer. Whether we like it or not, the subject has been broached. When we are tucking their wet-haired, squeaky-clean bodies into bed and a quiet voice asks, "So, Mom, does God float or walk up in heaven?" that's another perfect opportunity to begin a spiritual discussion with our sons. We want them to have the answers they're looking for, so sometimes we have to plow through our hesitation and find something reasonable to say when the questions start.

Second, we are usually the ones who haul their bodies to church on Sunday mornings. Maybe we had Sunday school lessons or learned the catechism, and we want to pass a religious foundation on to them. It's usually mom who is the conscience of the family and understands that sometimes, when life beats you up, you've got to have God to hold on to. During tough times, we have looked for answers. Sometimes those answers came from Sunday school lessons learned long ago, like "kill them with kindness, thereby heaping flaming coals upon their heads," and sometimes they came from believing that God is real and good and is there to help us. We want our boys to be prepared for life. Getting them to church helps them accomplish that.

Third (and this may make many fathers mad), perhaps our faces reflect the humility of God a bit more clearly than men's. This humility is born from the fact that most women are forced to adapt and change more frequently than men. We get pregnant and gain sixty pounds during our pregnancy, give birth, and then lose the weight. We work, take maternity leave, then go back to our jobs or become stay-at-home moms after having been a working woman all of our adult lives. I added up the average number of changes that mothers go through over their lifetimes and calculated that we undergo a major life change about every three years. Having to adapt to change makes us malleable but tough. Women tend to face their difficulties head-on because we know that enduring bruises in silence doesn't work as well as talking about them. Our sons see this. They see us bend and shift and communicate our thoughts and feelings. They watch how we respond: Do we turn to friends? Do we pick up the phone? Do we pray? They watch because they instinctively know that we can show them what to do when they are in trouble.

Faith Takes Him Deeper—and You Are His Guide

For many sons, curiosity can begin as early as age three. A hamster dies and they mourn, asking, what will happen to Slinky now? Will he rot in the ground, fly to another planet, or evaporate into the clouds? Even preschool-aged boys will surprise you with their thought processes, and will question more abstract concepts like what lies beyond the stars or how can God be real if He's invisible. Other boys might begin this intellectual quest around second grade, or the moment they experience hardships, like being bullied or watching parents divorce. If a young boy's world starts to crack around the edges, he begins to see that trouble sits next to happiness. How close will the two get? he wonders. And how will he cope?

We have to keep an eye out, because while boys see mom as the source of answers to their spiritual questions, this is also the time when they begin to worry about losing you. When they begin to realize that life brings pain as well as joy, they also then understand that their mother could get hurt, or even die. This can be terrifying, but many young boys are reticent to mention their fears out loud. So we mothers need to recognize that inside his tender little heart are worries that he can't articulate. That's why it is important that we take the lead in addressing spiritual issues; because he can't. We must have our radar up so that when fear or disappointment strike, we are ready to engage him with some answers about God and how He can help him weather the storms.

If we are ignorant, or afraid to address spiritual issues with our sons, they will turn to others to find solutions, and while that may be well and good in some situations, it may cause trouble for particularly vulnerable boys. They will be looking for answers, and they will find them. They might turn to coaches or teachers, but they might also turn to their friends. And some friends will have plenty of information to teach them that will make your hair stand on end. For instance, I have seen numerous teen boys who, when struggling with school, girlfriends, or home life, turn to friends for advice. Sometimes these friends don't have the boy's best interests in mind and their solutions will be more harmful than helpful, like offering drugs to help them "get through" the tough patches in life. So we mothers need to be there to offer help first. The most powerful thing that mothers can do is to give our sons solid emotional, intellectual, and spiritual roots.

Realizing that we are our son's spiritual mentor is daunting. We are his first experience of God, yet our first awareness of our own spiritual lives was long ago, so as adults we may feel confused about how to talk to our sons. What we must do is look at life through the lens of a little boy; think of him as someone pulling at your pant leg. He doesn't hear the homily we hear or the Bible lesson from the pew. He just sees his mom and makes some very simple decisions about God based on what you say and do. For sons of all ages, faith begins in that basic manner.

An Awareness of God Is Good for Boys

Kenny's mother taught him about God. Now in his forties, Kenny agreed to sit down with me in order to give me a glance into his relationship with his mother. Right after I thanked him for allowing me to interview him, he told me that he was nervous. Peculiar, I thought. Why would he be nervous? He wasn't sure, but I suspected that he was worried I would peel scabs from some old wounds. He was right.

Kenny told me right off the bat that he adored his mother. She was a teacher, very religious, and cared for anything that was breathing, especially if it limped. When he was growing up, creatures and folks of all ages came and went from their home. Usually, the family was never forewarned; his mother was always collecting needy folks. I probed for any tone of lingering resentment and I can honestly say that I couldn't find any. Certainly, if it had been there, Kenny had rid himself of it.

Kenny described his mother as boisterous, outgoing, and firm. She teased him frequently, and while he said that he liked her style of affection, I wasn't convinced. I could swear I heard his voice break when he told me some of the "jokes" she had cracked when he was only twelve. "Oh—you're just the family La-Z-Boy," she'd say, and then poke him in the side with a smile that said "you know I'm kidding—sort of."

I knew before I interviewed Kenny that he was a man with a strong Catholic faith. He spoke openly about it and seemed excited to discuss this part of his life. Equally important, he seemed proud to tell me that he had gained his faith from his mother. As a child, Kenny's mother regularly took him to her charismatic Protestant church. By the age of fourteen, Kenny said he'd had enough, so he stopped going. His friends didn't go to Sunday school, his sports events were frequently held on Sundays, and he just thought that his mom was too old-fashioned making him go. And after a while, he said, he began to doubt God. As a young teen, he became aware of the suffering in the world and began to question two things. First, he wondered if God was real. Second, if He was real, why wouldn't He do anything about all the starving people in the world? Because of this, he told me, he "left religion and God behind" until he was well into his twenties.

His mother, Caroline, continued to take folks into their home throughout his teen years. She told him that Jesus would have helped them, so she wanted to do the same. One might think that a teenage boy would have sneered at his mother's behavior and beliefs, but Kenny didn't. Even though he had cast aside church and religion, on some level he knew that this was important to his mother and that helping those who were less fortunate was the right thing to do. I could sense the pride he felt at his mother's example of faith and kindness toward others.

Learning that he left the church at fourteen, I was curious how he had circled back around to it. He immediately told me that his mother helped him find his way back to God. Since I had assumed that he left church because his mother had burned him out on religion (this was my bias, I later realized), how was it that she helped him find his way back? What did she do to transfer spiritual anchoring onto her son?

"You see," Kenny began, his tone turning abruptly somber, "when I was ten, my sister was diagnosed with cancer. It was hell for my mother. For years, my sister lived through chemo; she lost her hair and she endured a lot of physical pain.

"My dad couldn't handle her illness. All of the responsibility fell onto my mother. I felt so bad; I could see how painful it was for her but I couldn't do anything about it. But what I also saw was that after years of caring for other people, having her own daughter get sick forced her to love on a different level."

Kenny's voice grew quieter and harder to hear. It was clear he loved his sister and I could sense that even though she'd died many years before our conversation, talking about her death was difficult for him. I offered to end the conversation but he insisted that we could continue. I was glad, because as a mother, I wanted to know how his mother had gotten through such anguish. My questions became selfish because that's what happens to us mothers. We want to know that we could survive, if the unthinkable happened to us, God forbid. So we ask those who have gone through the hell before to pass on their survival skills. And I could tell that Kenny's mother definitely had those. Seeing her skills in action had changed his life, and little did I know that hearing her story would change mine as well.

"I will never forget the last day of my sister's life. She was only twenty-one," he began. "She was in the hospital and my mother held vigil over her. I didn't hear my mother complain, oddly enough. I would have thought that she would have screamed at God, but I don't think she did. Just moments before my sister died, she got out of bed and stood up in front of my mother. I watched as my mother wrapped her arms around her and told her goodbye."

Kenny became silent again. I imagined his mother holding his sister and I imagined myself doing the same to one of my own precious daughters. Would I have had the strength to hold my daughter in her dying moments and not scream at God? Even the thought made my heart race. Part of me believed that I would go crazy if one of my children died.

I said nothing and waited for Kenny to continue. "My mother sat back down and my sister slipped away. I can honestly say that the look on my mother's face was one of complete calm. Her skin, her eyes, everything about her exuded peace. I think what she was really doing was handing my sister over to Jesus. Yes, she was saying goodbye, but I believe that in her mind, she needed to literally take hold of my sister and then hand her over."

As a physician, I've witnessed a lot of death, and I can honestly say that I have found many deaths to be "holy" experiences. My own father lay in a coma for several days before he died. Just before he took his last breath a nurse saw him open his eyes with a startled look. He was looking at the ceiling. She was so taken aback that she asked, "Wally, what do you see?" She said later that the look on his face revealed that he was seeing something beautiful. I have had children with terminal cancer lie in hospital beds and tell me that angels came to their rooms at night. One twelve-year-old boy said to his mother, who wasn't particularly religious, that Jesus had come to him in the night and told him that everything was going to be okay and that he didn't need to worry about death or his mother. The next day he told his mother that she needn't fear for him. Because of these experiences, Kenny's story felt very familiar to me and it was easy to believe him when he told me about his mother's peaceful posture as his sister was dying.

At some point in our lives, each of us wonders about the afterlife. We ponder the existence of heaven and ask ourselves if God is real, because we need to know what happens when we die. We want to know if the spiritual world is real or if it's just a figment of our imaginations. We want answers because we want a reason to hope. I highly recommend Dr. Eben Alexander's book, *Proof of Heaven* (a national bestseller), because it gives us a peek into the afterlife. It is a book offering profound hope because Dr. Alexander's testimony confirms the reality of heaven.

"That's when I went back to God," Kenny said. "I was in my thirties by then. My mother never told me that I should go back to church or anything, but as an adult man, when I saw the strength that she had as my sister died, I knew that the God she believed in was real. My father didn't have that kind of faith and he couldn't handle my sister's death. Witnessing the difference in the responses of my father and my mother made me realize that what my mother was onto with her faith wasn't 'pie-in-the-sky.' It was real and I wanted it. But I wasn't comfortable going back to the church that I grew up in, so I started going to Catholic Mass. I've never stopped."

Numerous studies over the years have revealed that a belief in God helps keep our sons on the right path. In 2001, the National Survey of Youth and Religion research project, headed by Dr. Christian Smith of the University of Notre Dame, was started. The first findings were released in 2005 in *Soul Searching: The Religious and Spiritual Lives of American Teenagers,* written by Christian Smith and Melinda Lundquist Denton. After the release of *Soul Searching,* the study continued. More of their research was released in 2008 in *A Research Report of the National Survey of Youth and Religion.* Below is a summary of some of their findings with regard to the influence of faith in God and religion on the behavior of teens. The studies found that faith improves a teen's chances of staying away from all of the high-risk stuff in life: drugs, drinking, sexual activity, and truancy. And having faith improves their self-esteem and lowers the risk of depression.

Consider the following startling numbers about teens who have a faith in God, as reported in their studies:

- 54 percent of teens devoted to God say they are "very happy" while only 29 percent of disengaged say they are "very happy"
- 47 percent of religious teens think about the meaning of life often while 26 percent nonreligious teens think about it
- 1 percent of religious teens got drunk every few weeks during the past year while 10 percent of nonreligious kids got drunk during the same period

- 3 percent of devoted teens get C's, D's, and F's while 14 percent of nonreligious kids get the same
- Of kids who occasionally smoke marijuana, 1 percent are devoted teens, 13 percent are nonreligious
- Parents who report teens are rebellious: 3 percent are devoted, 17 percent nonreligious
- 95 percent of devoted teens feel it is important to wait until marriage for sex; 24 percent nonreligious believe the same
- 3 percent of devoted teens believe that it is okay to have sex if one is emotionally ready; 56 percent of nonreligious believe the same

When it comes to a mother's relationship with her son, faith helps there, too.

- 88 percent of devoted teens feel extremely or very close to their mothers while 66 percent of nonreligious feel the same
- 80 percent of devoted teens say they get along extremely well or very well with their mothers; 51 percent of nonreligious feel the same
- 93 percent of devoted teens feel that parents love and accept them a lot for who they are; 74 percent of nonreligious feel the same

In addition, an excellent study reported in the prestigious *Journal of Adolescence* in April of 2007 found similar results. "Adolescent Risk Behaviors and Religion: Findings from a National Study" concluded that their "findings demonstrate that religiosity, measured as perceived importance of religion, attendance in worship services, and participation in religious youth group, significantly contributed to explaining variation in six youth risk behaviors (smoking, alcohol use, truancy, sexual activity, marijuana use, and depression). Increased religious perception and increased religious behaviors are generally good predictors of decreased youth risk behaviors. Of course, like all youth, religious youth do engage in risk behavior, but the likelihood of their involvement in risk behaviors is less than those of less religiously active youth."

Seeing this data may cause different reactions. It can make some of us feel guilty; if only we took our kids to church more, knew more of the Bible, we'd be better moms. Or the reverse could be true. Some might say that such studies are contrived by religious people with an agenda to push. But I have seen the studies and looked at the figures and am convinced that allowing our sons to express their spiritual nature and explore a relationship with God is good for them. We all know the bad stuff out there, just waiting to influence our boys in the wrong way: violent video games, music with lewd and demeaning lyrics, movies that send the wrong message about sex and violence, peer pressure from the wrong crowd, drugs and alcohol. From the time he is ten until he's twenty-five, we live with a simmering fear that our sons will fall into one of these destructive habits. (I use the age of twenty-five as the mark of true adulthood because we know that areas of a boy's brain aren't fully developed until his early twenties.) But I believe that good parenting can't come from fear; it comes from acting out of strength. For instance, we can see all of the dangers our sons face, but we also know that if we enable them to have a strong faith in God, we can help keep them on the right path. This is one way we can turn our fear into actionable strength.

Interestingly, if you look deeper into this data, you will find that the roots of spiritual development are strongest if they come from home. If it is our role to be the teachers, the nurturers of our sons' faith, the next reasonable question is: How do we do that? First, we have to realize that we set the model for our sons; if we don't have a spiritual life, chances are neither will he. If we declare a lack of faith, he will feel the same way. I believe it is our responsibility to leave the door open to our children to make their own choices. It is especially important in the realm of religion and spirituality. If you are religious, you can skip the lectures and live your faith in front of him because he already knows what you believe. He's now watching you to see your faith in action. You tell him it is important to be patient because God tells us to be? Terrific. Your son knows whether that's working for you or not. If it isn't, he's not so sure about God (or what He's teaching you). And if you tell him to pray for a friend in need, he's grateful for the thought, but whether he actually prays or not might depend upon how he sees the ways in which you use, and believe in, prayer.

The bottom line is, your little boy (or grown son) starts looking for God in you. He might be interested in learning about the God who is "out there," but as a small child, that's too abstract. He wants to know if God makes his mom a nicer person. Then, maybe, he'll try Him out. My best advice to moms who want to teach their sons about the character of God is to say less and do more. Here's the good news: Being God to your little boy or your teen son can change his life. It can literally keep him from going over the edge. That's what Jackson told me about his mother.

THE FACE OF GOD

I met Jackson at the Austin, Texas, airport. I jumped in his cab, barked out the address to my destination, and settled in to text some colleagues from the backseat. But when he started chatting, it was clear that he wasn't going to let me get my work done. He wanted to know how my day was going, if I'd been to Austin before, and where I was from. For some reason I buried my New Englander instincts to keep my eye on work and ignore his question. Instead, I decided to engage back. When I inquired about his day so far, he responded that he was glad to be alive. I am embarrassed to say that when I studied his ripped driver's seat and heard the axles clanking beneath me, I wondered why this man, steering what I guessed was his life's savings down the freeway, was so happy. So I asked him.

"Oh, missus," Jackson said, "I got a great life." He detailed the successful lives of his grown daughters, and his wife's rheumatic illness, which was improving, and did so with a tone of profound appreciation. My writer's curiosity took over and I asked him where he grew up and how he had come to have such an upbeat outlook on life. I really wanted to know what made this kind man tick.

"Oh," he began, clearly enjoying the opportunity to talk about himself, "I don't know if you want to know about that. It's pretty rough stuff." Now I had to know.

"I grew up in a really tough neighborhood up there in New York City. There was gangs, crack houses, and almost ev'ry night I heard guns shootin' when I went to sleep. I liked goin' to school cuz I got decent meals and saw some of my friends. I liked some of my teachers, but they couldn't do much teachin' cuz some of them kids were outa control, if ya know what I mean. They were troublemakers." Jackson drove slower down the freeway. I didn't mind, even though I might be late for my meeting. He told me about his sister getting sick and going to the hospital when she was ten and about his three brothers who slept in the double bed with him. Then I started to ask him some more specific questions, and I struck gold.

"So," I tentatively asked, "how did you survive so well? I mean, any boy in that situation could have completely gone over the edge— ended up addicted to drugs, killed in a gang—you know what I mean."

"Oh, that's easy," he answered. "My mama. She's my hero."

"Jackson" I said, "I'm researching mothers and sons. Would you mind telling me more about your mother and your relationship with her?" I thought that he was going to drive off the road, he responded so enthusiastically.

"Of course, missus, you ask me anything you want. My mama— she kept us alive. She still keeps us all goin'. My daughters, me, my brothers. She's eighty-two and she still spits nails."

I wanted to ask what she said to him, what opportunities she gave him, what was his dad like. I never got to because once Jackson started talking about his mother, he lit up like a Christmas tree. He oozed affection for her.

"My mama was one tough bird, let me tell you. As far back as I can remember, she made us go to church ev'ry Sunday and sometimes in the middle of the week, too. She didn't give us no choice—we just went. And we never crossed my mama, that's for sure. If we didn't do what she wanted us to do, we would get a beatin'."

"What do you mean she would give you a beating? Would she really hit you hard?" I held my breath and waited for his answer.

"Naw, my mama loved us kids. She never hit us; she just told us that she would give us a whuppin' if we didn't mind her. She just liked to talk, but we knew she didn't want us to cross her. No, sir."

Jackson veered back toward his churchgoing days. "My mama worked two, sometimes three jobs. I could see age taking over on her face. By the time she was thirty, she looked fifty. She worked hard for us kids. We didn't have a father, at least one that was around, but we knew that she wasn't going to let any of us go down the dark way. She told us that God had a plan for us. She told us that He was our daddy.

"When I was a little kid, that kinda talk confused me, but when I got older, I knew what she meant. God was her strength and she wanted us kids to know that, too. She made us learn our Bible lessons and asked us questions about Elijah, Abednego, and Meshach at the dinner table. I liked it cuz none of our friends got quizzed by their mamas. I felt that she knew we were smart and that God did, too. All my life my mama kept telling me, 'Don't you go do stupid stuff now. God's watchin' and he's got better plans for your mind, your skills. Don't you go disappointing me and God.'"

Jackson put his turn signal on and exited the freeway. I didn't want to go to my meeting. I asked if we could keep driving and talk just a little longer. "I got all the time in the world, miss, when it comes to talking about my mama."

"Didn't you resent your mother pushing you when you became a teenager?" He looked at me as though I were speaking Latvian.

"Resent my mama? Are you crazy, miss? My mama loved us. She loved Jesus and her church family. If she hadn't taught us that God is real and good, we might not be alive! We would have all ended up like many of our friends. Dead. In prison. Dealing drugs. My mama fought hard for us kids cuz she loved us so much. When she told us about Jesus, we believed her cuz he gave her jobs, he gave us money, he gave my mama the spirit to keep going."

I was dying to meet Jackson's mother. She had something that I wanted. She was a survivor, a woman of a faith so deep it had saved her kids, according to Jackson. He told me that he went into the military and rose up through the ranks over twenty-three years. His brother found his way to college and none of his siblings had ended up in gangs or gone "the dark way."

My final question: So, what is your relationship with your mother like now?

"My mama, she's the queen of the family. She teaches my kids about Jesus and I tell you that if God wore lipstick, He'd wear the shade my mama does, she's that close to him. My girls are crazy 'bout her. I got three daughters and they're very smart. One's in med school, one's got two kids and a nice husband, and one's working for a big company up in the North. Yep, they're good girls. Every time they come home to Austin, they always go to see their grandmother cuz they love her. They know she's tough and that she loves them. And you know what, missus? They all go to church, too, cuz of her."

I thanked Jackson for the privilege of entering into his life for a brief time. Though I will never meet his mother, she changed me. She challenged me to be wiser and to understand that every time our sons look at us, they just might be making some decisions about God.

FAITH GIVES HIM A DEEPER IDENTITY

Growing up in America in the twenty-first century looks glamorous on the outside, but the truth is, it can be tough for our boys—particularly those who are lucky enough to come from a family with comfortable means. As much as we mothers struggle to have a solid, healthy sense of our value and worth, our sons do so tenfold. Having a lovely home, giving our son a car, making sure that he has the best hockey coach, paying for private school or a college education—all of it can be a blessing, but it can also be a curse for our boys.

Young boys think pragmatically. If they are unhappy, they feel that all they need to do is buy something, eat something, or go somewhere and their happiness will return. In the short term, this can work. But as adults, we know this: Those beautiful homes and that money in our bank account brings only very limited happiness. Every one of us struggles at some point wondering what life is really about and what it is that gives us our deepest joy. Many turn to faith to find these answers. And in an increasingly material world, we owe it to our sons to give them a guided tour through their spiritual dimension.

Every mother makes laborious decisions when it comes to raising our son. We think hard about the school our son should attend, what sports he should play, and which friends are good for him to be around and which are not. We can be consumed by every detail, every dollar spent. That's how we are wired: We love deeply and we worry passionately. But it's important to step back from the details of our days and take a look at the grand scheme of our sons' lives. Before they grow old enough to leave home, we must ask ourselves what character qualities we want to nurture and what we want to teach them about faith and God.

To figure out what we believe, we can start by asking ourselves the big questions. First, do I believe that God exists? If I do believe so, on what grounds do I believe? Do I have evidence? Once you establish this fundamental premise, push yourself further for answers (because your son will ask questions). If you believe God exists, then you must ask, what difference does that fact make in your life? Should it make a difference? Then find out what you believe God's character to be like. Young boys are wonderfully curious and adventurous in their thinking, so you need to be able to discuss deep matters with your son.

If you live in a religious home, be sure to be crystal clear with your son about the fundamental tenets of your faith. Teach him who the prophets were and tell him stories of the great forefathers. Many mothers are squeamish about telling some of the more gruesome stories in the Old Testament. When I was teaching our son about the underdog David slaying the giant Goliath, I was upset because he didn't want to know about David—all he wanted to hear about was how long it took to get Goliath's head chopped off. I wanted, of course, to drill home the moral of the story—that God helped the righteous, the underdog—and my son wanted to hear all about the gory details. So I indulged him and he paid attention, and we talked about the stories in their entirety.

We need to remember that young boys process information differently than we do and that's fine. There are points that they will initially miss, but we need to plant those seeds anyway. As they mature, the stories will retell themselves in their developing minds and take on different meaning.

If you follow the Christian faith, be ready to help him understand who the disciples were, why Christ came to earth, how he was born, and most important, why he was born. Yes, you can leave your son's religious education to pastors, priests, or rabbis, but this is important material. So you be his teacher, too.

The truth is, there are a lot of questions that we can't answer, but that's okay. The great mystery of faith for any of us is that we can only know things incompletely. We should teach our sons from a position of strength and boldness, not from the fear that we don't know everything. I encourage you to dig for your own answers rather than settling for others' answers. I consider C. S. Lewis the perfect example of this: He was someone who refused to accept others' beliefs about God, faith, and religion. When he was an atheist, he learned everything that he could about God in order to prove that He wasn't real. That's how this brilliant man ultimately became a devout Christian and scholar: He pushed himself to find answers and found some completely unexpected ones. We need to search for our own answers, and then pass them along to our sons. We can't make them believe, but when we present our case, passing along the answers we've found in our own lives, we encourage them in two ways. First, we show them the importance of challenging ideas and beliefs and searching for answers on our own terms. Second, we give them a belief system to either choose or reject.

The remarkable thing about sons is that, when it comes to very important topics like God and faith, they want to hear what their mothers have to say. Some information they internalize and incorporate into their own belief system and some they hold at a distance to decide upon later. Since your son is scouring you for clues as to what you think—and don't think—about God, be clear about what you teach him. Asking questions and finding answers is not only intellectually stimulating; it is fun. Talking about your faith, and your reasons for having it (or not having it), will lead to some of the greatest conversations you will ever have with your boy.

Be a Bold Mom, Not a Wimp

I have witnessed a trend evolving in young mothers that disturbs me: Many of them refuse to trust their instincts. A couple of decades ago, mothers could be overly bossy and controlling. Some of us grew up with mothers like this and we determined that we would never be so overbearing. This is a good thing, but in trying to avoid being too repressive, many of us have gone to the opposite extreme. We are so afraid to make mistakes that we don't listen to our gut when it tells us to act. For instance, I have had mothers tell me that they don't want their son to go to a friends' house and watch a movie but then immediately ask me if I thought they should let him go. I ask these mothers, "Why are you asking me? You just told me what you want. You don't want him to see the movie. So, say no."

Others have told me that they want to take their sons to church but that their husband doesn't approve. It's an issue they feel strongly about, but when I ask if they have challenged their husbands on it, they say no. When I ask why, they respond that they don't want to make waves in the family.

Repeatedly, mothers pull away from acting according to their instincts. We should never ignore our instincts, because they help us make better decisions. Mothers are uniquely wired to love, protect, and guide our sons, and listening to our gut is one of the most important things that we can do for them as we raise them. If we, who know our sons better than anyone, refuse to do what is right and good for them, how will they learn? The short answer is, they won't. I fear that many mothers have become so afraid of doing the wrong thing and thereby alienating their sons, that we fail to do many of the right things that will strengthen our bond with them. Our instincts are sometimes our only guide and we must listen to them.

When it comes to religion, we can become almost paralyzed by self-doubt. We not only fear teaching our sons the wrong thing; we fear having them feel as though they are odd or prudish at school because they may believe different things about God than their friends do. We desperately want them to fit in with friends and we certainly don't want them to feel like outcasts among them. Life for kids is hard enough, we reason. So we often forgo making them attend catechism or youth groups because we don't want them to become the "geeky" kid. To whatever extent religion can turn our sons into awkward kids, we won't have any of it.

And of course, there are other worries. What if we teach them to have faith in God and they rebel? What if we teach them the tenets of our faith and we don't get the facts straight? What if, as I've just said, we make them go to church and their friends make fun of them and then they feel isolated at school? But—we must stop worrying and start acting. The best way to get away from fretting is to begin doing something. When it comes to faith, the first thing that we must do for our sons is to be clear about what we want them to believe and what we don't want them to believe. And to do this, we have to be clear about our own faith.

Many mothers I meet decide that they want their children to grow up with the freedom to choose their own religion. I understand this, but the truth is, your kids will choose anyway—whether you want them to or not—because faith is an intensely personal thing. Every son grows up and makes his own choices; from the type of pants he wears, to whom he will marry and where he will live. Decisions about his faith are the same. At some point, what you believe won't be enough for him. He will need to know deep in his soul what he thinks about God. In the meantime, though, you must give him the choice to believe. Boys who grow up knowing nothing about God have nothing to choose from. If they don't know the difference between Catholicism, Judaism, Mormonism, and the Muslim faith, don't have any details at all about different religions, they end up with a giant vacuum to be filled, and no clue how to do so. It's very much like taking a ten-year-old American boy to downtown Prague and telling him that he can go anywhere he'd like. He would look at you with a blank stare. "But Mom," he'd say, "I've never been to Prague before and don't even know the street names." So it is for boys who grow up without any understanding of the tenets of your faith.

Exercise God

I speak to many parents around the country and most want to know what they can do to boost their child's self-esteem. Mothers, in particular, want to know what they can do to make their kids feel better about themselves and have healthy self-confidence. Some of the answers are obvious: We figure out what our sons are good at—whether it's sports, or art, or music—and then sign them up for classes to show them their own talent and help it grow. We are planners and doers and we want to make life work out well for our sons. Once we recognize their skills, we pour our money and energy into developing those talents. We drive them to the rink at 4 A.M., sit at the back of the bus on those weekend rugby matches, and then, of course, we drag them on college tours with the prospect of underwriting their choice, just to help them take what we hope is the best path possible toward their future.

But, as discussed, when we believe that our son gains self-confidence primarily through achieving certain goals, we fail him. The truth is, doing well academically, artistically, or athletically only helps boys know that they can perform; it doesn't make them feel valuable as human beings. What does make them feel valuable? Love and affirmation from us. Physical affection, a long-suffering listening ear, a readiness to talk at 3 A.M., an ability to let them go through their own changes. Those things show our sons that we love who they are, not what they do. When we support their talents, but withhold the other things, we raise high performers and achievers, but that's it. Many young men grow up to make a lot of money and land prestigious jobs and so look quite successful from the outside. But many of these men end up lonely and wanting, feeling that they are loved for what they've accomplished. How can any son—whether he is a child or an adult—have a healthy sense of self if all he knows is that his mother likes the way he "succeeds" (that is, performs)?

And don't we mothers feel the same way? We too want to know

that God loves us whether we succeed, fail, get fat, or become exhausted or depressed. And we especially need that comfort in the moments when we feel that we may be the worst mothers in the universe. We want to know deep in our souls that someone loves us just because we exist. Similarly our sons want to know—need to know—that if they did nothing else for the rest of their lives but sat in a closet, we would adore them. We must exercise the love and complete acceptance that God gave us toward our sons, so that they can understand exactly how unconditional our love for them is.

Many of us mothers say that we love our sons unconditionally, but the truth is, we're pretty poor at it. We may say that we are being loving when we push them to achieve more and more, but what we're really communicating to them is that the only way they will meet our approval is to ante up. Of course we want our sons to be successful. But the expression of our love to our sons must never come only with their successes. Sadly, I hear many boys say that the only time they feel approval or love from their parents is when they are on the football or soccer field. We mothers may feel that we are being supportive with our sons when we show up at their athletic events or concerts—indeed, we are being supportive—but we must be very careful to make sure that we express love to our sons when they perform well, poorly, or not at all. A son needs to know that he is loved regardless of what he does.

When so much of our interaction with our sons revolves around their performance or schoolwork, I encourage mothers to intentionally find opportunities to show their love to their sons apart from these. Henry's mother, Linda, was good at this. Henry was an awkward boy who was a mediocre soccer player and struggled academically in school. One might look at him and think that he had a poor self-esteem, but in fact, he felt very good about himself and about his life. His mother single-handedly raised Henry after his father divorced her when he was two. He never knew his father and what little he did know was positive, he said. His father played semipro baseball for a few years and Henry thought that was pretty cool. But, his mother told him, life became tough for his dad (though his mother never gave details) and he couldn't cope with family life.

When Henry was eight, he was in a near-fatal car accident. His mother was not in the car and learned of the accident over the phone. For three weeks Henry stayed in the intensive care unit and his mother thought she had lost him many times during those weeks. Her life consisted of her and Henry. Her parents had passed away and she was an only child. If Henry died, she believed she would lose her mind.

During his stay, Linda told me that she prayed her heart out. "I never really knew if God was real or not," she confided, "but I was desperate. I didn't know what to do or where to turn. I just poured my heart out to God and asked for help."

Over the weeks that she leaned on God, Linda said that she felt his presence. She had others pray, too, and after Henry came out of his coma, she believed that God heard her desperation and answered her prayers.

When Linda took Henry home from the hospital, he had some minor memory issues and needed help with his speech, but within a few months he was back to himself. But it was when I spoke to her a few years after the incident that her words really struck me.

"I can't believe that after I came home, how quickly I felt pressure to get life back to normal. I wanted Henry to ski, play baseball, or go to soccer camp. Maybe that was how I could make pretend that the accident never happened. But it did. And I never wanted to forget the greatest two lessons of my life."

I asked her what those lessons were, and how she kept from jumping back aboard the "crazy train."

"The first lesson I learned was that God is here. Okay, he's invisible—but until Henry was in the ICU, I never paid any attention to him. I'll never do that again. The second lesson was that Henry is a gift to me. He's not something I need to show off or shine. He's my son—my son. And I always want him to know that he is the apple of my eye because he is mine. Does that make sense?" she asked.

Her words made more than good sense. They showed great wisdom that we can all learn from. Linda simply loved Henry. She took him camping when other kids went to soccer tournaments and taught him to pitch a tent and fish. If he got a bad grade in school, she took it in stride and never made him feel as though he disappointed her.

Linda continues to treat Henry, now fifteen years old, as if he had fallen from heaven itself. And the fact that he landed in her home is all that matters to her. From Henry's perspective, he knows why his mother loves him. She loves him because he is.

Putting yourself in your son's shoes can be an enormous eye-opener when making decisions about how to parent. Not only will it help you make better decisions, but it will pull you closer to your son and, most important, genuinely build his self-confidence and sense of value.

Practicing a faith in God is not only good for our boys; it can be a lifesaver for us mothers. Being a mother can be a lonely and tough job—especially for single moms. Acknowledging this need for faith is hard for those of us who want to be strong and self-sufficient, but who are we trying to kid? We are mothers to some incredibly great boys, boys who need a whole lot of advice, love, and support. And in order to give those things to our sons, we need the same. The best way to give advice is to have received it from a wiser person. The best way to love our sons better is to have been extraordinarily loved ourselves. And the very best way to support our sons is to know what it feels like to depend on someone and receive support. God, I believe, offers all of this and more to any of us mothers willing to take a risk and ask Him for it.

CHAPTER 6

Give Him an Ax

Strength. Ability. Maturity. Your son wants them all, starting from the time he is a toddler. Your job, as his ardent supporter, teacher, and number-one fan is to make sure that he embraces his strengths at different stages of his life. As he grows, your job is to draw out his natural abilities and then help him develop them so that he can feel independent and competent as he matures.

So what does it mean to "give him an ax"? This metaphor represents the times throughout his life when you bestow upon him your "blessing" to be more independent. When you do this, you will give him tools (sometimes literal ones, other times cognitive or emotional ones) to understand his own capabilities. Then you must help him exercise those capabilities in a way that reinforces his independence. This may be as simple as giving him an Erector Set when he is five or six and letting him put it together on his own. When he cries in frustration to you that he just can't get it, you send him back to the table to try again. By doing this, he hears from you that he is capable of figuring things out.

When he is in junior high, this may mean giving him a lawn mower and telling him to ask neighbors if they need their lawn cut. You will literally put a machine in his hands that could cause him bodily harm, but you show him how to use it. You teach him to respect its power. Then you add that you have confidence in his physical strength to handle the machine carefully and in his mental maturity to be cautious.

As we challenge our sons with new tools, it is important that we continue to teach them how to use them. It would be foolish to just hand our son an ax and say, "Go cut some wood." Our job is to give the tool and then instruct them in how to wield it. Many women may not know how to swing an ax, so they find a competent instructor and have him or her show their son what to do. If the "tool" you give your son is a less tangible one—like helping him overcome stage fright during performances—you talk him through what he may feel during the performance or what he is worried may happen during the show; then you challenge him to focus on the performance, not on the people watching him, give him tips about decreasing his anxiety, and remind him that if he does forget a line, it's okay. Only then do you put him on the stage.

Such moments are critical for a son as he develops through boyhood and then into manhood, because they help him understand two things. He learns that he is strong and that he can have control over his life, his impulses, his feelings. Mothers must teach sons that yes, they can be in charge, even in a culture that tells them that they aren't expected to be, a culture that in fact readily assumes they are *not* in control.

The trickiest part for us mothers is making sure that the challenges we give our sons are age appropriate. Often a boy's desires to do things independently are way ahead of his abilities. When he's a child, his brain, body, and psyche have not fully grown and he knows it, even as he wants things he's not ready for, including independence. This can lead to feelings of frustration for him. Every boy needs a sense that he can be in charge of something, even when he is only two years old. Think of the first temper tantrum that your son had. He threw himself on the floor of the grocery store not to embarrass you (well, maybe not) but to protest your authority. He wanted something. You told him no. He couldn't reach it himself. The frustration between wanting to take control and his body—and you—not allowing it made him want to explode. He cried, screamed, and flailed all because he wanted you to know that he needed power and independence.

It is no different when he is sixteen. He has temper tantrums at that age, too, but they are louder and fiercer. He no longer throws himself onto the floor, but maybe he grabs the car keys and storms out, slams his bedroom door, or hurls insults at you. The frustration he feels at sixteen is the same as what he felt at two, but it is more intense. It's important for you to understand that these episodes are completely normal and have a sound psychological foundation, because then you won't take his behavior personally. Developmentally, boys progress through stages where their minds mature before their bodies. At three, they want to pedal a two-wheeler because they know that "big kids" ride two-wheelers, but their nervous system hasn't quite caught up to the point where riding one is possible. When he is thirteen, he wants to play M-rated video games because he knows that "mature" guys play them, but when he does, he has nightmares. At seventeen, he wholeheartedly believes that he can stay home alone for the weekend and ensure that no uninvited guests come over to your home. Alas, he is usually wrong and some very serious trouble can follow.

As his mother, you understand all this and, in order to be accommodating and make his life a little less frustrating, you give him choices. I hear mothers tell their eighteen-month-old that yelling is not appropriate and that he should choose to use his quiet voice. I hear them offer their six-year-old the option between playing basketball or trying the violin or the piano. As mothers, we hope the opportunity to make decisions will allow our sons to feel more in control, a bit more adultlike. Sometimes these tactics work, but often they don't. Young boys really have a hard time knowing what they want, or what is best for them. Sometimes giving them a choice only frustrates them more. So what is a good mom to do?

ARMING YOUR SON FOR LIFE

Giving sons a sense of power and control is very important, so we need to be thoughtful and deliberate in doing so. We don't want to frustrate our sons more (that makes life harder for both of us) but we want to give them an increasing sense of independence as they grow. Sometimes there are choices we make as mothers, made out of love certainly, that can unintentionally cripple our sons emotionally.

As our sons pass through the early elementary years into the middle school years, they live with a strong internal tension. They depend on us and want our comfort, but they don't want anyone to know it. At some point in their development, they even try to convince *themselves* that they don't need us. During those early years, boys get the external message that leaning on mom is a sign of weakness and in order to be a man, they need to break away from us. Regardless of what we think, or what we try to tell them, this feeling is pervasive among their peers. Some young boys don't like their moms to drive them to school; they want to ride the bus, proving to their friends that they don't need Mother hovering in the background. When it comes to sports, they want us to be their number-one fan, but they don't want us to be Team Mom or like us to always be talking to the coach about their games. That kind of involvement from mom can be enormously humiliating for sons. Our intentions in involving ourselves in our son's activities may be purely affirmative, but this doesn't mean that our sons will perceive them as such.

I have seen numerous mothers at their son's soccer or baseball games yelling at the opposing team or scolding coaches for not playing their son enough. I have seen mothers finish their son's school projects or lie to the principal that their son was not at a party drinking and therefore should be able to play on a football team, when he clearly had been, in spite of knowing that drinking was against the team rules. When we do these things for our sons, we might feel as though we're helping them, but really, we are doing the opposite. When we cover for them, we communicate that they need *us* to fight their battles, that they cannot depend on themselves. If we aren't careful, these feelings can persist into manhood.

As hard as it is for us to swallow, as our sons mature they will depend more easily on their fathers than they will us. The bottom line is, a son will perceive his father as stronger than his mother. He wants—and needs—to see his father as stronger because that's his role model for his own impending adulthood. He doesn't want to think of his mother as stronger, because this threatens his masculinity. He wants to be stronger than his mother in many ways—either physically, emotionally, or intellectually—and he needs this for healthy ego development. This doesn't mean that he is chauvinistic; rather, it means that he needs to identify with his male father more than with his female mother in order to figure out his own masculinity. Mom's love and protection were all well and good when he was a baby, but the minute he perceives himself as "different" from mom—that is, male, not female—when his mother bails him out, it makes him feel enormously weak. (Having his father bail him out is tough for him, too, but he feels much worse when his mother does.)

The Mistakes We Make When We Mean to Love

When Tim was a senior in high school, he played varsity soccer. His mother, Brenda, worked part-time as an accountant, but when she wasn't working, she was supporting the team. She drove to all the events, brought food for the team, and cheered loudly at every game. She prided herself on knowing all the players. She also spoke frequently of the great relationship she enjoyed with Tim, saying that the two were very close.

Tim went out one Saturday night and partied with his friends. A few of his team members were at the party and they all had some drinks. Tim got drunk and called his folks at midnight asking for a ride home because he didn't want to drive. The next morning, Brenda told him how proud she was of him that he called for a ride. When Tim got to school Monday morning, his soccer coach approached Tim and told him that he and the other team members who had been drinking at the party were suspended from the team for two weeks. That evening, when Tim got home and told Brenda what the coach had done, she hit the roof. She phoned the coach and insisted that Tim play. He had simply been acting like a normal teen, she said, and after all, no one got in trouble and no one got hurt. He was a good kid. What was the big deal?

The coach felt so bullied by Brenda that he gave in and let Tim and the other partying team members play. I spoke with Tim shortly after the incident and I could feel his embarrassment over what his mother had done. He was seventeen years old and he watched his mother manipulate the coach and disregard the rules (rules to which Tim had agreed when he joined the team). He also received two dangerous messages that Brenda had never intended: *You* can't handle consequences, so you need Mom to get rid of them. And the coach's rule doesn't apply to you, even though you understood it and agreed to it. These kinds of lessons are the last ones we should be imparting on our sons' impressionable teenage minds.

Let's examine what this scenario would have looked like if Brenda had responded in a healthy way. What if, instead of coddling her almost grown son, she had given him an ax to use on his own behalf? She could have said, "Tim, you're a man and this is life. You can deal with the consequences of your choices." He would have had a fit, probably yelled about how stupid his coach was, but when it was over, you can bet that he would have learned a powerful lesson: I need to start acting like a grown-up. And I can. You can bet that lesson would have helped Tim mature into a better student in college, a better worker at his future job—and a better husband and father.

Lana also made the mistake of protecting her son, Richard, from experiencing the consequences of his behavior. With the best of intentions, she, like Brenda, wanted to preserve her son's good reputation. But she did this one too many times.

Richard was shy and introverted. He had a few guy friends but mostly hovered on the periphery of many circles of friendship. When he was sixteen he started dating a girl and Lana was thrilled. Richard fell hard for this girl. He spent every evening texting or calling her. On weekends, the two were inseparable. Being close to her son, and excited about the fact that he was dating, Lana spoke frequently to Richard about his relationship. She asked how he felt and encouraged him to be a gentleman to his girlfriend. Soon she started to cross boundaries without realizing it. She was so excited to see her son happy that she inadvertently projected her own hopes onto him. In her mind, she had the two of them getting married, and began pushing them to commit to a more serious relationship than either was ready to have. She encouraged them to spend more time together and coached Richard on how to express his feelings. Unfortunately for Richard, she made the mistake that many enthusiastic mothers make, perceiving her son to be far more mature than he actually was. He related to his girlfriend as a sixteen-year-old, but Lana encouraged him to act as though he were a grown man.

One day, Richard's girlfriend called it quits. Richard was crushed and Lana was furious. How dare this girl dump her son? While Richard holed up in his room, needing some alone time, Lana fumed downstairs. What could she do to remedy this? How could she restore her son's dignity, she wondered? She had an idea. She opened up Facebook and wrote on Richard's girlfriend's wall. She didn't ask Richard's permission before doing this (mistake number one), and she wrote publicly that Richard was too good to deserve to be dumped. She called the girl a few names and signed off.

You can imagine what happened. Richard's friends read the post; some of his guy friends chided him and some girls laughed at him, too, though some felt sorry for him. Not only did Richard undergo the pain of the breakup, but now he was humiliated in front of his friends. His mother's actions made him look, and feel, weak.

If we look back at Richard's relationship with his girlfriend, we can see where Lana made mistakes. First, she was emotionally overinvested in the outcome. She worried about him because he was shy and when he began dating, she was so excited that she projected her own enthusiasm onto her son. She should have sat back and allowed Richard to figure out how he felt rather than constantly convey to him how *she* felt and how she thought he should feel about the relationship.

Second, she really overstepped her boundaries. She jumped into the middle of his relationship and coached her son on what to do and when to do it. Certainly, mothers should give advice, but Richard didn't ask Lana for hers. It is best for us mothers to watch and wait and then give our opinion when it's needed, rather than take over right from the beginning. Her intentions were good but she was far too aggressive.

Third, Lana spoke for her son; she didn't let him speak. She had no business writing on his Facebook wall and she had no business saying mean things about his girlfriend. This was supremely embarrassing for Richard. We must always remember to act like parents, not friends to our kids. By writing on his girlfriend's Facebook wall, she spoke for him just like one of his friends might have done. Every mother is tempted to act as her son's friend in order to stay emotionally close. We fear that if we act like adults then our sons will feel distant from us and they might feel that we don't understand them. But acting like their peers always backfires.

Lana emasculated her son at an intensely low point in his life because she felt protective of him (this is normal) and she wanted revenge (this is a normal feeling, too). Her mistake came when she *acted* on her impulses. Her behavior taught Richard two very harmful life lessons: 1) You can't speak up for yourself and 2) you need Mom around to help you with your relationship issues. Moms, many times, we simply need to back off. Be there for your son *if* he wants to talk. Look at his Facebook account, but *never* write on his wall or those of his friends.

When we prevent them from experiencing consequences or negative situations, run interference for them, or rationalize to ourselves why they need us to intervene, advise, and protect, we create an unhealthy dependency that will affect them for a long time. Sometimes they need to endure punishment or get through a difficult time in order to grow and understand themselves better. By backing off, we hand them their own power. And the great news is, backing off isn't terribly hard, if you know a couple of secrets.

AXES COME IN DIFFERENT SHAPES AND SIZES

First, regardless of his age, give your son physical challenges. Boys respond very well to demands of this kind because anything they can master physically makes them feel tough and strong. One of the best and easiest ways to do this is to give your son chores. Have him do yard work on a regular basis or help you out around the house by doing dishes or taking out the trash. Tell him that you need his help.

He may whine or grumble, but don't pay attention. Make him help you in the garden, ask him to go the grocery store for you, or you can opt to do what I did with my own son: Ask him to start supper. By doing this, my son quickly grew into a terrific cook. When he was old enough, he would buy the groceries (with my credit card), bring them home, and start dinner, because sometimes I'd have to work late. This was not only fun for me; it will make him a terrific husband one day. So be creative with your son when you look for work for him to do. Don't limit him to traditional male jobs. You would be surprised how many ways there are for your son to use his physical abilities. And remember, asking him to do physical work isn't punishment; approach him with it as if you are asking him to do a favor, because you know how strong and capable he is.

Second, as your son matures, you need to communicate to him that he can do many things without your help, because—and I know that this hurts—in an older son's eyes, needing your help means that he's a wimp. When he is three, having you help him cut with scissors is acceptable, but when he is thirteen, having you jump in and do his homework for him at his first sign of confusion makes him feel inadequate. I know that many schools are so demanding that many kids need a parent's help. I don't agree with this. Having mom or dad routinely help causes a young man to feel that he can't accomplish things on his own. Needing mom and dad's help every night does not make for healthy independence and it certainly hurts a boy's self-confidence. So if your son routinely needs help, talk to his teachers. And if you do help, make sure that he has worked hard at it before he asks for help, because when a mother rushes in to do for a son what he can do on his own, he feels weak and emasculated. Unfortunately, with the best of intentions, we do this all the time. As mothers, we become so used to aiding and nurturing our sons that it can be very difficult to know when to withhold our help. That's why we must be very cautious. We must watch our sons and challenge them in age-appropriate ways.

In the same manner, we must be attentive enough to recognize when our sons do actually need help. For instance, if a son is struggling with schoolwork, experiencing depression or anxiety, or having trouble in his relationships with friends, although it is good to teach him to first try to handle the issues on his own, if he finds that he can't, we must ensure he feels comfortable asking an adult for help.

Tom's mother knew how difficult it could be to withhold help. When Tom was only eight years old, he got into an argument with a classmate because the other boy criticized Tom's younger brother. Tom didn't like the insult and told the boy to come over to his house after school to duke it out. Late in the afternoon the doorbell rang, and Tom's mother answered. On the front stoop stood the boy who had called her younger son names at school. She greeted him and asked if she could help him.

"Yup. I'm here to fight Tom," said the youngster. She was surprised and paused for a few moments.

Then, she calmly spoke to the boy. "Oh, I see. Well, Tom's in the backyard. You can go around the side of the house." She closed the door and, sure enough, the other eight-year-old walked to the backyard and found Tom. As the two met, his mother watched from the kitchen window. She saw them exchange a few words and then they startled to wrestle. No punches were thrown, but after they rolled around on the ground for a bit, Tom's mother came out and declared that the "fight" was over. She told the classmate that it was time to go home.

I have to confess, as a mother, when Tom told me this story, I gasped inside. If a little boy came to my door wanting to fight my son, I can't say that I would have allowed it. I probably would have brought the two boys into the kitchen, offered them something to drink and maybe some cookies to put them both in a good mood, and discussed the situation with them. I would have tried to convince them that settling an argument without fighting was a much healthier way to handle conflict, or I would have acted on plan B: Leave the boys out of it entirely and give an angry call to the visitor's mother.

Fortunately for Tom, I wasn't his mother. When he told me this story, many years after it happened, he said, "My mother was my hero. I looked up to her even as a young child and when that boy came to my door, my life changed. Instead of telling the boy to go home, my mother sent him out back because she knew that I needed to defend my brother. She knew that my pride was at stake and she wouldn't take that from me. After that fight was over (and it really wasn't a fight after all) I felt on top of the world. Not only could I handle myself, but I saw that my mother believed it, too. Her actions told me, 'Tom, you can handle anything. I believe in you.'"

Clearly excited to tell the story, he continued about his mother. "As I got older, I felt so grateful that she did that. When I was in college, I remember sometimes feeling insecure about my studies. Whenever I did, I'd call my mom and she would tell me that I could get through. She was my inspiration. When I left for college, my mother went back as well and then went on to law school. She was brilliant and is currently a judge. Seeing what she did and understanding how much she believed in my abilities to accomplish the goals that I'd set for myself inspired me to go to law school. Those ten minutes of my life changed me and they changed my relationship with my mother. I am so grateful for what she did that day."

We mothers parent from our instincts and this usually works quite well. However, when it comes to parenting our sons, we need to understand the difference between what they need and what we want to give them. That's the key to raising fabulous sons. We have to understand that as women, we see things differently than men do and that our sons need us to act in a way that emboldens them, not weakens them.

In many ways, sons can be delightfully easy to parent. They're often physically restless and need to move a lot, so you can just send them outside to work off their energy. When they are upset, they usually get over it quickly and move forward as if nothing happened. Most boys don't hold grudges, because they simply can't be bothered to. They go on about their business. If there is a problem, they like to find solutions and get the issue resolved. We need to remember this and not interfere by trying to get them to approach problems the same way we do.

When it comes to empowering our sons, we have a lot of options. Like Tom's mother, we can make the decision to let them act on their own impulses and not jump into every argument they have. We can let them struggle on the field (without yelling at their coaches), and we can ask them to do chores that require them to use their physical strength like taking out the trash or raking leaves. We can make them ride their bikes to school instead of expecting us to drive them or have them help their grandparents run errands. Everyone benefits!

But there are other wonderful ways we can hand our sons the ax they need to navigate their way through life. We can teach them to intellectually challenge themselves. Rather than indulging them by giving in to their desires to watch television or play video games, we can hand them age-appropriate books to read and then ask them what they thought of the story. Or better yet, read the book along with your son and discuss questions or thoughts either of you may have about the story as it progresses. Think for a moment what life is like in your house at five o'clock in the afternoon. You have just gotten back from picking one child up from play practice and you're taking a few minutes to rummage through the refrigerator to figure out what in the world to have for dinner. You groan because you have half a pack of lettuce, a few carrots, and only enough hamburger for two. The inevitable hits you: You need to get back in the car. Your son watches you do all this. You tell him that you're going to the store and he groans because he's starving. Then you feel guilty because you really should have been more organized and gotten food the day before (we're always feeling guilty about something).

Your son is also anxious because he has two tests tomorrow and he's nervous. He needs your help to study because he just doesn't understand his algebra. He climbs up onto the sofa and begins to play with his PSP to pass the time while you're at the store. You know he needs to get his homework started, but you don't want him to get frustrated with it, so you let him play the video game.

What did you just do? Your decision told him, "You really can't understand math without me, so wait. You need me. I don't want you to get impatient and since I'm a good mom, I'm going to help you avoid that. Play the game."

This may appear trivial, but from a young boy's perspective, it is a big deal. You are creating a thought pattern regarding what he believes about himself. Sitting on the couch, he feels that he can't deal with frustration and he can't do intellectually challenging tasks without you. You, on the other hand, are tired and you don't want an argument. You just want to get dinner on the table. But with a few tough rules (you battle for them at first, but the battle passes once your son accepts the rules, which he will, if you stick to them), you can ensure that your boy feels *more* capable, not less so.

Teach Him Confidence

The coddling begins early. Talk to any good high school teacher and he or she will tell you that one of the biggest obstacles young men face is being disabled by a loving mother. When our sons are in first or second grade we see them struggle with new ideas and we want to help them out. At first, we coach them in how to do their math problems, and before you know it, we're starting and finishing dioramas, art projects, and history reports. We feel we have to "help out" because the world is competitive and we don't want our sons to fall behind. But when we do this, we communicate to our sons that their work simply isn't good enough without our assistance. By the time they hit fourth grade, many of us have fostered an unhealthy dependency in our sons.

Many mothers feel stuck between trying to teach their sons how to do things on their own and not wanting them to be at an academic disadvantage because other parents of his classmates are doing too much work for their kids. I feel that in situations like this, mothers must go to the teacher and address the problem. The truth is, kids may get better grades if their parents are doing their work, but in the end, everyone loses. The boys who do their own work may get lower grades, and the boys whose parents do their work get higher ones, but the latter never learn what their true capabilities are.

One of the main reasons moms step in and do too much for their sons is that they see him struggling in a certain area and think that picking up the slack for him is the solution. Maybe our son is strong academically, but he seems physically different from the other boys in his class; a bit chubby or athletically clumsy. We desperately want our son to be respected and accepted by his peers, but too often we try to force him to be something he's not, encouraging him to play ball when he'd rather read or suggesting he try out for a team sport when he doesn't want to. Feeling sorry for our sons because they don't fit into the "norm" is different from feeling empathy, and they soon get the message that they are deserving of pity.

Empathizing with a son who lacks athletic prowess, academic strengths, or social skills means that we understand his difficulties and recognize that they will make life more challenging for him. Empathy allows us to be sensitive to his issues, but not take on responsibility for them. It brings us to the point where we can understand the struggles our son faces, but ensures that we keep up healthy and appropriate boundaries when dealing with these struggles, boundaries that are critical to the healthy development of his identity as a man.

Let's say that your son is athletically challenged. He really wants to play football but is rejected time after time by coaches who say that he isn't good enough for their team. In this situation, an empathetic mother would help her son understand that she knows he wants to play football but since that isn't an option, she wants to help him find a better place for him to use his energies (don't say talents because that might not be accurate). By handling the situation in a matter-of-fact way and helping our son see that he has many other ways to enjoy himself, we teach him that not being talented in football isn't a big deal. Empathy allows us to understand his situation but not handicap him by overreacting or making him feel like a failure.

If, however, we respond to this situation by feeling sorry for our son and becoming defensive, we communicate to him that he is at fault somehow. Why else would we feel sorry for him, he wonders. Sympathy can cause us to try to prove to our son that he really isn't a failure. The problem is, our boys see right through this. Even their young minds can reason that if being good at football isn't a big deal, why does Mom get so upset about it?

When we move from empathizing to sympathizing with our sons, we get into trouble. Where empathy keeps us from taking on the responsibility for their problems, sympathy does not. Sympathy woos us into feeling sorry for our boys. And the moment that pang of feeling sorry for our sons takes hold, we put them in a bad position because now we perceive them as the underdog, the boy with the broken wing. Once we cross over to seeing them as disadvantaged, we begin to treat them as such. A boy will pick up on that feeling and then there's trouble. No boy wants to feel that his own mother believes he is weak. At first, the sympathy may feel good to him; he will recognize that his mother loves him and cares for him. But over time, the sympathy can be crippling. Most good moms don't see this coming. We simply watch our sons, pick up on the difficulties they are having, and want to make their lives better. If they are vulnerable to being bullied, we want to make sure that no one hurts them. If they aren't very popular with other kids in their class, if they have a learning disorder, if life just seems to be unfair to them, our instincts are to step in and make things work out for them. But we must be careful. If you find yourself constantly making excuses for your son's behavior or defending him to others, ask yourself whether you are feeling empathy or pity. Then remind yourself that feeling sorry for him never leads to anywhere good. It only hurts him.

If your son lives with a perceived (or real) disadvantage, challenge him to live as normally as possible with his difference, or even use it to make himself stronger. You will probably feel that you are acting against your maternal instinct by doing this, but that's okay. It's still the right thing to do.

When Quinton was a freshman in college, he began experiencing intense anxiety, often waking up at night with panic attacks. At first, he didn't call home to tell his mother, Andrea, but soon the attacks became so severe that he was unable to leave his dormitory. When he finally told her, Andrea immediately drove three hours to his school to meet with him and help him figure out what to do. Quinton wanted to drop out. He was embarrassed to let his roommates or friends know what was happening. When Andrea arrived, she found him anxious, thin, and pale. Over the next several days, they talked about his anxiety and they made a plan for him to see a good counselor and a local doctor. Andrea told me that at first she felt so sorry for Quinton that she wanted to pack up his things and bring him home. She said that she hurt so much for him she became nauseated and couldn't sleep.

While she was with him at college, he admitted to her that he had been smoking a lot of marijuana just to get through the day. He had even been caught in town with the drug and was put in jail for several days. He said that he had been too ashamed to call her. But he just couldn't stop smoking because he felt so terrible and the pot helped. She understood, she said, because he was in such turmoil. But she told him that taking drugs was in the past.

When Andrea got home, she called me because she wasn't sure that she had done the right thing. "At first, all I really wanted was to bring him home. I didn't even really condemn his smoking. I knew it helped him and he was having such a hard time of it. Then something happened to me as we spent those days together. I so desperately wanted to tell him that he could quit school, but I didn't. Instead I told him that yes, he was having bad anxiety but he was going to be okay. We found a doctor and a counselor and I told him that he needed to finish the last six weeks of school. I said that life is hard but that what he had was treatable and that I would do everything I could to help him recover."

As a mother, I understood her impulse to excuse his use of marijuana and even feel sorry that he got caught and spent time in jail. And I can say that I, too, would have been tempted to plunk his nineteen-year-old body in the car and drive him home. But as a physician, I can tell you that she made exactly the right decision for Quinton at that juncture in his life. Yes, he had bad anxiety, but when she approached it in a matter-of-fact manner and helped him devise a plan to treat it, he was relieved. If she had gone to him and told him how terrible she felt for him and how awful it was that he had to suffer panic attacks, and how he should just come home, he would have sensed her pity for him and this would have made his problems much worse.

When she told her son that he most surely had the emotional stamina to finish the year, she communicated to him that in spite of his anxiety problem, he was strong. She also told him that while she understood it, smoking pot was not acceptable even when he was feeling anxious. In other words, she communicated high expectations for his future without condemning him. Although she felt tough and coldhearted, she did her son an enormous favor. She gave him an ax when he needed it most.

Teach Him Responsibility

Because men usually aren't the primary caregivers in the home, they feel safe allowing their identity to be bound in their work, which is the lens through which most adult men see themselves. Even when boys are young, they see their father's identity as strongly tied to his profession. They learn that working is part of being a man. Work builds strength of character in boys because it allows them to feel accomplished and proud of themselves. As they mature through their teen years, healthy psychological development depends on transitioning from being dependent on mom to being independent, and having the responsibility of some kind of work allows this process to happen.

Boys as young as six or seven years old will feel better about themselves knowing that they are relied on to do certain things. But for many of us, handing our young son a list of chores makes us feel guilty. *We* are the caregivers, the ones who run our households and provide a nice home environment for our families. Asking our sons to work can feel counterintuitive. What we need to realize, however, is that while boys may complain and grumble, they need chores to do, tasks of their own, in order to have a sense of belonging. Even young boys need to feel that they are an integral part of a unit and that they are needed. When boys aren't asked to do anything at home (whether they are paid or not), they feel that they are not needed. A boy who has no responsibilities may behave like a spoiled brat, but really, he is acting out because he is a frustrated, sometimes lonely, boy yearning to belong in an important way to his family.

I encourage mothers to begin finding small chores for boys to do as soon as they are big enough to handle them. As boys mature, the work should become more difficult, more frequent, and thus more meaningful. The work can be divided up between chores at home and a paid job outside the home. This is particularly important for single mothers for several reasons.

First, single mothers usually feel more guilt because the father isn't around and many try to compensate by making life easier for their sons. Their guilt causes them to work harder and ask less from their sons. But in that situation, both mother and son lose out. The son loses the very important realization that he is needed and that he has an important role in the family. And mom loses out because she is constantly overworked and exhausted. So for those of you who are single mothers or mothers who receive very little support from your spouses, please don't deprive your sons of all the benefits they receive through the years by working. Before they leave home, it is imperative that they have a strong sense of accomplishment and contribution, because as they mature, they begin to bind their identity up with their ability to produce good work. Boys who work hard feel better about themselves. Strong mothers teach them that, yes, they are always loved unconditionally, but also that working hard is vital for them.

Many mothers "protect" their sons from doing chores, reasoning that boys need to spend their free time on sports and other extracurricular activities so that they can get into a good college, or simply to just have fun. While I understand the desire to help position sons to achieve long-term goals, we mothers must remember that uncovering a passion or skill does our sons no good if they don't know how to cultivate a work ethic. Yes, they can learn discipline on a football field, in a classroom, or in a concert hall, but in those environments they are learning how to get better at something through discipline and practice and thus to see a clear improvement in their performance. Work that is separate from sports or other self-centered activities teaches sons how to persevere simply because it's the right thing to do. If they spend the afternoon raking leaves, they won't receive accolades or a clear sense of some improvement in a skill, but they will get a feeling of accomplishment and the pride that comes from helping others and being responsible.

Many mothers have come to believe that our lives are about giving, providing, and handing things to our sons. We do this because we have seen our friends do it and because we feel some peer pressure to do the same. And some of us do it because, well, it's just easier than fighting with our boys. Our sons will at times argue about helping out around the house and sometimes it's easier to just do the chores ourselves and skip the hassle of trying to force our reluctant boys to do them. In my experience, energy is the primary limiting factor to great parenting and I completely understand this. But what we need to remember is that getting boys *started* on this path is the tough part, the part that requires the most energy. Once they are used to working, life gets easier. We won't have to prod and fight for years to come; all we need to do is invest the initial energy to launch them down that path. Boys will argue forever about not doing chores if they know arguing is going to get them out of it. Once we let them know that we refuse to relent, and communicate that work is just a part of life, they give up and their responsibilities simply become part of the rhythm of their lives.

I am often asked by moms how much work boys should do at different ages. If you are unsure what you should ask of your son, here are a few guidelines for chores and tasks around the home that I recommend for boys.

For preschoolers: Give them one chore in the house that they must do a couple of times per week. Maybe it's to help move a wet load of clothes from the washer to the dryer, to help pick up toys, or to help you sweep the kitchen floor. The important thing is to pick a chore that he can do over and over. This helps him get into a routine and builds the foundation of work being a part of life.

For the elementary school years: Give them a chore that must be done at least three times per week either before or after school. It doesn't have to take long. He can sort through the recyclable materials in the house, clear dinner dishes, set the table, etc. Ideally, the chore should be something that not only helps him, but also benefits everyone else in the family. This makes him feel that he is an integral part of the family unit.

For junior high and high schoolers: Boys should have daily chores and can begin to pick up work outside their homes. If your son is too young to work at a store, then he can ask neighbors if they have yard work, painting, or other household chores that need to be done. Perhaps there is an elderly couple that needs their driveway shoveled in winter or their lawn mowed in the summer. I'm not advocating that boys spend their entire summers working and never having fun, but it is certainly possible to combine the two. The important thing is that during these crucial years when sons are developing independence, they have some work which gives them a sense of capability and autonomy. These are both extremely important qualities for adolescent boys to obtain. And a job can keep them out of trouble. In my twenty-five years of working with boys, I have found that those who work or who have something that they feel invested in drink less, have better self-esteem, have lower rates of depression, and have a happier outlook toward life in general. With that as a basis, they are then much better prepared for their future years when they no longer live with you.

Good Boring Jobs

One of the great disservices that we nice mothers do for our sons is that we try so hard to keep them from being bored we end up overscheduling them. When my own son was a teenager, I wanted him to figure out if he'd rather be a professional soccer player, go to the Olympics to compete in tae kwon do, become a neurosurgeon, learn how to lead a group of students in the wilderness (like his father had done at his age; here's a tip: *Never* make him do what his father did), or become a chemical engineer. He needed to try out all of these things in order to pick one, I reasoned, so how in the world did he have time to work? In my mind it was my job, as his very good mother, to make sure that he got his future figured out before his sophomore year in college.

My intentions, as his doting, overzealous mom, were good, I guess. I wanted the best for my son. But what my instincts (and friends) told me was best for my son, wasn't. He needed a job and he needed to learn how to cope with boredom more than he needed to figure out whether or not he was good enough to be a professional soccer player. A good mother would make him figure out how to manage the daily stresses of life (like what to do when he's bored) before pushing him to find out what he wanted to be when he grew up. But, ugh. I didn't want to. I wanted him to be super-active because I believed that's what great moms did for their sons: give them opportunities, good times, adventures and activities, leaving no room for boredom.

Fortunately (for me) I figured out a way to combine responsibility with fun when his aunt needed help in her coffee shop one summer. Making coffee is kind of boring when you're a senior in high school, but I can tell you that overall, it was a wonderful experience for him. I saw his demeanor change. He continued to play soccer, but something about helping his aunt, getting up and going to a job that was albeit a bit dull, working hard, and being committed to a schedule made him happy. He often came home from soccer or from summer school (yup—I threw that in there to get him amped up for college) in a sour mood. But when he came home from work, his mood was upbeat. He *expected* work to be boring, so he made it fun. Soccer practice, on the other hand, was supposed to make him stronger, a better player, and it cost money. When it failed to deliver (which it frequently did), he felt disappointed. Working in a coffee shop never failed to deliver because he *made* it what he wanted it to be.

Push Him into Battle

Anyone who has spent any time around a male, regardless of his age, knows that every now and then boys just need a fight to win. Sometimes the fight is physical; often it is mental. Either way, boys are wired to want to control situations and people and, in particular, to defend what they believe is right. This is tough for many moms because we aren't all wired this way. Sure, some of us can be very assertive, going to battle when someone we love is threatened, but in my experience, boys are generally more prone to waging wars than are their sisters.

Watch any five-year-old boy who goes outside to play. Within minutes, he will find a branch or a stone to fight a bear with. He will build things and destroy them moments later only to rebuild them again. Boys are gross-motor people and many times this manifests itself in a desire to fight off enemies. We need to be ready to embrace this instinct and channel it in a healthy direction. This is important not only to help a son get rid of energy, but also to build self-confidence. Contrary to what you might believe or read, playing video games with war themes in no way satisfies your son's need to have a battle to fight. Violent video games, violent movies, or songs with violent themes cause boys to become desensitized to others and act more aggressively as they get older. It does not teach them compassion or give them a sense of their own, masculine power. We have numerous studies documenting the damaging effects of violent media on boys.[1] We know that watching violence repeatedly over time causes boys to act out more and be more aggressive.[2] Engaging in violent media does not assuage his desire for fighting; it only desensitizes him.

Many mothers ask me if I think it's okay for their young boys to play war games with plastic figurines. Some are concerned when they see their sons and the other boys in the neighborhood playing games where one group represents the villains and the other the heroes. Often boys will pick up sticks and fashion make-believe guns, causing their mothers to worry that they have the next Unabomber on their hands. To these mothers, I say, relax! There is an enormous difference in the effect that engaging in make-believe has as compared to playing violent video games. The former utilizes a boy's imagination. It allows him to release some of his fears and apprehensions. Bruno Bettelheim wrote extensively about a boy's need to read fairy tales that deal with good-guy, bad-guy themes, because hearing a story that deals with right and wrong, a story with a hero and a villain, allows a boy the opportunity to resolve internal conflicts about good and bad or right and wrong on his own. With fantasy, he can imagine himself as the knight who saves the girl in distress. If he has read about a cruel king who is mean to his subjects, he can recognize that perhaps he, too, behaves badly when he has angry feelings toward people in his own life. Because he can actively recruit his imagination, he is able to process deeper thoughts and feelings that are perhaps conflicting. He may imagine himself as the king riding through the woods with a sword at his side and a horse beneath him. He may feel how powerful he would be as king. He would be nice, he thinks but he understands why the king is mean. Then he wonders if being mean is fine, because the king was mean, or should he be nice like his mother has told him? The conflict over his wanting to be mean like the king or nice, like his mother says to be, grows. He ultimately decides to let the king stay mean and that he will be nice, because life works better that way. This is just one example of how fantasy allows a young boy to resolve conflict in a healthy way.

This doesn't happen when boys use video games and act reflexively; they absorb messages and imitate behaviors but they never process issues on a deeper level.

Teaching sons to be assertive and to fight for what they believe in takes on many forms. An important part of a boy's self-esteem is built by learning how to defend himself and stick up for what he believes is right. Does this mean that we are to teach our son to knock kids down on the playground if they take a swing at him? No. But it does mean that we teach our son what to do if he feels he is being taken advantage of, demeaned, or bullied.

We have become so afraid of insulting others that we have made our sons feel that they can't defend themselves and worse—that they don't need to defend those around them who are being victimized. I have listened to recordings of boys bullying others. Often, what is as disturbing as hearing the voices of those who are taunting is the lack of defense coming from the boys who are standing by watching. Being mean is easy. Intervening and defending those who are wronged is hard. And I can tell you that if you want to raise a boy who grows into a man who feels good about himself and about life, teach him how to fight for those who need his help. If your son is tall and bigger than most of the other boys in his class, teach him to watch out for the smaller boys or those who are considered nerdy. As he grows older, encourage him to be chivalrous. When he's in high school, teach him to keep an eye out for girls who may be pushed around by others. And when he is in college, encourage him to offer to walk his coed colleagues across campus if it's late at night. By helping others, he will feel better about himself and learn to be more selfless.

Fortunately, we can teach our sons to be *mentally savvy*. The best place to start is to alert our boys that many of the messages coming at them on a daily basis about being popular, sexy, aggressive, or disrespectful to girls can affect the way they see themselves. So we must first try to uncover what these messages are and then help our sons fight them off. This is a wonderful way for boys to engage in "battle," if you will. Here are some of the most common toxic messages that boys receive, which you can help them fight. I have collected all of these from the young men I have seen over the past twenty-five years. Your son may struggle with some or all of them. You'll easily be able to tell which ones hit home with him.

1. *I'm not as smart as the rest of my friends.*

Most boys mature more slowly than girls, particularly in the early elementary school years. Boys often catch on to reading later than girls, have more difficulty paying attention in school, or have trouble with the sciences and math. If they are in a coed class, they will quickly pick out the girls who are faster learners. Since they don't understand their own cognitive developmental process, they conclude that they are stupid. Significantly more boys than girls are marked as "learning challenged" or as having ADHD by the time they are in the first or second grade.[3] The feelings of inferiority and the lack of self-esteem such a designation can cause can stick for years. I have had boys tell me that a teacher once told them they were poor readers in an early grade and that the humiliation they felt at this stayed with them all the way through high school.

I am extremely cautious when it comes to labeling boys in the early elementary years as having any learning issues, because in many cases, they simply need more time to mature. I encourage you to be the advocate for your son and make sure he gets the growing time he needs. If a teacher or doctor wants to label him as having difficulties, that person should be able to prove it. Because once a boy is diagnosed, there may be no going back.

The best thing to do with any boy is to avoid using words like *smart* or *intelligent*. You simply don't know, in those early years, what his intellectual capacity will be. It is just as harmful to tell a child he is gifted before you know enough about it as it is to label a child as having learning difficulties.

If your son does worry that he can't keep up at school, especially compared to the girls his age, you can help him challenge his feelings about not being smart. Teach him that when those thoughts come into his mind—that he can't do something or isn't smart enough to solve a problem—they are just thoughts, not reality. Teach him that he can ignore those negative ideas or fight back at them and make them go away.

2. I'm not as likable as my friends (and therefore I don't fit in).

If your son feels this way his self-esteem will be poor, regardless of his age. Therefore, you must do two things to help him combat this idea. First, if his father is willing, ask him to increase the amount of time that he is spending with your son. Boys (particularly teen boys) get an enormous boost to their self-confidence when they see their father paying attention to them. Second, see if you can tease the idea that he is unlikable out of him and then help him reverse it. This is important because boys need to begin to separate how they feel about themselves from what's really true about themselves. Boys may feel unlikable when they are in fact *very* likable. Point out to him what is genuinely wonderful about him. Is he courageous, patient, empathetic, or a good brother? Try to highlight character qualities in him that you are proud of rather than things that he does well. He doesn't want to be likable because of the things he *does,* but because of who he *is.*

Then teach him that even if there are kids in his class who don't like him and have been mean to him, that doesn't mean that he is unlikable; it may simply mean that they aren't the nicest kids. As you help him identify ugly thoughts, also help him replace them with positive ones. Again, this requires a lot of patience, but over time, it really works.

3. It's okay if I get bullied.

Many fathers have commented to me that being bullied is simply a part of life for a young boy. It's part of the establishment of the pecking order, they reason. While this may sit all right with some fathers, it certainly doesn't sit well with mothers. We are the protectors of our sons from a very early age, and we feel that it is not only our right to protect our sons; it is our duty.

Stories about bullying have become far more prevalent in the news these days, either because bullying has become more common or because we are only now reporting on it. I think it is a combination of the two. The last decade has also seen the creation and rise of In ternet bullying. Boys can now bully another child in front of a huge audience of friends through Facebook posts, tweets, or YouTube videos. No longer is the victim humiliated before a few familiar peers— now he or she is embarrassed in front of hundreds of other kids. This makes the emotional pain of the bullying that much greater.

Shame and humiliation are two of the hardest emotions for boys to deal with, because they are so complex. They impact his self-esteem, his beliefs about himself, and his beliefs about those around him. Every good mother wants to protect her son from these emotions, but doing so can be tricky. If we aren't careful, we can intensify a boy's humiliation by trying to fight his battles for him long after he's old enough and mature enough to handle it himself.

There are several important things that we can do to help prevent our sons from being bullied and to help them recover if this does occur. First, we must teach our sons to be politely assertive. Some boys are naturally bossy; others are more sensitive and quiet. Without changing the personality of a boy (which we can't do anyway) we can influence how he interacts with his peers. We can train him to speak up for himself without being overly aggressive. The best way to do this is to ask him from an early age about his feelings and wishes. For example, after visiting with extended family, we can ask our son what he liked most about the visit and what he didn't like. By asking his opinion about important matters, we communicate that his words and thoughts have value. This doesn't mean that we ask our boys what they want all the time and then give it to them; it simply means that we care about what they think and feel. A boy learns that he, too, should value his own thoughts and feelings. By asking him to verbalize both positive and negative feelings, we are helping him practice saying things that he might not otherwise articulate.

Teaching your son not to be afraid of bullies is also very important. Bullies prey on kids who are quiet, compliant, nice, and, sometimes, a little different from the rest of the class. They may pick on the smartest boy, the one who wins all the awards. And sometimes they just pick on the one who lets them get away with it. Bullies tend to stay away from kids who will challenge them. If a boy stares a bully down, the bully will most likely move on to an easier target.

You should always be on the lookout for signs of bullying, particularly because boys often don't tell their mothers when it happens to them. The older the boy, the less likely he is to tell his mom. You must be diligent in your detective work. Watch for signs of withdrawal, or of suddenly not wanting to go to school. If your son rides the bus, he may refuse, seemingly out of the blue, to get on it. If he is bullied on the playground, he may ask to stay indoors all the time. Remember, bullying makes boys feel humiliated and weak, and when these feelings settle inside, they make boys feel miserable. But since boys don't easily come out and state that they feel humiliated and embarrassed, the pent-up emotions come out "sideways." For instance, a boy may become sullen, his grades may drop, his interest in doing activities that he previously enjoyed may vanish, or he may suddenly have angry outbursts for no reasons at all. All of these are signs that he could be feeling some humiliation, and when you notice them, you should prod a bit to see if he is being bullied.

If you find out that this is indeed what's going on, you first need to assess the situation. It's important not to overreact, since that will make any problem worse. For instance, if one boy continually accuses your son of cheating, that may not necessarily constitute bullying, especially if your son knows the boy and doesn't care about what that boy says. If someone calls him a name and he calls the offender a name back, that may not qualify, depending on the context and what the insults were. Defining whether your son is feeling bullied really depends on the effect that the bad behavior from the offender has on him. Often boys banter back and forth and no one gets particularly offended because they know one another well and feel that they are on equal social footing. Sometimes in our fervor to stand up for our sons we make small matters much larger than they really are.

If you have determined that your son is truly being humiliated, that is when you need to step up to the plate. Find out the details from the teacher or adult in charge. If they don't help you resolve the issue, or if you feel that the bully hasn't been adequately reprimanded, go to the principal. If the principal fails you, then go to the other child's parents. I encourage both parents to be involved in this process if possible because sadly, many authority figures listen to men more than they do women. The more you can present a united front as parents, the better.

Let's turn the tables for a moment. What if you find out that your son is a bully? Universally, parents believe that their son could "never do mean things" to others. This denial is ingrained in almost every parent I see. What is it in us parents that refuses to see all sides of our children? We want them to be wonderful because they are a reflection of us, and we want to think that we are wonderful. But we must get over this. Humility helps us realize that our kids can face the same struggle we do to always be kind and nonjudgmental. As badly as we don't want to see their faults, we must, because in order to help them grow up into happy, responsible adults, we need to help them confront and reverse bad behaviors.

If you hear accusations about your son being a bully, first verify them. Ask his teacher, or another parent you trust. Don't ask his friends, because they may not tell you the truth. Then ask your son if he did what others have accused him of doing. This is tricky because he will be defensive (if he's guilty) and he may lie. He doesn't want to disappoint you and he also doesn't want to suffer the consequences. You may need to ask several times over several days, but find out the truth.

Once you determine that he is doing cruel things to others, he must learn some lessons. Being mean always hurts him and it hurts others. If you fail to teach him how serious being mean is by letting him off the hook, you cripple his growth. So don't let that happen. Discuss his behavior, tell him why it is absolutely unacceptable, and then come up with appropriate punishment. This will require him to humble himself and feel humiliation. He should apologize (in person is best) to the victim and to the victim's parents. Then he must be made to work, lose something that he enjoys, or be put on probation. If his behavior is such that he is suspended from school, then make sure he puts the time off to use. He should not be allowed to just stay home and watch television or play video games. This is hard for parents and takes some tough inner fortitude, but it is one of the kindest things parents can do for a child who's acting out.

But most important is to get to the root of the behavior. Why is he being mean? Without treating him as a victim (because this paralyzes boys, too), talk frankly about feelings. Why is he in turmoil? Why is he so angry? Does he not feel compassion or empathy? You may need a professional to help you, because most parents can't elicit this kind of information from their kids. You are simply too close to them, so ask for help. But whatever you do, *never shy away from the truth* of what is happening and what your son is doing. Keeping your eyes wide open is one of the best parenting skills you can acquire. Your child will never lead a healthy, happy life if you allow him to deny what is happening.

4. In order to be cool I need to have sex with a number of girls.
Mothers can underestimate the loud messages that teen boys receive about being sexually active. It often seems that men who have sex with multiple women are more macho. As his mom, you know a whole lot better. There is tremendous pressure on boys to have sex before they graduate from high school. And, very important, many boys feel bad about themselves if they aren't having sex or if they have had sex and it ended up being a bad experience. I see the latter situation quite frequently in teen boys.

We need to be ready to tackle sexual issues with our sons. It's tough and uncomfortable but it has to be done, not just because there is an epidemic of sexually transmitted diseases out there, but because many teen boys feel poorly about themselves if they perceive that they aren't as sexually active as their friends. In fact, often boys will boast about the number of sexual partners they have had (whether they are being truthful or not) to make themselves appear more macho than their friends. If a boy believes that having sex makes him more manly and he believes that his friends are more sexually active than he is, he can feel inferior. And this can color a boy's feelings about other things as he grows up. But being too sexually active at too young an age can also harm his future personality. Quite simply, if your son seems to be struggling with this issue, find a time to sit him down and talk about the positive aspects of not being sexually active. Tell him that he probably will feel out of the loop with many of his friends. And there certainly is no harm in telling him that many boys (even his friends) lie about how many partners they have had. Show him that by holding off on sex, he has more self-control and values himself more than they do. Never talk about sex in a negative way; always be upbeat and positive. If he senses that you are a sex hater or that you feel it is disgusting, he'll tune you out in a nanosecond.

Remember, you can give him a perspective about self-respect and sex that a man can't give him. As you teach him to respect his own body, tell him how to respect a woman's body. And tell him why. His friends will probably talk about girls in a condescending way, boasting that they "made it" with one girl or another. When he hears this, he may feel that it's wrong to talk about women that way but become desensitized because so many of his friends accept this kind of talk. So tell him that it isn't acceptable. If he has a sister, ask him how he would feel if his friends were talking about her that way. The protectiveness he feels if he imagines them talking about his sister (or other close female relative or friend) is something he should feel toward all women. So encourage him to treat women well. I can promise, when he hears it from you, it will resonate on some level and he won't forget.

If his father is around, it is important for him to weigh in on sexual issues with your son. Boys look up to their dads when it comes to many issues—especially sex. But often fathers hesitate in talking to their sons about it; they either feel guilty because they had sexual encounters when they were young that they regret, or because they are simply shy when it comes to talking about sex. It is very important for your son to know, however, what his father thinks about *him* having sex. Sons don't really care what their dads did as teens; they care what their fathers think about what they are doing now. So encourage your husband to talk with your son about putting the brakes on.

You can broach the subject of sex by asking your son if his friends are dating. If he says they are, tell him that you know that many kids his age are sexually active and then gently ask if any of his friends are. Don't act as though you think these are "bad" kids; just ask in a matter-of-fact, nonjudgmental tone. From his response you'll be able to pick up on what his thoughts about sex are, and you may even be able to figure out if he's having sex himself. Either way, the most important thing is to keep the conversation going. (More on the subject of your son and sex will follow in Chapter 8.)

Your son might feel awkward, but his awkwardness should not stop you from talking, because the topic is important. You can ask questions sideways if you prefer, rather than straight on. For instance, you can say, "If I were in your shoes, I'd have a tough time figuring out what to do with girls. Some guys are having sex and some aren't. I also know that sexual activity can make guys feel better or worse about themselves. Has that ever happened to you?"

Most likely your son will avoid the conversation, but keep talking anyway. Boys are squeamish when it comes to talking with their moms about sex, but again, even if he doesn't respond, keep going. Tell him that many boys feel they need to have sex in order to be cool. Tell him that this isn't true. If he does feel weird about himself or concerned because of a sexual issue, stress that those are just thoughts and he can change his thoughts. In all of these instances, it is vital that you arm him with the tools to combat negative thoughts and replace them with positive ones. This is one of the most powerful lessons that you can ever impart to your son.

─────

We need our sons to be able to fight and stick up for themselves when they have to. They need to have the confidence to trust themselves, even when we aren't there. There's not a lot of positive reinforcement in the messages society sends about teenage boys. Well-meaning teachers label them with learning problems too early, friends at school can turn into bullies at a moment's notice, and fathers who bail on their sons can rip the center right out of their being. Moms who continually jump in to save their sons and fix their problems also send a message: *You can't do it without me.* The great mom is one who hands her son an ax, teaches him how to use it, and then steps backs and lets him.

CHAPTER 7

You Are His Connection to Dad

When I was a young physician, I worked with a pediatrician thirty years my senior. He was short, a little thick in the waist, and brilliant. He had a demeanor that said, "I love listening to you." We would scurry past each other in the narrow halls of our office and each time I saw him, he would have a smile on his face. I learned as much from him in the one brief year we worked together as I did in three years at the busy children's hospital I later moved to. Here's the most important lesson he taught me. He said, "Meg, if a mother brings her child to you and says there's something wrong, stay in the room until you find out what it is. Mothers know their children better than anyone, so listen to them."

Being a young mother myself at the time, I loved that advice. Time and again I have found it to be true. If a mother insists that something is wrong with her child, then she's usually right. In my practice, I have worked hard to not only listen to mothers but also help them know their own kids better, because as a pediatrician, the best thing I can do for any child is to help his or her mother and father. I can give a child antibiotics or asthma medicines and advise them about the horrible hazards of smoking, but as much authority as the title "Doctor" gives me, the ones whom a child really listens to are mom and dad.

Recognizing the power of a parent in a child's life was a turning point in my career because it shifted my focus. Pediatricians are trained to focus on the child. We are taught, especially when dealing with teens, that we may be able to get through to a kid when a parent can't. We are trained to be the child's ally; if a fifteen-year-old girl wants birth control, we'd better give her a prescription for oral contraceptives if her parents won't get it for her themselves. But while this may help her avoid an unwanted pregnancy, which is important, what that girl really needs is a support system—someone to openly discuss with her why she wants to be sexually active. She needs them to help her understand that her need for male love and attention can be met in healthier, less dangerous ways. In other words, she needs emotional support from an adult (hopefully a parent) to help her navigate sexual pressures she feels in her peer culture. If I do things for their child without their knowledge, I'm not helping the girl strengthen her connection with her parents, which is what she needs in the long run. Thanks to my one year spent working with my wonderful colleague in a pediatrics office, I learned to always pull mom and dad into the conversation. I will tell you that 99 percent of the kids I work with love it when I do this because they *want* to be close to their parents. They don't want to be hiding things. Helping mothers and fathers connect with their children is the greatest gift and the best health-care plan I can give to the kids in my office.

At home, mothers must sometimes play a similar role in terms of bringing the father into the conversation. If you adore your child and want what's best for him or her, always remember to include dad. Your children are looking to have a great relationship with their father. Sometimes this is particularly difficult for boys and you can be the key component in making it easier. Boys need close relationships with their fathers, but since they often don't know how to facilitate this, you must. As I said, I have learned that the best thing I can do for my pediatric patients is to help their parents, because if parents are healthier, the kids are healthier. The same is true in your home. If you help your son's father and have a healthier relationship with him, you give your son a tremendous gift. And if their relationship is a strong one, you will have a lot less to worry about.

I fully appreciate the difficulty many of you mothers have in hearing this, but my job isn't to make your life easier; it's to make it better. I am convinced that if your child is happier, then you will be happier. So I am willing to say tough things like this: You can't be everything to your sons. We can only give so much as mothers; even if you are the best mom on earth, what you can provide your sons is, by nature, limited. This isn't a criticism; it's merely the truth. Your son wants a solid relationship with his dad because he needs his dad. The more you can do to help the two grow closer, the better parent you will be to your son. If you want your son to grow up to be a good man, he needs to have a relationship with a good man; he needs to experience what it's like to watch a good man speak, conduct his business, and interact with his family. When he sees a man speak respectfully to you, he learns that women are to be respected. Since boys are highly visual, seeing a good man in action helps him learn how to behave better than does simply imagining how a man should act.

Of course, if you're a single mom, you are worried now, especially if your son doesn't have a father in his life. Or if the father he has is not a good role model. You are thinking that your son is doomed. But don't be anxious; he isn't. There are many things that you can do to help him, and we will address these later in the chapter—so hold on! For you mothers who have a husband or an ex-husband who is involved in your son's life, I firmly believe that if you shift your perspective of your role in your son's life from one where you do it all to one where you do your part, and then help your son's dad do his, you will change the course of your son's life. Nothing matters more to a boy than having a good relationship with his father. Forget sports, what college he goes to, what courses he takes, or what his grades are. We all spend too much time helping our boys improve those aspects of their lives and forget what is far more important to them—helping them feel great about themselves and about life. But this is no small feat. It takes a lot of grit. Lucky for us, that's what we mothers do really well—the tough stuff.

WHAT WE WANT FROM OUR SPOUSES

Most men simply don't place enough importance on listening to the women (and kids) in their lives. They listen to colleagues, male friends, and some older folks, but they're not very good at listening to those closest to them. My husband, for example, is an internist, and he loves what he does. He's patient and kind and many of his female patients tell him their problems. Over the years, this has been tough for me, because when he comes home he doesn't have the energy left to listen to a word I have to say. Maybe you are one of the lucky ones whose husband comes home at the end of a workday, hands you a glass of wine, asks you how your day was, and then actually looks at you while listening to your answer. If this is your husband, he is a rare bird and you are one lucky woman. The rest of us, however, must contend with repeating ourselves and sometimes chasing after husbands to get them to hear what we are trying to say. Listening simply doesn't come naturally to most men. This wouldn't be a problem if it weren't for the fact that there are loved ones in men's lives who often need their undivided attention. Wives need to connect with their husband; children need to connect with their father.

As wives, we want our spouse's ear because it makes us feel valued. We are wired to desire intimate connections with our loved ones, and we need to have an ongoing dialogue and exchange of ideas because that's how we foster intimacy. Some marriages break up when one spouse refuses to listen, and this is for good reason. When one partner won't listen, that person is saying, in essence, "What you have to say and how you feel aren't important. Therefore, you aren't important." Men don't have this need to the same extent, so it is difficult for them to understand how very important it is to us to have their undivided attention at times.

Sons have the same need for connection that we do. Yes, they are male, but when they are young, they need their father's attention, acceptance, and approval. If they receive these things, then boys can mature into adulthood with a healthy sense of value and self-respect. If they don't, they can face some trouble down the road. Some serious trouble. That's why sons need us to run interference for them.

Even though their fathers were once young boys with the same need for connection, they forget what it was like to desperately want their father's ear. And if they never got attention from their father, a boy will very likely grow up to be a man who will fail to provide that attention to his son. The whole concept will be foreign to him.

At this point you might be wondering what you can do to influence the father of your son. We are taught that we can't change people, that we must accept them as they are. To some extent this is true, but there are some very important things that we can (and must) do to help our husbands parent our sons. It can be a bit tricky, but with a few tweaks and a little insight, any mother can help her husband (even her ex-husband) be a more accepting, loving dad. And who among us doesn't want that? To understand how we can help our husbands parent our sons better, we must first recognize what our sons need from their fathers.

WHAT BOYS NEED FROM THEIR FATHERS

Understanding the Blessing

Gary Smalley and John Trent wrote a book a number of years ago called *The Blessing*. In it, they discuss a son's need to receive what they call a blessing from his father. And attention *is* a blessing. Watch closely how your son talks to his dad. Look at the expression on his face when he tells his father that he got an A on a test or that he made the soccer team. The expression says, "Dad, don't you think I'm wonderful?" Whether your son is eight or eighteen, something inside him is driven to find out what his dad thinks, feels, and believes about him. He needs to know if his father respects him as a male. It is often true that when a boy is very young (two to seven years old), he may feel that all he needs is his mother. We can love, nurture, soothe, and discipline our little boy, and, for a time, this can be enough. But once that boy turns eleven or twelve, we become the enemy overnight. Not only are we no longer enough; somehow we have turned into the person who just doesn't "get" it. The reality is, he doesn't want closeness with a woman (for the time being) because he has to figure out what maleness is all about. And he doesn't want us to help him get there; he wants his dad to.

There's another reason boys need their fathers when they are teens. Because they are visual creatures, they need to see a man in action. They need to watch their dad talk, play baseball, and conduct himself at work or with his friends. Boys want to see their dad live life in front of them so that they can internalize their dad's behaviors and in essence "try on" manhood. And as a father sees his son imitate him, he will notice and approve (or disapprove); in other words, he will either grant the blessing or he will reject his son. Of course, the healthiest thing for your son is to get his dad's blessing. We can't make this happen but we can help it along, or pick up the pieces when it doesn't. Either way, we need to be waiting in the wings to help sons navigate this sometimes tricky territory with their fathers.

Sons who leave home with a deep belief that their father approves of them are bound for a bright future. You can spot these young men quickly. They exude self-confidence, they believe in their capabilities, and they enjoy life. They can take the knocks life gives them in stride and get back up because they know that they are strong. Their dad communicated that to them somewhere along the way.

Boys who leave home without the blessing of their father suffer. Many wonder if they have any value at all. Others doubt their abilities, even if they are clearly accomplished in certain areas. I have seen outstanding athletes who go off to college to play Division 1 sports suffer from low self-esteem because they feel that they had never earned their father's approval. Boys who have unfinished business with their fathers carry the pain from that forward for many years. Fortunately, a father can give his son the blessing in very easy ways. Paul did this for his son Freddy. When Freddy was twelve, he struggled with sixth grade. His friends rarely included him in activities outside school and his grades went down. He didn't like his teacher and therefore had trouble paying attention to what she was saying. He didn't want to do his homework and the worse his grades got, the madder his teacher got at him.

Paul recognized Freddy's struggles and decided to help out. Rather than bringing up the problems directly, he simply asked Freddy to join him on the weekends while he did chores. When he went to have the oil changed in the car, he asked Freddy to come along because, he said, he "just wanted his company." Occasionally Paul left work early and picked Freddy up from school and took him to an early dinner. He began giving his son the blessing by simply showing up in his life more.

But Paul didn't stop there. Once he had established a pattern of being a little more involved, he started talking a bit more deeply to Freddy. Paul told me what he said to his son and I will paraphrase him here.

"I told Freddy that life throws you curveballs and that he was getting his first major one. His friends weren't nice and I told him that he would meet many others in the future who also weren't nice. I told him about guys rejecting me when I was young and about some who still do. Then I told him that no matter what life threw at him, he could handle it. He was strong and resilient. Then I told him that regardless of the difficulties he had, I believed in him. And no matter what mistakes he made, which kids disliked him, or what happened with his grades, I would always be proud of him because he was my son and I loved him for who he was."

For many boys, simply hearing that their father is proud to be *their* father is enough to extend the blessing.

The Gift of the Blessing #1: Acceptance

When your son is a little boy, he constantly checks if dad is noticing him. Does dad see him kick the ball or make it a hundred feet on his two-wheeler? Does dad notice that he made a friend, colored in the lines for the first time, or brought his library book back on time? If so, does dad (and this is really important) approve of what he saw? If the answer is yes, then your son feels good about himself and therefore about life. He can move forward feeling confident.

As intently as your son watches his father for positive feedback, he watches just as carefully for negative feedback. If he got an A on a test and his father just shrugged his shoulders, the boy will feel that his effort wasn't good enough. The A doesn't mean anything because it seems that, in his father's eyes, he missed the mark. If his father watches a hockey game where he scores a goal but then tells him that the goal was great but that he could have made two, he removes his skates feeling like a loser.

A father's words are powerful. Every encounter with his dad makes a boy feel either better about himself or worse, depending on his father's reactions. Every day, a boy tries to figure out more about himself and more about life. He is maturing, changing, watching his own character unfold, and trying to decide who he is and where he fits. Much of this is learned by what his father believes about him. Does his dad like what he sees? If he does, then the boy integrates that acceptance into his person. His dad's approval of his behaviors, accomplishments, and even his feelings are very important, because once he believes he has his father's approval in these, then his self-esteem and belief in himself skyrocket.

Unfortunately, the same is true when a son feels rejected by his father. When dad disapproves, your son can carry negative feelings about himself for years to come. Of course, a father isn't going to like everything his son does as he goes through life. He may dislike a hairstyle, disagree with his choice of friends, or disapprove of his academic path. Does this mean that it is inevitable that a father is going to scar his son for years to come? Not at all. A father can disagree with his son's choices but instill in him a deep sense of self-worth. The key is that he needs to let his son know early on that he approves of him as a person, even if he doesn't agree with all his choices. He must communicate to his son that he accepts him as a unique, irreplaceable part of his life. When a dad teaches his son that his existence is a gift and that as his dad he cares for and cherishes that gift, he is free to disagree with his son's choices later in life without scarring the boy.

One of the best ways for a father to teach this to his son is by encouraging him during times of failure. For instance, if a boy flunks an algebra test after he has studied hard, misses the winning penalty kick for his soccer team, or gets dumped by his girlfriend, if his father comes to him and lets him know that regardless of his "failures," he (his father) believes that he is fabulous, then all will be well. Moments of perceived failure are the best times for a father to show his son that his love for him is unyielding. This is how a father can lay down a deep foundation of love and respect toward his son, and when he does this, even when the boy is still at an early age, the lessons will carry that son into manhood.

Gift #2: Admiration

Even very young boys need a sense that they can do something extraordinary. Three-year-olds are aware that they are little, but they still long to be admired. The difference between approval and admiration can be subtle, but it is important. Boys need a sense that they have something worthwhile to offer those around them. They need to feel special and looked up to. When our boys are still very young, we moms can help them with this. All we need to do is show them that they can do something we can't. For instance, watching them pick up a worm or frog and put it in a box gives us an opportunity to express admiration. "Ugh, I can't stand touching worms. It's really great that picking it up doesn't bother you like it does me."

But as our sons get older, we can tell them until we are blue in the face that we find their drawing skills or their courage admirable, but the weight that our praise carries becomes limited simply because we are female. Sons don't feel competitive with us because we are women. But they do feel competitive with their dads. It's a guy thing; one Y chromosome needs to know how it stacks up against the other Y. When a son sees that his dad carries a sense of admiration for what he does, feels, or believes, he feels larger than life. Every son needs admiration from his father because in his eyes, his dad is smart, strong, and wise. If he gets his father's respect, he doesn't need anyone else's.

As I said above, it is important to differentiate admiration from approval. When a son believes that his father admires him, he has a sense that his dad respects and looks up to his decisions and behaviors. Approval, on the other hand, is the understanding that his father agrees with his actions but doesn't necessarily think more highly of his son because of them. Both are equally important.

Gift #3: Attention

We women know too keenly that men have difficulty paying attention to those around them, wives and girlfriends included. We become easy to miss because we are familiar to them. Day in and day out, we are there; it's easy to take us for granted. It may make us mad when it happens, but we are adults and can understand and put it aside. Our young sons cannot. All they know is that they want dad's attention, and when they don't get it, rather than sitting back and recognizing that dad is busy or preoccupied, they feel rejected. When a son runs up to his dad and asks a question and sees his father walk away without hearing or responding, he feels that he did something wrong. His question was stupid, he thinks. That means he is stupid. And since (in his mind) he is stupid, he might as well give up trying for dad's approval.

Giving your attention to another person is the primary form of communicating your love to them. You can't kiss someone without noticing them. A mother can't give her son a hug without stopping what she is doing in order to wrap her arms around him. To your son, having your attention means that he is seen and loved. I can tell you that kids crave attention so desperately that they will do anything to get it. If dad doesn't give enough attention to his son and show that he loves him, the boy will go to extremes to catch his father's eye. Recently I spoke with a seventeen-year-old boy who told me how it felt to be in that situation. His mother had left his father five years earlier to start a new life with another man, someone with whom she argued less and got along with better. This young man understood why his mother had left his dad, but he hated it. He spent weekdays with his mother and her boyfriend, and since his father lived only one town away, he stayed with him on the weekends. He felt as though he had no home, and he simply couldn't get his emotional footing.

Because of his anger over the situation, he fought with his dad most of the time they were together. He made new friends in his father's town that his father disliked. He hung out with them whenever he went to his dad's and he admitted that he did it because it made his father mad. He got in trouble with the law and ended up in jail for driving drunk. He came to see me one particular day as a follow-up to a car accident. (A week earlier he had rolled his SUV and ended up in the emergency room.) As I asked him questions about the accident, he answered in a way that intrigued me. Rather than describing the details of the horrific event, he kept telling me how his dad had responded.

"Were you driving drunk and that's why you got in the accident?" I asked.

"What difference does it make if I was," he said. "I was a couple of miles from my house and when the cops came to the scene, they called my dad and he wouldn't come."

The young man went to the hospital for tests and fortunately wasn't seriously injured. When I told him that he was fortunate, he stared at me. "Who cares? What do I have to live for? My mom's downstate and my dad's too busy with his work. They want nothing to do with me." He stared into a corner.

When a boy doesn't get attention from his father (regardless of his age), his bearings are ripped from him. Without his father's attention, he feels that the very core of his life is off balance and uncentered. He can't figure out what he is good at or what he wants, and he certainly can't figure out what he should be doing. The only thing he knows how to do is act in a way that will get his dad's attention. As he sees it, even bad attention is better than none at all. And if the attention doesn't come, he can even go as far as harming himself to get some response.

Being a really good mother to our sons means recognizing what we can and can't give. As mothers, we can't act as a substitute for a dad, and no, we can't *change* their fathers. But that doesn't mean that we can't influence our husbands (or sons' fathers); show them how to give our sons approval, admiration, and attention; and even explain why it's so important they do this. When we respect the intense male dynamic that exists between father and son, we can inspire a closer, healthier relationship between the two. The best ways that we can do this are by never driving a wedge between a father and son and by never talking against a father. We must always remember that a son *needs* his father—even if they have a strained relationship. We may get angry at our husbands and distance ourselves from them, but our sons feel differently than we do. We must always separate our own feelings from those of our son. When we do, we can help our son recognize his feelings toward his father and help the two of them have a better, stronger relationship.

Issues Fathers Face

When Dads Orbit

During the early years of a boy's life, parents tend to be extremely busy. They may be trying to establish careers, make ends meet around the house, care for multiple kids, or watch over aging parents. Life can often feel out of control. Since women are taught that we multi-task well and since we are usually required to do so more often than men (even if we're not good at it), we learn to attend to our kids' needs more quickly. We sleep less soundly because we are wired to hear our kids in the night. On a playground, we can differentiate our child's voice from another's when he calls out, "Mom!" We know the difference between a sad cry and a mad cry. We listen to kid talk coming from the backseat of a car because we are conversationally oriented; since we need to talk more than men, we naturally spend more time listening, too.

Even at work we think about what goes on at home. I have worked as my husband's partner in medicine for many years and I will tell you that in that time I have done the lion's share of cooking and grocery shopping, usually planning these things during brief, free moments at the office. For instance, I often skipped lunch at work in order to have time later to stop by the store on my way home and pick up groceries for dinner. I am not alone. Most mothers do the same. Is that wrong? Not for me. My husband isn't a good cook and I love spending time in the kitchen with my kids. We have had great conversations over the years while cooking. We have figured out boy-friend troubles, decided which college works well for whom, and gotten into fights and made up, all while dying Easter eggs or making gingerbread houses or pasta dinners. Our kitchen is where life happens and I decided early in my marriage that I wanted to be smack in the middle of it.

More mothers than fathers make the conscious decision to be with their kids full-time, especially during their children's early years. And because dads know that mom is home with the kids, they feel secure that the children are being taken care of, enabling them, subconsciously or not, to pour themselves into their work. We only have limited hours in a week and we simply can't be concentrating on too many things at the same time. But since it is usually mom who decides to give up work time in exchange for time with their kids, dads end up missing out. The more they focus on work, the less they focus on home. It is easy to get swept up in a pattern of concentration in one area of our lives and forget about the others.

Some mothers feel jealousy toward their husbands because they spend more time at work and don't have to contend with screaming kids. They often feel neglected by men who work too much and pay little attention to them or to the children. I understand this. My husband worked insane hours for many years while our children were young. He was trying to get a medical practice established and that took a toll on our family. But I had also worked an incredibly demanding schedule during my pediatric residency training several years earlier while he stayed at home with our children. I can say that I wouldn't trade one hour of being with my kids for anything. Yes, the person working outside the home often becomes hyperfocused on the job and ignores the family, and this is never right; but sometimes it just happens. We who bear the burden of being ignored must be assertive and point out the situation. Then we must ask what we can do to make some changes. And if you are the one working outside the home and finding yourself too focused on work and ignoring those at home, face it. Do something about it, because you are missing out. Work makes us money and sometimes boosts our self-esteem. But relationships give us life.

Psychologically, dads and moms with careers have difficulty transitioning from work to home. Their bodies walk through the door at the end of a workday, but often their minds don't. There are tricks we must all learn when moving from work to home. We must literally learn to compartmentalize our thoughts. We need to train our minds to shut down work thoughts and ramp up concentration on what's happening at the house. When we walk through the door and our kids come running, we know we need to pay attention . . . and it's hard.

When life is exhausting during the early years of parenting, working, and career building, blame gets passed around. Couples fight over who should do what, why, and especially why not. Dads criticize moms for not paying enough attention to kids, work, or the house, and moms scold dads for the same. Each feels that they are doing more than the other. The truth is, in a busy home, both parents are working very hard and couples need to give each other a break, if not for their own sakes, then for the sake of their children. When we mothers are criticized for forgetting to do something, we get mad and fight back. When we criticize our husbands for never being around, they stay away even more. Neither of these reactions helps the marriage or the boys who sit at our feet and watch the Ping-Pong ball of blame. What does help is a very simple trick. Giving grace.

I think of grace as a kindness that a person doesn't deserve. When one partner feels as though she's doing the bulk of the work, but gives the other partner a pass, she's giving grace. When the other partner feels underappreciated, but decides not to act on it, he's giving grace. Think of the last mistake you made. If a loved one came to you and said, "I know that you messed up but I'm here to help, not criticize you," how would you feel? Chances are, you would want to be nicer to that person. You would want to be more engaged and spend more time with them. When a secure mother sees a failure (or perceived failure) in her spouse and gives him a pass, the whole dynamic in the family shifts. If a husband doesn't come home until eight every night and misses putting the kids to bed, your blood begins to boil. I get it. I've been there. But when we stop and make a decision to focus on the good that a dad brings to the family, rather than focusing on how he lets everyone down, we begin giving him grace. This not only helps us have a better relationship with him; it also sets an example for our kids to do the same when they are older. (And, for the record, reminding your husband that he doesn't deserve the forgiveness nullifies the whole grace part!)

I realize that the idea of choosing to do this seems to make many women angry. Some of you may be thinking, "You just don't know how ugly life is at my house. My husband is an alcoholic and there's no way I'm giving that a pass." Or perhaps your husband is abusive. He screams at you and your kids and his temper is out of control. I'm not talking about excusing that kind of bad behavior—particularly behavior that is harmful to you or your children. Rather, I'm saying that in situations where a father is a good man clearly trying to do a good job, we help him do a better job when we choose to focus on his positive attributes rather than the negative ones. Doing this takes a conscious effort because we naturally become defensive when we think we are being cheated.

There is a simple exercise that can help us begin this process. When we have a critical thought about how our husbands (or ex-husbands) let us down, are we going to let that thought out and complain to our husband or are we going to supplant it with a less critical thought? Sometimes we have no choice. If a dad does something outrageous and harmful, we must confront him, but usually this isn't the case. Most often our criticisms are small. They just feel big because we are exhausted. Or they feel overwhelming because we lack perspective. The truth is that for most of us, a lot of the criticism we levy doesn't gain us or our kids any ground. It only makes life tougher for everyone. When we take charge and decide to extend understanding and kindness to our husbands and manage some control over our negative thoughts, our sons win.

When a boy lives in an environment where he feels that his dad orbits the home, only shows up at night, and is gone—or inattentive—most of the time, he loses. Many fathers live on the periphery of the family either because they work long hours or because they don't know what their role is at home. Some dads might not know how to relate to their kids (maybe their parents never related well to them) or they simply feel uncomfortable in their role as fathers. When men are unsure how to parent, they pull back. I see this all the time with fathers and daughters. When daughters hit their adolescent years, fathers often feel insecure with what to do and what not to do. So rather than try something only to have it turn out to be the wrong thing, they do nothing. They back away. They stop talking to their daughters. They stop hugging them. The daughter, who already feels terribly uncomfortable with herself, feels worse because it seems that dad doesn't love her anymore. You can see how things become messy very quickly—all because a dad retreats when he really should be moving forward.

The same is true for dads during the early years in their sons' lives. Many dads simply don't understand how much they are needed. They feel confused about our roles as mothers, and it isn't uncommon for them to feel jealous toward us. I have met many fathers who say that they wish they had the closeness with their kids that their wives do. But they can! We need to recognize that often dads aren't involved not because they don't want to be, but because they don't realize how important they are, and because many dads simply don't know what to do with their kids. And in order to help our husbands relate better to our sons, it is important for us to understand our husbands' insecurities, hesitations, and even their history. Many fathers want better relationships but are afraid to express warmth and affection to their sons for fear of appearing weak. Others want to talk to their sons but don't know how. It may be that simple. Still other men may not know how to relate to their sons, because their father never related to them in any meaningful way. So we can help them by giving pointers and encouragement.

Every Father Had a Father

In light of what we now know a boy needs from his dad in order to be emotionally whole, you can perhaps begin to see why your husband acts the way he does. If he never had his father's blessing, he may feel tremendously insecure. If he felt rejection rather than acceptance from his father, how will he act toward his own son? He may criticize others constantly (particularly his son, who reminds him of himself as a boy) or he may work exhaustively trying to prove that he is successful and able. A man who never got enough attention from his father may crave excessive affection, both physically and emotionally, in order to fill the emptiness he feels inside. For many men, pain from their relationships with their fathers comes out sideways. They may not know why they rage, but you might be able to see that it is tied to a deep-seated fear that you, too, will reject him one day. You may notice that whenever he is around older men, he brags about himself, trying to garner praise because he feels he still needs it. Watch your husband closely and you will begin to see the motive behind many of his behaviors, and recognize that some may very well be linked to wounds from his relationship with his father.

This is an important exercise because many times we observe our husbands' actions from a self-centered point of view; we assume that they behave badly because of something we've done. Very often, it has nothing to do with us. The same goes for our sons; when dad acts harshly toward his son, or criticizes him, it may be because that's how his father treated him, not because of something his son said or did. Remember that men do what they know. As a mother, you are in a perfect position to watch your husband's behavior toward your son and recognize what is good parenting and what behaviors stem from his childhood. You don't want to flood him with psychobabble and you most certainly don't want to be the psychological police of the family. But you can position yourself to help your husband be a better dad if you watch, listen, and try hard to understand his relationship with your son as it relates to his relationship with his own dad. You'll be amazed at how clearly you will begin to see patterns of his dad's behavior in his treatment of your son.

One of the best things mothers can do is talk to their husbands about their husbands' relationships with their own fathers. We must be sensitive and cautious when asking husbands about their fathers, because if they had a bad relationship, they can become defensive and shut down. It helps to ask very simple and nonthreatening questions like "What kinds of things did you do with your dad when you were growing up?" or "Did you and your dad spend much time together when you were a kid?"

As you listen to your husband's answers you will hear his feelings. He may reflect on their activities with a warm tone or he may disconnect emotionally right away. If his father never paid attention to him, you will see hurt on his face. Watch closely and use his expressions as a guide to whether or not you should keep going. One of the greatest values in having your husband talk about his own father is that it not only lets you have a peek into what he experienced; more important, it allows him to see how his father parented him and it helps him discern exactly how much he is or is not repeating his father's parenting patterns.

———

Alyce was an astute mother. She brought Kyle to see me when he was fourteen because she said that she was worried he was depressed.

When he began ninth grade, he started a new high school, which was three times the size of his junior high school. When he got there, his grades dropped and he began hanging out with a new set of friends. He got his ankle tattooed against his parents' express wishes. Even his clothing changed. He went from wearing khakis to oversize jeans that showed most of his buttocks.

"I don't know what happened to my kid," she cried. "I feel like he just changed overnight. He doesn't come home until late at night, he won't do his homework, and whenever I ask him what's wrong, he just stares at me like I'm something from a horror movie."

As Alyce talked, I watched Kyle. He sat stone-faced beside his mother, clearly embarrassed and a bit agitated. When I asked him to tell me what was going on, he wouldn't answer. For a full forty-five minutes he refused to talk, even though I asked his mother to leave the room so we could speak alone. At the end of the visit, I asked his mother to do some detective work. What was happening at school? Was a girlfriend involved, or had he started taking drugs? Essentially, I advised Alyce to look for clues to explain Kyle's behavior in the sphere outside the home—I figured the culprit must lie among his friends or at school, perhaps even an incident where he was molested or bullied. I tried to think of everything. Fortunately, she thought more outside the box than I did.

When she returned with Kyle a few weeks later, she told me what she had found. Kyle was a nice kid in class. His teachers didn't have any complaints other than the fact that he lacked motivation. But they assured her that a lot of boys his age shared that problem. As far as friends went, he only had a few, and some smoked weed and some didn't. No hard drugs or drinking. No girlfriend, no bullies, and as far as she could tell, he hadn't been the victim of any type of abuse— recently or in the past.

But she had noticed something else. "Kyle's dad, Carl, hasn't been himself lately," she told me. "His own father died a few months back and he won't talk about it. He never used to drink but lately he's been coming home and throwing down a few beers. He doesn't get drunk or anything, but drinking gives him a meaner edge than he normally has."

I looked at Kyle as she said this and his eyes welled up. I asked Alyce to explain. "It's just the three of us at night and sometimes he gets tough on Kyle. Carl tells him that he'll never amount to anything because he won't do his homework. When Kyle comes home late, Carl goes into his room and accuses him of doing drugs or sleeping around. I just don't get it. He never did stuff like that before."

By this time Kyle had tears streaming down both cheeks. They were falling onto his black baggy pants and he made no effort to wipe them away. Suddenly he looked six, not fourteen.

"Kyle, does your dad yell at you a lot?" I asked.

"I don't know," he answered. I asked if he wanted his mother to leave the room and he shook his head.

"What did you and your dad use to do for fun?" I asked.

He seemed relieved by the levity of the question. "A lot of stuff. Nothing big, but we'd go to the racetrack on the weekends sometimes. We used to work on an old car we have in the shed. Lots of stuff, I guess."

I asked what he and his dad did together now and he stared at the wall.

"Nothing. He can't stand me," he said curtly.

"Why do you think your dad doesn't like you anymore?" I asked.

"Why should he?"

"What did you do?" I pressed.

"I don't know. Doesn't matter. Nothing I do is right. I mean, I don't have to do *any*thing anymore for my dad not to like me." In fact, I found out, Kyle really hadn't done anything wrong. His problem was that he was the son of his father who was hurting over the death of his own dad. Before her second appointment, Alyce had called her sister-in-law to ask why Carl was taking his father's death so hard. Alyce learned that when her husband was a child, his father criticized him relentlessly. He was a good kid, her sister-in-law said, but their father never encouraged him. Rather, he picked apart every mistake Carl made and told him that unless he worked harder, he was never going to amount to anything. The relationship was so painful that Carl distanced himself from his father. In fact, until his father died, Carl had rarely spoken to Alyce about the man.

"Could it be possible that Carl's dumping all of his hurt about his own dad onto Kyle?" Alyce asked me.

"I think so. Do you think you can talk to Carl about this?" I replied.

Alyce went home and talked with Carl. As she later described to me, she carefully asked him how he was taking his dad's death and she told him that she was willing to talk anytime he wanted. What was particularly beneficial in her approach was that, rather than insisting they speak about how poorly he was treating Kyle, she first acknowledged that her husband was in pain. Then she gently pried and found out that he felt terrible guilt over his father's death. He couldn't stand him. He had never told her so, but couldn't keep it in anymore. When his father died, Carl felt awful that he'd never tried to reconcile with his dad or even bothered to be nice at all. He also hadn't helped his father financially, and he thought he should have.

Over the next weeks, Alyce listened to Carl, and she also told him that Kyle was hurting, too. He needed his dad now. He didn't need a better teacher, different friends, or another sport. He needed his dad. Once Carl realized that he had been taking his anger at himself and his father out on Kyle, he told his son that.

You can write the rest of the story. Kyle's grades improved. His demeanor changed almost overnight and his depression lifted. Sometimes the answers to our son's problems are staring us in the face, and unless we are savvy enough to keep our eyes open, we'll miss them. The best part, too, is that many times their problems are much easier to solve than we think. Kyle didn't need a psychiatrist or a counselor. He simply needed his dad back. And his mom helped him get that.

There are many things that can create distance and discord between our sons and their dads. Often, neither of them recognizes the causes, but as in Alyce's case, we mothers see things that fathers can't see. We don't need to have a Ph.D. in psychology, but we do have to be open-minded. This is the toughest part. Our inclination is to home in on our husband's faults and start the blame game rather than stand back and figure out what is best for our sons. We want our husbands to *change* so that our lives will be better, but that isn't what we should be focusing on, nor is it realistic to think that's going to happen. When it comes to our sons, we must put their needs first and help make their relationships with their dads stronger. When we make this a priority, life changes for everyone. Here's where we can start.

WHAT WE MOTHERS MUST DO

Be Inclusive, Not Exclusive

From the time our child is an infant, the message that we send, and in turn the role we accept, is that we are the sole source of everything good in that child's life. But is it really smart to believe that if you don't, say, breastfeed for at least a year, you aren't a great mom? We hear from our friends and well-meaning physicians that the best mothers offer their kids the best of everything, always. If he cries as an infant, pick him up, because it is vital to meet all of our child's emotional needs 24/7. When he is two, rather than saying "no" when he makes unreasonable demands, we must redirect our son's interests so that he doesn't hear anything negative from our lips. We are to constantly bolster self-esteem, provide meals that are made from scratch (using organic foods of course), and ensure that our son gets into the accelerated reading group in second grade (and if he can't, then find him an excellent tutor). We are to work extra jobs to pay for his high-priced shoes and jeans, be the cool mom whose house all the teens want to hang out at, and make sure that our kids connect well with us at all times. We are the happy police and we will do whatever it takes to keep our kids entertained. If they need to spend a year abroad, we pay for it. If they need a nose job, we pay for it. New equipment for a sport he wants to try out just to see if he likes it? No problem.

If all this sounds excessive, that's because it is. We want so badly for our sons to be happy, we have jumped on the crazy train. I understand, because I jumped on it along with everyone else. But I'm tired, and I'll bet you are, too. It's time to recognize that we can't *do* it all, we can't *buy* it all, and that the only other ingredient in our children's lives that is as important as we are is their father.

The healthy way to view our son's needs is to recognize that he is born into a family unit. He belongs not just to us, but to others as well; his father, grandparents, aunts and uncles, cousins, and siblings. He needs them in different ways than he needs us, but those ways are terribly important. When we parent as if those people don't really matter, we parent exclusively. Subconsciously, we cut our son off from an important source of influence and love. And when we do that, our son loses. But when we shift our perspective and learn to parent inclusively, our son wins. And so do we.

What would it look like to parent inclusively? Let's consider the first year of your son's life. You might decide to breastfeed but also to pump or bottle-feed. That way, your husband can help with feedings during the day or night, giving the two of them the opportunity to bond. You might choose to shift your work schedule and your husband's so that he is home more with your son while you are at work. More dramatically, you might choose to believe that you need time alone and your son needs more time with your husband, and have the two spend a night away or spend a night away yourself. And when it comes to important decisions, don't discount the input of others just because you feel you know best.

In other words, parenting more inclusively means letting go of some of the control that we long to have over our sons' lives. It means being willing to not always have our way with his life and trusting others—especially his dad—to do as good a job as we can. Many mothers may say that they want this but their body language communicates something altogether different. I have been guilty of this myself. I would tell my husband that he needed to spend more time with the kids, of course saying it in a way that made him feel like he wasn't doing his part. Then, when he would take the kids somewhere, I would criticize how they were dressed, what they did, and how he handled the outing. Being a nonconfrontational sort, he would simply throw his hands up and shake his head. What I learned is that while I wanted him more involved, I parented as though I were the only one who knew how to do things right with our kids. So why in the world would he want to cooperate?

It may be a generalization, but I believe women are more prone than men to bossiness and are bigger control freaks. Of course, that stems from wanting everything to be perfect, but we have to learn that our way is not necessarily the best way. Sometimes we hide behind the guise of being the better parent because we feel threatened; we worry that if our son grows closer to his dad, we will lose him. We worry that the two of them will forge a bond that will exclude us. But the only thing that will happen if your son develops a healthier relationship with his dad is that he will have a healthier relationship with you. You don't have to compete with his father. Your son is bound to you by a love that feels very different to him than his love for his dad. So never feel threatened. When a boy has a solid relationship with his father, he feels better about his life. Since he is happier, he will relate to you better. When his father meets the needs that must be met by him, your son won't turn to you to try to have those needs met. This frees you up to focus on being simply his mother.

From your son's earliest days, think about the fact that you and he are bound together in a unit—a community, if you will. His dad is in that unit and your son wants you all to be together. He wants dad inside the community, and regardless of how you feel toward his dad, all of your lives will be richer if you help make that happen.

Sometimes being more inclusive means backing out of the way. Make sure that dad's opinions count when it comes to parenting and let your son see that you pay attention and respect his dad's thoughts and feelings.

Teach Him to Turn to Dad

Many conscientious mothers sabotage their son's relationship with their dads because they take over. I have found myself interrupting my husband when he is talking to our son about important issues. I would hear the two of them discussing something, disagree with how my husband was handling the conversation, and swoop into the room. I would sidle my way into the conversation and everything about my body language would communicate to my husband, "Move over, I've got this. I know how to handle this better than you do."

Have you ever found yourself interrupting an otherwise good conversation between your husband and son? Or taking control of an important decision such as choosing his school, or giving advice about dating, drinking, or sex? Teaching our sons is wonderful and I'm not saying that we shouldn't do it. Of course we should, and it's our job, but many times we usurp our husband's influence by answering all of our son's questions and always being the one to attend to his needs. If we want to help our son grow closer to his father, sometimes we need to swallow hard and tell him to seek his dad's advice. Doing this accomplishes three very important things.

First, it tells your son that his dad is important. He learns that his dad has a lot of good advice to give and that his advice is trustworthy. When he learns this, he looks up to his father and feels better and more secure about his life.

Second, it makes the two of them communicate. Working through a problem and communicating helps them grow closer, and it helps set the precedent for their relationship in the future.

Third, it makes the dad feel needed. When fathers feel needed in their relationships with their kids, they parent better, and become more confident in their parenting. This is especially true if a mother is strong-willed; many fathers feel inadequate and in my experience, when dads feel insecure, and afraid of screwing up or doing the wrong thing, they simply vanish into the background. This timidity can easily be mistaken by your son as a lack of caring or lack of love, which is the last thing you want.

So what do you do if dad is not available? Many mothers simply have no choice but to spearhead the resolution of the son's problems. When your son starts maturing and wishing for a father who could help him, you can tell him, "I'll bet you would like to have a dad who could help you. I'm sorry that you don't." Again, if there is a way where you can recruit a good adult man to help, do it. Your son will love you for it. If an uncle, grandfather, rabbi, pastor, youth group leader, friend, even has good, solid character, ask if he will spend time with your son. This may feel awkward at first, but do it. You might simply ask if your son could tag along to a movie with him. If he has kids, ask if your son could join him on an outing or help around the house sometime. Be creative. Many men feel appreciated when asked to share themselves with younger kids, because knowing that you think they have something important to offer makes them feel valued.

Practice Applause

Many mothers aren't long on applause when it comes to the men in our lives. We are tired; we work extremely hard and get frustrated that we don't have more help. Single moms feel as though they get beaten up every day. Mothers who work outside the home feel resentful if their husbands don't work, or work too much, and vice versa. We get mad, sad, and annoyed easily, and all of this is normal. Unfortunately, our loved ones are the ones who pay the price for our grief. We don't yell at coworkers; we yell at our kids. We don't criticize a girlfriend of ours for being late, but we bark at our husbands when they make us wait for dinner. Loved ones have to live with our good *and* bad sides because at home we are our real selves.

Most of us mothers, though, work hard to keep our frustrations away from our kids. Yes, we lose it with them on occasion, but we try not to. Our husbands, however, are another story. They forget to put the toilet seat down. They don't bathe the kids enough, or ever. They don't do the classroom-mom thing. They don't do as much house-work as we do, etc., etc. Complaining is as natural as breathing air to exhausted women. In fact, we have made husband-bashing a national pastime. How many Internet jokes do you see regularly about men who are lazy, stupid, or drink too much beer? And try to pick up a decent Father's Day card. All you will find are two types: ones that are scripted in flowery letters, filled with euphemisms about perfect dads, and ones about dads who hog the remote, never mow the lawn, and watch too many sports on television. Seeing such stereotypes rein-forced has an impact on how sons view their fathers and themselves.

Ask yourself how you would feel as a mother if you saw such jokes about yourself. If I saw Mother's Day cards filled with cartoon char-acters of women who shop too much, talk on the phone too much, or watch too many TV shows, I'd feel terrible and furious!

Giving praise rather than criticism makes us happier women. Try it. If you speak more positively, you will feel more positive. Changing the way we talk changes the way we feel. Challenge yourself to an experiment for two weeks and see if you don't feel better. When you are ready to criticize your husband, stop. Instead, say something nice to him. Find something—anything—to compliment him on. If you have a real beef with him, talk to a friend. I can guarantee that over time, complimenting your husband on his parenting will make him a much better father.

Deirdre's life changed when she tried this approach. Married for fifteen years, with three children and a full-time job as a letter carrier, she hit her early forties feeling miserable about life. She found herself daydreaming about being divorced. Sometimes she imagined herself buying a plane ticket to a sunny California spot and living there all alone. When she had these thoughts, she felt guilty.

We were chatting one day about her depression and I asked about her kids and her marriage. "Everyone's fine. They all seem to be doing well. The kids' grades are good. Sports are going well and Matt's job is fine. But he's just not really into home life, you know what I mean?"

"Sure," I told her. "What do you guys do on weekends? Can you spend any time together?"

"I wish!" she groaned. "He's up at the crack of dawn fishing with his buddies. He's so selfish, really. I'm left to haul the kids to their soccer games, sleepovers, you name it." Deirdre sounded exhausted.

"Are you bitter toward Matt?" I queried.

"Bitter? I'm beyond bitter. We've argued so many times over fishing that he doesn't even hear me anymore. Yelling doesn't work. Threatening to leave doesn't work. I've even tried telling the kids to talk to him and ask if he'll do something with them on the weekends."

I sympathized with Deirdre. She was a hardworking woman and a good mom who felt stuck. I also knew Matt and wondered why in the world he was acting so selfishly. Why would a man leave his family every Saturday to fish for the whole day and pay no attention to his kids? Was he simply a jerk?

We finished our coffee and I suggested that she get some help for her depression. She really was spiraling downward and I knew that her life would just get worse if she didn't take action.

"Here's the deal," I said. "You're depressed. I've known you for a long time and you've never been this negative about life, your kids, yourself, or Matt. There's a whole lot that's good about your life but you can't see it now. Yes, your husband's being incredibly selfish but you can't change that. You're exhausted and there are a few things that you *can* do about that. You need some help. Medications are good and there are some really good counselors who can help you pick your way through this. In the meantime, I think it might help for you to begin each day by focusing on a few great things in your life just to help you get through the day. Make a list. Write them down. Like: Your kids are good students. You have a nice home. Your dog likes you."

Deirdre chuckled but got the point. She left that day and I didn't see her for a few months. We had one of those relationships that spanned time and distance. We didn't need to talk every day or even every week. Several months later, we picked up our conversation exactly where we left off.

"Well," she announced, "I think my depression's doing a lot better." We always cut right to the chase, leaving the small talk behind.

"Wonderful," I said. "How did that happen?"

"I took your advice and went to a counselor. I saw my doctor and we talked about medication. That was all helpful, but the most amazing thing was Matt. I think he saw that I was hurting. I tried that thing about writing down what I'm grateful for, to see if it would work. Then I decided to go one step further. I chose to find something positive about Matt and tell him every day—or maybe it was every other day. Like, I told him that he's a good listener (when he listens—but I didn't add that part!) with the kids. I told him that we wished he was with us when we went for ice cream after soccer games on Saturday. You know, I said it like I really meant it—not like I was trying to make him feel guilty. He seemed to respond, so I kept it up for one week, then another and another."

Deirdre was applauding Matt by giving him verbal praise in spite of her anger and bitterness toward his absence on weekends. I admired her self-discipline.

"That must have been really hard," I told her. "I mean feeling so upset and down and saying nice things to him when you were mad that he was never home."

"Yep. It was really hard. But here's the cool thing. I had nothing to lose. I'd tried fighting and he only fished more. So I decided to think about his wonderful qualities. He is kind. He is patient with the kids and when he's with them, he's a really loving dad. So I told him that. The thing was, once I started, I found that it wasn't that hard *and* I started to like him more. Can you believe it?"

"Yes, I can."

"For some reason, we all started to get along a little better. And you won't believe this. After about six weeks, we all woke up one Saturday morning and Matt was home. He was in the garage working on his car. When one of the kids asked why he wasn't fishing, I heard him say, 'Aw, I just didn't feel like it today.' To tell you the truth, I felt kind of mad. I had gotten so used to him being gone that I had a hard time adjusting to him being around! At first I thought, 'What was he doing home on our Saturday?'"

When we change the way we talk, we change the way we feel. But there's more: We also change the ways others behave around us. I'll bet if we could hear Matt's side of the story we would find that much of the reason he left on Saturday mornings wasn't that he was a selfish jerk. He might have felt unwanted. He might have believed that no one needed him at home. I'm not sure. But I do know that Deirdre changed the dynamics of her relationship with her husband and her kids' relationship with their father by making one simple but very difficult change: She focused on the positives in her life, and made an intentional habit of praising her husband regularly.

Giving our sons' fathers applause changes them. Men who feel encouraged are far more likely to parent better than men who feel beaten up at every turn by their wives at home. Yes, we are communicators by nature, but tweaking *how* we communicate can have a strong impact on our loved ones. One of the best gifts we can give our sons is to praise their dads. Happier dads mean happier sons, and that is the ultimate goal of us moms.

However, I know many mothers live with particularly stressful challenges. Many parent their sons alone. Others contend with an ex-husband who won't support her or their son. Some mothers strongly disagree with the lifestyles their ex-husbands expose their sons to, like too much drinking, or women coming and going from the father's home. Some contend with fathers who abuse their sons. I have seen mothers desperate to keep their sons from bad or dangerous influences. The following section is for those who have particularly difficult issues.

A Word to Single Moms

Many mothers have real problems with the fathers of their sons. Maybe your husband is out of the picture, or maybe he is in the picture but is a bad influence. If that is the case, take heart; you are not alone and there are several things you can do to help your son. Let's first look at mothers whose sons' fathers are completely absent. Here are a few tips that may help you.

Don't go it alone. Chances are good that you've been trying to be both Mom and Dad. Stop. You can only be a really good mom, and that's enough for your son to turn out really well. Many great men were raised by mothers who parented solo. The key is accepting that you can't do it all, and that no matter how wonderful a mom you are, your son needs healthy interaction with men. His peers don't count. He needs adult men whom he can observe. Find a grandfather, uncle, coach, pastor, or teacher in his life whom you trust. Make sure that you know the man well before you ask his help because certainly, you don't want your son to spend time with or learn to look up to a man who will hurt him. Then find ways for your son to be around him. Invite him to dinner. Ask him to take your son camping, or along for some other activity that interests him. After the two are together, talk about that man to your son. Keep an image of him alive in your son's mind. When difficulties come up, ask your son what he thinks that man would do. What would he say? How would he decide what is best? By doing this you are helping your son create the picture of a man with integrity, courage, kindness, and dedication (and any other attributes that you believe a good man needs) in his mind. As he matures, he can draw on that image to make decisions.

Most single mothers I have met feel guilty because a man is not involved in their son's life. So do the best you can to help him spend time with a man you respect. If, however, you can't find a man to help with your son, remember to still acknowledge your son's need to have a man to look up to. Boys are visual people and they need to create a mental image of a good man to follow. If that image is all he can have, then help him create one. Talk about how he thinks a smart man would make decisions, how a patient man would act, or how a man with great courage would respond under pressure, especially when certain situations arise. For example, if his friends ask him to go to a party where kids are drinking, and he knows he shouldn't, ask what he thinks a courageous man would say. If his girlfriend breaks up with him, ask how a forgiving man would handle the situation. Once you look for opportunities like these moments for him to create a mental picture of a strong role model, you will find them everywhere.

If you are uncomfortable asking him about how an anonymous but good man would react, then draw on one of his heroes. If he loves reading about a past president or loves a character in a novel, ask him how those men would respond. A word of caution here: Be careful whom you choose because many boys look up to men who aren't men you want your son to emulate. For instance, many boys revere actors, athletes, or musicians whom you don't necessarily respect. So avoid allowing your son to use them as examples. If they want to use them (and many will) as men to imitate, continue to talk up men with greater character qualities. You don't need to constantly criticize their idols; simply bring up different ones whom you want him to admire.

Be careful how you speak about your son's father, and even men in general. Many women whose husbands or boyfriends have walked out on them carry a lot of hurt and anger toward those men. This is natural. But you must remember that your sons parrot many of your thoughts and beliefs, and if he hears you talking negatively about his father and other men often, he will begin to feel negatively about men as well. More important, he may start to feel negatively about his own manhood, and psychologically that gets very messy. So when you are upset about men, don't vent in front of your son. *Acknowledge his need for Dad.* One of the most painful things we can do to our sons when we parent exclusively is to try to convince them that they need only us. Since in their hearts they can't help but have a deep longing for a father's affection, they will ultimately wonder if that means something is wrong with them. Moms are grown-ups, so in our son's eyes, we are right. When we communicate that our son needs only us and that they will do just fine without a dad, we are in essence telling them that their desire for their dad's attention and love is silly, and wrong.

Tell your son that you understand his need for his dad. Tell him that you are sorry his dad isn't available. Talk with him about what it would be like to have his dad around. Don't be afraid of bringing his deeper needs out into the open, because doing so will help him face them and let him begin to heal. Hiding his feelings and needs is what gets him into trouble, and doing so may set him up for depression later in life. The way to be an extraordinary mom is to help your son understand his needs and then acknowledge them. If they aren't met, help him grieve, but also do something more: Help him to see that although his dad isn't around, he does have Uncle Mike, his pastor, his coach, or his grandfather. Tell him that no, they aren't his dad and they never will be, but they can still be men who will love and care for him.

For mothers with an ex-husband who is a bad influence

Pick your battles. Mothers coparenting with fathers who do bad things have a tough road, but there are some things to do that will help smooth it out. One of my close friends coparents with an ex-husband who gambles and frequently has girlfriends spend nights at his home. There is nothing she can do to stop these behaviors and the courts have given her ex-husband partial custody. So she found a different way to work with her ex-husband even though she is very angry with him. She decided to be courteous with him and see if they could negotiate what their son will be exposed to and what he won't while he is with him. And she respectfully asked him if there were certain things he would like her to do with and for their son while she was with him. Understanding that she wasn't in charge of what their son did while she was away from him, she acknowledged that she was willing to help her ex-husband feel honored and respected. Then she told him that she would do those things for him if he would do a few things for *her* while their son was at his home. She asked that his girlfriends not spend nights when their son was at his home. Then she asked that he go to casinos on the nights when their son wasn't with him.

By telling her ex-husband that she recognized he had wishes for their son that he wanted honored while he was away from him, she then felt heard when she asked the same from him. Negotiating in a respectful way can really help make life easier and less stressful for children caught in the middle. One of the most important rules is to pick the battles you are willing to fight. Try making a list of three (or so) rules—things that are important to you. For instance, you may want your son's father to avoid drinking, having girl-friends spend the night, overly criticizing your son, or taking him to casinos, as my friend did. You will know which specific rules are important to you. Then ask your ex if you can talk and negotiate some things about your son's care. Share your list with him and then ask him to tell you the top three things he would like to see you do with your son. Then tell him that you will honor them. Let him know that you are willing to work with him because you respect him as your son's dad.

Honor your son's need for his absent dad. A father may be alive but never engaged with a son, or he may be present but never emotionally involved in any way. Either way, a son needs to know that you recognize his need for his father's involvement since a son is connected to his dad for life. No matter how badly his father has acted, a son lives with an ache for his missing dad. Even if he wants to hate his father, maybe for the way he treated you, he can't because he needs something from him. He may never get what he needs, but he won't be able to resolve that in any significant way if all he hears from you is criticism about his dad, or if you fail to acknowledge *his* feelings because of your own.

Your son knows what bad things your ex did (or does); you don't have to tell him. What your son may need to do is discuss his own feelings of disappointment. If all you do is talk about *your* feelings, it puts your son on the defensive and he will stick up for his dad rather than open up about *his* hurt.

When your ex misbehaves, criticize the behavior, not the man. This is really tough, but train yourself to let your son know that it's his dad's behavior that is bad, not the man himself. When negative incidents happen, talk to your son about them. Tell him that his dad's behavior was completely inappropriate and let your son know that he is in no way responsible for it.

For instance, if a father leaves home and has a series of live-in girlfriends, your son will most likely be upset. And he should. This is the behavior of an adolescent, not a mature, responsible man. This will come up in your conversation with him and I would encourage you to say something like "What your dad chooses to do isn't healthy. It hurts him, it hurts you, and I don't agree with it. He's a good person, but I don't think what he's doing is right." Then leave it at that. If your son senses that his dad disgusts you, he will become defensive and say that his dad is right. So always try to keep your son from being in a position where he needs to defend his father to you.

———

Helping our sons grow into great men is not a task for wimpy moms. Fortunately for our sons, most of us are anything but wimpy. It takes courage, tenacity, and a bit of chutzpah to raise strong men, but that is part of the joy of being the mother of a son. And one of the most courageous things that we mothers can do for our sons is acknowledge their need for their fathers (or good men) and help them have better relationships with them.

CHAPTER 8

Sex on the Brain and What My Mom Says

S o you think that, because you are the mom, you can't influence the decisions your teenage son makes about sex? Think again. Your beliefs about sex and what you teach your son regarding those beliefs are more powerful than you can imagine. All mothers need to be aware of the fact that when a son is formulating his decisions about sex and shaping his ideas about his sexuality and the way he sees himself, he will always factor in what you think and what you've told him. In fact, the formation of his sexuality and how he feels about it is largely dependent upon cues that he receives from you regarding his value and his manhood.

OUR BOYS AND THEIR SEXUALITY

The development of a boy's sexuality is a complicated and sophisticated process. We moms would like to see it as pretty straightforward, but, just like healthy psychological development, the maturing of a man's sexuality is influenced by genetics, the attitudes of loved ones, social pressures, life experiences (including negative ones, such as abuse), and many other factors. As a matter of fact, Dr. Armand Nicholi, a learned and wise professor of medicine at Harvard Medical

School and author of *The Harvard Guide to Psychiatry,* told me that he believes the complete formation of one's sexuality doesn't occur until the end of the teen years. That's because it is a beautifully complex process, which involves numerous dimensions of a man's character. Based on my experience with teenage boys over the past twenty-five years, I would certainly agree with Dr. Nicholi.

The sexual identity of a man is defined by how he sees himself as a sexual being. It is a bit different from his broader identity as a man, which defines who he is as a person. For instance, men see themselves as sexual beings interested in sexual activity that connects them on emotional, physical, and intellectual levels to their partners. Their larger identity as men includes their sexuality and encompasses every aspect of who they are. For instance, a man may identify himself as his father's son, an engineer, a loving father, and a devoted husband. Within those contexts, he is a man deeply connected to his wife through his sexuality. Let's say that this man had a medical disorder that prevented him from having sexual activity and even lowered his desire to have sex. Would his identity as a man be diminished because he felt that his sexuality was compromised? No. His larger identity as father, husband, engineer, etc. would continue to give him value as a man. Consider priests. They have a strong identity as men who are sons of God, loving, caring to their parishioners, and deeply devoted to the God and the people He calls them to serve. Within their identities as these men, they each have their own sexualities but they choose not to act on their sexual desires. We can see that the sexuality of a man is part of his core identity as a man, but it is not the whole of it.

Teen boys have an emerging sense of who they are as men even while their sexualities are still developing. The truth is, most teens grapple with who they are as sexual beings on a daily basis and this is how it should be. Boys don't simply wake up one day and know who they are sexually. Sexuality, just like a boy's identity, takes time to develop and emerge. Most important, a boy's sexuality is linked to his ability to trust, to love others, to like himself, to express himself, and to regard himself as valuable. It is enmeshed with every aspect of his character: If he is patient, he will be patient sexually. If he is kind, he is likely to express kindness during his sexual activity; on the flip side, if he suffers from rage, the chances are likely that his rage will come out during sexual activity. A man's sexual confidence will inform his overall personality, as well. For example, feeling sexually confident will make him feel more courageous in other things. In fact, it is difficult to disconnect other aspects of a man's character from his sexuality. So, when it comes to raising healthy sons, we mothers need to understand that helping them mature into men who feel strong and good about themselves as sexual beings is paramount. The daunting question for us is, how in the world can we do this?

First, we must accept that regardless of whether or not we like it, our role as mom means that we *will* influence our son's sexuality. It will happen whether we try to make it happen or not. And since this is the case, we should learn to exert our influence in a healthy, positive manner. The good news is that it's simpler than one might think. The first thing to know is that we will actually have an easier time of it than will dad, because our son will never compare his masculinity with ours. Because we are women, our sons will not see us as a "competitor," and therefore will be more accepting of our point of view. Our job is simply to love, direct, challenge, and buoy his masculinity at every turn. And these are things we can do.

The process starts from the time our son is born. Once he enters our world, he will immediately know whether we love and accept him or if we reject him. When we pick him up and he smells the scent of our skin, he learns that smell means Mom and the smell of Mom soothes him. The smell means that he is safe because when he cries, it comes back to him again and again. When he is a toddler, he runs away and waits to see if we watch where he goes and if we'll come to get him. He turns a corner and wants to hear us call his name. If we do, he feels loved and (depending upon his mood or temperament) will either run farther away to test us more, or come back toward us to be comforted. All he needs to know is that we were paying attention. When we pay attention, he learns that he's a person who deserves to be cared about.

As our son matures into his early elementary school years, there will be changes in his everyday world. For example, he will learn that he can no longer go into the ladies' room with us. For many mothers, this can be a terrifying moment. When my son was in second grade, he and I were traveling to Boston and we had a layover in the Detroit airport. I begged him to use the bathroom on the airplane before we landed but he said he didn't need to. But sure enough, the moment we set foot in the airport, he needed to go. He appropriately refused to go into the ladies' room with me (even though I offered to pay him five dollars) and insisted on going into the men's room. I wrung my hands. I told him exactly what to say if a stranger began talking to him inappropriately. For the first time in his life, he strutted into the men's room all alone, the heels of his light-up sneakers winking at me as he walked away. I stood as close to the entrance as was socially acceptable and made sure to yell loudly. "How's it going?" Ten seconds. "Need any help?" Ten seconds. "Uh—I didn't mean that—um—just waiting here. Take your time."

The poor kid. It's a miracle he even was able to pee. When he emerged from the men's room, I made a face and asked if he had washed his hands. He shook his head. Ugh, now I had a problem on my hands. Should I send him back in and go through the torment of waiting all over again, or just live with filthy hands? I quickly found a sanitary wipe and made do with that.

As he matured, I asked my son if he remembered those early times when I fretted over sending him to the men's room alone, and he told me that he most certainly did. Every detail. He told me that I had indeed embarrassed him but that he also remembered me explaining my fears to him. And now he could understand my perspective. Had I irreparably harmed his sense of independence and masculinity? No. At least, that's what he tells me now. We can even laugh about it.

A son's masculinity isn't shaped by our sitting down with him and presenting our clearly articulated beliefs in a few sessions; it is shaped along the way by everyday experiences. When they see how we react in different circumstances—like how and when we let them use public men's restrooms—it gives them messages about their sexuality. At eight years old, my son had a very clear sense that he was male and didn't belong with the girls anymore. He used urinals; *girls* used toilets. He needed to separate from me and see that I trusted his ability to be independent. As he matured, he was learning that being different from me was a good thing. It made him feel strong. It made him male. I didn't handle his first (or subsequent few) visits to the men's room alone well, because I let my fears over what might happen overwhelm my trust in my son. But over time, I learned to be comfortable letting him go. After all, he was fine; I was the one with the problem. And by gradually accepting this fact, eventually I learned to be fine with it, too.

Our sons pass through many different stages as they grow up, both emotionally and physically, and we must teach ourselves to let them take their own steps into their manhood. I don't know if I've ever met a mother who is completely comfortable doing this, but at a certain point, we must put aside our fears and let them do what is best for them. If we don't, we communicate to our sons that being male is frightening and may even be dangerous. And if we send this message, the health of our son's sexuality will be threatened. So, as they make their way into the adult male world, the best thing we can do is stand in the wings, and react to their performance in the healthiest way that we can by being supportive, loving, and trusting in their capabilities.

Our Sons Are Under Sexual Assault

I will be the first to admit that I was more nervous about my daughters being harmed in high school than I was my son. I worried that a guy would slip something into their drink and assault them sexually, or just be too aggressive or demanding. My daughters, while very capable and assertive, seemed more vulnerable to me than my son. When it came time for him to maneuver his way through high school, his six-foot-one frame made me feel secure in his ability to take care of himself. So I relaxed. But I wasn't paying close enough attention to all the unhealthy messages that he would be bombarded with every day—and many of the messages involved his sexuality.

Take, for example, video games that combine hypersexual imagery with violence. Teenage boys love to play these types of games. The sexual content is bad enough, but when the sex is married to violent behavior, boys get the message that it's okay to dominate women. Now, the boys themselves, and even parents, may argue that video games are just that—games. That they know what happens on the screen isn't real, and so playing such games doesn't affect them. But I don't believe this is the case.

Boys are hardwired to be visual people. Unlike girls, when boys see sexy images, they have difficulty looking away. That's why pornography so powerfully affects many men. The pull of sexually graphic imagery can feel so strong that a boy will be unable to break his focus on what he is seeing; and the sex and violence involved in pornography or even in R-rated movies or mature video games can titillate boys to the point of addiction. Because they are highly visual, boys gravitate toward looking at sexual imagery in its many different forms, and unfortunately, many are all too available to them. There are scantily clad women in television ads, in MTV clips, in movies, and on the Internet. Finding pornography or even happening upon it can happen in a click or two of the mouse for most twelve-year-old boys. They can become addicted without even realizing what's happening.

When I speak to teen boys across the country, I talk frankly to them about how they are wired and I tell them to be very, very careful when it comes to viewing sexual imagery. Adults might think that seventeen-year-old boys would roll their eyes when I say this, but I find that most don't. Most of them sit up and listen because there aren't many adults talking to them on an honest level about their feelings toward sex and media. I tell them why they are wired to want to look at pornography. Then I tell them how easy it is to become addicted to viewing and how this can lead them down a very dark path.

Before I leave this topic, I want to add an interesting conversation that I recently had with my friend and colleague Dr. James Dobson. He is a child psychologist who hosts a radio show called *Family Talk*. We were discussing an interview he had many years ago with serial killer and rapist Ted Bundy, who was sentenced to death in 1979. Before Bundy died, Dr. Dobson was granted a meeting with him. He told me that he will never forget Bundy's chilling words about pornography. He told Dobson that he believed that pornography was the start of much of his sick and sadistic behavior.

Clearly Bundy was a man with mental illness. Will watching pornography make most boys act like him? No. But let us never be cavalier about the dark influence that it can have, no matter how mildly it manifests itself.

Boys can also become hooked on playing video games whether the games are sexually charged or not. (If the games are laced with sex, the addictive potential of them is that much greater.) Again, this is because boys are so visually oriented. Many become attached slowly. They come home from school and play an hour or two of games just to unwind. Then two hours turns into three or four. If parents aren't careful, boys can be playing up to eight to ten hours a day without realizing it.

I have seen an increasing number of teen boys addicted to playing video games and there is a growing body of research to support my experience. One study found that almost one-tenth of children and teens who play video games are classified as addicted.[1] This means that they need more gaming time to feel satisfied with playing and if the games are taken away, they become highly agitated. Many end up playing well into the night because they say they just can't stop. Is it the images, the sounds, the violence, or just the act of playing? We don't know. But physicians everywhere are seeing more teen boys than ever having difficulty tearing themselves away from their screens and consoles. And since this may not be something we mothers naturally understand, we need to be very savvy about the possibility and take steps to prevent it.

Sons, Sex, and the Preteen Years

Around age ten, most boys become very curious about their bodies. They start to have erections. They begin to feel sexual urges and wonder what they are. It is fairly usual for boys to ask their friends to touch or kiss their penises when no one is looking. Because boy-to-boy experimenting is not uncommon, moms need to know how to handle such situations; what we say and how we react has an enormous impact on sons. And why should it be us, not dad, who handles this type of situation? First, mom is probably the one who gets the upsetting phone call from another mother or a teacher. Second, our sons will likely feel less embarrassed if we discuss this kind of situation with them because we are so different from them physically.

So, if this happens with your son, don't freak out, and don't jump to conclusions that are irrational. Boys are curious about their bodies. Having one or two mutually agreed-upon encounters with a boy who is the same age isn't unhealthy and doesn't constitute sexual abuse. It simply means that both boys were playing around with their bodies. If you react calmly and talk to your son in a positive, understanding tone, he will listen to what you have to say. If you get angry or cry, he will feel ashamed, and shaming a boy about his sexual interest never leads anywhere good. I encourage mothers to tell their sons that you know what happened may have felt *nice* and that curiosity is a *good* thing; then tell him that his body is private and he must protect it. Tell him he is wired to have wonderful sexual or physical feelings, but it's important not to share those feelings with other boys or girls yet.

If a mother reacts in a positive, loving, understanding way, these exploratory episodes usually pass. But as boys get older, numerous other issues involving sex arise, and again, these are all opportunities for a mother to roll up her sleeves and talk to her son in order to reinforce healthy messages about his sexuality. It's important to never underestimate the importance of the general messages you offer your son when he is little—you are strong, you are capable, you are independent, and so on—as these messages will begin to shape his sexual identity.

———

Maybe I'm overly sympathetic to certain issues, but I think the ages ten through twelve are rougher years for boys than their teen years. They still haven't grown tall. They still don't shave. Even their voices haven't matured and at times they probably think they sound like girls. They feel they are getting too old to want to be seen with their mother, but they still love spending time with mom because it feels so safe and familiar. Life is scary. Mom isn't. More important, the world, which expresses itself and its ills to our sons at this age, feels confusing and a bit gross. Sexual messages and images that they see in television ads, sitcoms, or movies aren't yet titillating—they're unfamiliar and confusing. A preteen boy understands that they represent sex, kind of, but he doesn't really know what that means because he isn't prepared for that kind of maturity. His testosterone levels are still low enough that he's not overwhelmed by desire. Yet if he's not interested in sex, he feels like something is wrong with him because he knows he's supposed to be interested.

At this age, boys are also exposed to violence, and while he has probably enjoyed playing cowboys and Indians or other war games up to this point, when the violence becomes more specific and visual— such as in movies or video games—it feels disturbing to him that down deep he kind of enjoys the experience. The struggle between knowing that something's bad for you and wanting it anyway has begun. He knows that *you* don't like the images he sees on television or hears referenced in songs, but he likes them and that makes him feel like a bad boy. But he also knows that you can't really understand how he feels because you're a girl, so maybe he's right and you're wrong. Suddenly you are the enemy. But that feels wrong, too, because when he was little (just a few minutes ago) you weren't the enemy, you were just Mom, whom he loved to go on errands with.

It would be 200 percent simpler to help our sons navigate the early and teen years if we didn't have televisions, iPods, or iPhones. But we do. These devices are the "anti-mom" voice and the trouble for us is that they talk to our boys all the time. Some things they say are good, but they can also crush the important lessons we are trying to teach. They are powerful. But we are more powerful. We must *never* forget this. What we must do, however, is create very clear rules about the use of electronics in our homes. I advocate making all cellphones "family phones," which are phones shared by parents and siblings, until kids are at least in their junior or senior year of high school. This lets boys know that they have no privacy with phones. Second, parents should have full access to all messages and texts on phones. Make it clear that this isn't because you don't trust your son; it is simply to help him stay away from trouble. Third, when it comes to video games, television, or any other "screen time" activity, set firm time limits, say two hours per day, when used recreationally. Many boys need to be on their computers for schoolwork but when it comes to relaxing in front of a screen, limit his use. I promise, he'll thank you later. Finally, I feel strongly that when boys have computers, they should only use them within earshot of you. Don't let your son take his laptop to his bedroom, close the door, and spend hours alone there. The temptation to wander into bad territory is simply too great for any boy.

Many young boys measure their maturity level and "coolness" by the ratings of movies they watch. Most in this preteen age group want to watch R-rated movies and think that PG-13 is for little kids. He thinks that if he's *almost* thirteen—especially if he feels mature (and what kid doesn't at least *want* to feel mature?)—then he should be able to watch R-rated movies. But just think what those R-rated movies expose him to: not only violence and sex, but violence without guilt and sex without love. It's the same with video games. Boys may begin playing games with some violence and sex when they are ten but by the time they are twelve or thirteen, the intensity of the sex and violence amplifies. All these visual stimuli engage their minds and stick in their memories, steering their sexual development. Who helps them decipher the messages they're receiving? No one. Even if he's with his friends, these are subjects he's not going to talk about in any depth with the other boys. He is alone with his feelings and sensibilities, and it all swirls into a vortex of confusion in his young, malleable mind.

I recommend that as his mom, you periodically tell him that you realize boys his age are running into a lot of sex in movies, etc. and that even if they don't realize it, the images affect them. Don't say it with a derogatory tone, but with an understanding one. In other words, you don't want him to hear unspoken accusations beneath your words like "you kids are all up to no good, watching bad movies with sex," but rather with a tone that conveys an attitude of "I realize that this is what comes up and I want to help you figure out how it could be negatively affecting you."

Explain to him why he is so drawn to them (he's visually wired that way). You can ask what he thinks about the messages in the movies. Does he think the messages affect him and his male friends, and if so, how? That said, many thirteen-year-old boys won't be quick to open up. The last thing your son wants is to hear you talk about sex, so don't expect him to respond. But *don't* let your son's lack of engagement deter you from telling him your feelings. They will resonate and stick with him even if he says nothing. Tell him that you don't like him to watch sexual imagery because you feel that it hurts him. It can make him objectify himself as well as women. Tell him that it leads him to wrongly believe that sex is nonemotional for guys and you know that it isn't. Tell him that he is a highly sensitive, thinking young man and that most sexual images in media convey that he isn't. Even if he says nothing in response, make sure that he hears you say that many messages undermine his integrity as a young man.

By fifth grade, most boys have sex education classes. In my capacity as a pediatric doctor and teen counselor, I visit all types of schools across the country and am often asked to review curricula used in sex ed programs. I will tell you that in general, sex education materials are outdated, particularly in our public schools. The process of getting material accepted by the school system—because it must meet specific criteria—takes a long time. In a world where statistics around sexual activity are changing yearly, most schools simply can't keep up. But even if they could, there's the war between parents and educators over what is being taught. Some feel that abstinence should be the only lesson; others believe that kids should be given comprehensive sex education and be taught how to use condoms, birth control, etc. Our sons are aware of these disagreements among adults and wonder why sexuality is such a loaded subject. So what we moms say and how we say it matters more to them than what they see written on a blackboard or in a textbook.

Personally, I believe in keeping sex education simple and fun. Because I see what really influences boys' decisions about sex, I know that moms (and dads, if available) hold all the cards. That being said, it is very important to know what your son is being taught at school. Ask to see the materials before the teacher teaches them. Realize, too, that many sex ed teachers in schools really don't want to teach that particular class; they've just been called upon to do so. (Why do PE teachers always get pegged? Does anybody know?) There will be some points on which you agree with the lesson and some on which you don't. Since it is your job to tell your child what *you* believe, don't bail out on this one. What your son learns about sex at this age is very, very important, so dive in and see what he's being taught, then adjust what he learns according to what you personally believe.

Most (like 99 percent) of the mothers (and fathers) I have met don't feel comfortable talking to their kids about sex at any age and often ask me how to go about it. Should the dad talk to the sons and the mom the daughters? Should they both talk? Each partner thinks the other would be the right one for the task. Here's what I tell them: Though both parents are usually chickens when it comes to talking to their kids about sex, one of them will be the bigger chicken. I usually suggest that the one who is least chicken take on the task. It doesn't matter whether the parent is male or female—what is most important is that the less uncomfortable one should do the communicating. Your discussions with your children about sex should be free of tension. Regardless of the content of the conversation, if the parent is ashamed, condescending, or defensive, the child will learn that sex is a negative, awkward topic and that an interest in sex and emerging sexual feelings are bad or at least "off-limits" as a conversation topic with either parent.

Though it could be either parent who is most comfortable, in my experience it is mom who is usually more conversant and available—so go for it! Take a deep breath and let your son know that at school he will hear all sorts of things about sex. He may see kids his age fondling one another, kissing, or even having sex. He will definitely come across it on television, and he might view pornography on his computer. Tell him that he will see, read, and hear things about sex that aren't necessarily true. Then tell him that you are the "go-to" person when it comes to answering his questions. Let him know that, since you are *old,* you know the correct answers. Tell him you can help keep him from getting confused; tell him you will talk to him about sex anytime, and that you will always do your best to tell him the truth. Even though you might be embarrassed, you need to pretend that you're not. This is very important because he will be embarrassed anyway. If both of you feel embarrassed, all conversation stops, but you need to keep the conversation going.

Between the ages of ten and thirteen, your son will listen to what you say because he doesn't feel like a know-it-all yet, especially when it comes to sex. There will come a time when your son is convinced he is smarter than you are and that all of the ideas floating in your brain are terribly outdated. It is crucial to start the conversation before he feels that way.

Knowing this paid off for Heather. When Sean was twelve, he and thirteen-year-old Julio were best friends. Heather and Julio's mother, Jessica, were also very close friends. As single mothers, they depended on each other for child care while they worked. Over the years, Sean and Julio became so close that they often behaved more like brothers than friends. While Heather worked a night shift at her job in the hospital, Sean would frequently sleep at Jessica's home with Julio and his two younger siblings. As an only child, Sean told his mother that he liked being there because there was so much commotion.

Both women appreciated their friendship because they not only found comfort and encouragement from one another; they saved money and the angst of worrying about their kids being with strangers while they worked. The arrangement seemed almost too good to be true.

During spring break of seventh grade, Heather took Sean on a road trip. Both were excited to get away from home, work, school, and the boring routines of life. They left on a Saturday morning to go to a nearby city, where Heather made plans to see museums, a play, and a few friends who lived there. She told me that the car ride into the city was fun and that they settled into their hotel and headed off for a nice dinner. During dinner, she noticed that Sean was acting strange. He was quiet and standoffish, and she was concerned that something was wrong. After dinner, she probed. At first, Sean denied any peculiar feelings, but the more he tried to convince her that he was fine, the more she became convinced that he was not. He was acting guilty, angry, and defensive, but she couldn't figure out the reason.

Heather decided that the best thing to do was to stop asking Sean what the problem was. So she changed the subject. Later in the evening, Sean reopened the issue with his mother. He spoke awkwardly, Heather told me. He stammered and said that he was worried about something but didn't want to talk about it. After many uncomfortable minutes, she told him to just blurt out what he was worried about. She learned over the next hour that Sean and Julio had engaged in four sexual encounters. Sean didn't want to give his mother the details, but he clearly needed to talk about the incidents. Wisely, Heather never pressed Sean for more information than he was willing to volunteer. She simply stayed calm and listened to her son to hear what worried him about the situation.

Sean told his mother that the two boys had touched each other and had done some "other things" (she later pieced together that the two boys had had oral–genital contact). Sean's biggest worry, she said, was that he was going to be physically harmed. He worried that he might not be able to have children and that he might have gotten any number of diseases.

"My heart started pounding in my chest," she told me as she recounted that Saturday night of their vacation. "So many thoughts spun in my mind. Had Julio forced himself on Sean? Did Sean feel ashamed, frightened, traumatized? What should I say to him?"

"So, what *did* you say when he told you about the encounters?" I asked.

"Nothing at first," she replied. "I just stared at him. I was mad, scared, and I felt like a total failure as a mother. I also knew that I didn't want to say anything that would make him stop talking to me, because I thought that it was a miracle he was even telling me this in the first place. So I listened and tried to act understanding. Inside, though, I felt as if I was being punched in the stomach."

Although their conversation had taken place two months earlier, Heather's face still expressed fresh pain when she related all this to me. Talking to our children about sex is tough enough, but talking to a son about an early sexual encounter that might have been traumatic makes the conversation much harder. I gave Heather kudos for keeping her wits about her. In fact, I told her that she did an extraordinary job handling a tough situation. I asked her more specifically about her response, not only over the subsequent minutes of that first conversation, but over the rest of her vacation with Sean.

"Well," she said, "like I said, I listened a lot. As Sean told me what he and Julio had done, I asked if he had been scared at the time. He said no. Then I asked if they both agreed to do things to one another or if only one of them wanted it. At first, he told me that all of the fondling was Julio's idea. But after a while, he admitted that he agreed to do things together because it felt good. Throughout the conversation, I was mostly concerned about whether or not he felt violated, or whether this was consensual."

Heather was completely right in her worries, and right to prod, gently, to find out if her son felt victimized, or whether he had participated willingly. She came to the conclusion that both boys wanted the sexual play and that neither forced the other. This was extremely important because many young boys at this age can feel physically or sexually threatened and the psychological repercussions of that can be quite severe. If, for instance, a young boy is pressured by an older boy to perform sexual acts, he can suffer serious mental trauma. Many boys won't tell anyone (even their mothers) if such an incident has occurred, because of the shame associated with the event. I have seen boys have all symptoms of sexual abuse even when the trauma appeared mild—he was told to pull his pants down, for instance, but no physical contact was made. So the issue isn't as much what happens during the encounter as the dynamics of the two involved. If a boy knows that he is on equal footing, psychologically and physically, and the play is consensual, he will not feel abused. If, however, he feels dominated in any way, regardless of the severity of the act he will feel abused. Heather watched for signs of abuse in her son—withdrawal, sadness, depression, falling grades, and anger outbursts, to name a few—and thankfully, found none. He had also never stopped being comfortable or protested spending time with Julio, which led Heather to believe that Sean was telling the truth about the acts being consensual.

The next thing that Heather did right was that she kept her cool and didn't act judgmental when Sean talked. If she had, Sean would likely have stopped speaking immediately, and more important, he would have felt a sense of shame that might have scarred him for a long time. Heather realized this and responded calmly and kindly. She said that after he told her what the boys had done over the four encounters, Sean was sobbing.

"My heart just broke," she told me. "He told me about these grown-up things that he was doing and as he sobbed, he looked like a little boy. I just sat with him and hugged him."

Heather had come to me because she was worried that Sean might have persistent worries or confusion and she wanted to talk to a professional about her concerns. Had she done the right thing, she wondered. In fact, she handled the situation beautifully, I told her. Here are a few of the things that she did very well.

First, Heather made time and space for her son to talk about something that was troubling him. Too often, because we are so busy multitasking, we mothers are too engaged in whatever feels most pressing at the moment, and so we may miss something important. We need to make time to look at our sons face-to-face, to see what they're feeling and talk to them about it. Then we need to make sure that we're really present with them during the conversation, relaxed and ready to really listen. Heather was lucky that she'd had this spring break "getaway" planned, giving Sean the opportunity to express himself in an intimate surrounding. But even if it's not a vacation, some mother–son time away from the house, face-to-face, can be really fruitful.

Second, Heather had proved to Sean over the years that she was trustworthy. Somehow he felt comfortable enough to come to her with something that is extremely difficult for a young boy to speak to his mother about. Some boys talk easily, but most don't. Therefore, it is imperative that mothers begin at an early age to let their sons know that they can come to them at any time about any problem.

When the conversation happened and Sean revealed his behavior,

Heather calmly listened and asked how *he* felt. Rather than telling him what he should or shouldn't have done, she continued to draw her son out by asking questions about *his* feelings. The conversation thus stayed about the boys and never became about Heather, which likely would have been another conversation stopper.

Finally, Heather reassured her son that he wasn't physically harmed for life. It is very common for boys to believe any myths they hear about sexual behaviors. Sean thought that by having another boy fondle him and kiss him on the genitals, he was not going to be able to have children when he was older. I have had boys Sean's age ask if masturbation damages their penises. Others have believed that they will go to hell if they masturbate. It is very important for boys to know the medical truth about what will and will not harm them. Not only does reassurance dispel shame; it alleviates unnecessary worry. I am not a theologian, but I do take the liberty of telling boys that they will not go to hell by masturbating. I tell them that every boy has wet dreams as he matures and if God created boys and their sexual functions, He would be a hypocrite to send them to hell for such a reason.

Teen Sons and Sex: What Every Mother MUST Know

Something happens to sons as they mature from the preteen years into the teen years. Because of the increase in hormones, the psychological maturation, and the cognitive changes they're undergoing, sons often verbally withdraw from their mothers as they try to assimilate to their rapidly developing minds and bodies. So it's crucial, as mentioned earlier, that the conversation about sex begin during the preteen years, when boys feel more open to talking—and listening—to their moms. But if you have a son who is already a teen and he has let you know in no uncertain terms that he has no intention of talking to you about girls, sex, or his sexuality, don't worry, there are things that you can do to get through to him and we'll discuss these in a moment.

First, let's look at some surprising facts about sex and modern life. The most recent data from the U.S. Centers for Disease Control and Prevention states the following:

In the United States, 20 million Americans every year contract a new sexually transmitted infection.[2]

50 percent of these infections are in young people ages fifteen to twenty-four. The same age group accounts for 25 percent of the sexually experienced population. Young people are disproportionately affected.[3]

People ages fifteen to twenty-four have five times the incidence of chlamydia than the rest of the population.[4]

Men have 5.6 times higher incidence of syphilis than women.[5]

Boys fifteen to nineteen have the second-highest rates of gonorrhea in the United States.[6]

One in 5 people over age twelve in the United States has genital herpes.[7]

Six million people under age twenty-five get genital herpes every year.[8]

These numbers are scary, but we need to know them because this is the reality of our kids' lives. As we help our sons navigate the teen years, we need to know what they are up against if and when they decide to start having sex. And we're really the only ones who will tell them. They won't learn the whole truth from sex ed, their friends, television, the movies, or pornography.

Teens and sex is a loaded topic. I know how complicated it is because I have reviewed school curricula, testified at a congressional hearing on the prevention of sexually transmitted diseases (STDs), and read and written extensively about the topic. I have personally spoken to thousands of teens about sex and have heard what they think, believe, and feel. The sad thing is, most of the adults in their lives *don't* talk to them. And I understand why. Sex is a hot-button issue and most adults don't want to deal with it. Because if we really begin dealing with serious sex-related health issues with our boys, we will also be forced to confront the companies that aggressively use sex to market products to our kids. If we held these companies accountable (just as we do with companies that market cigarettes to our kids) they could lose billions of dollars. Sadly, we are a country that cares more about making money than about keeping our kids healthy. Abercrombie & Fitch, for example, uses sex appeal to market to teens (many of their posters feature men without clothes on), as do most fashion brands that target young adults. Hollywood knows that all they need to do to increase revenue with any of their movies is to inject a salacious sex scene and kids (and adults) will want to watch. Video games use sex to market their products to boys because they realize that boys are visual and will get hooked on playing if sexy figures, references to sexual acts, and violence are on the screen.

Sex, Boys, and the Heart

Whenever I speak to groups of teens about sex (usually a mixed-gender crowd), I always talk about their feelings. I ask kids if they like having sex and how they feel afterward. And I have discovered a unique phenomenon: Each and every time I begin to ask these questions, I see girls and boys of all ages sit upright. Usually, the older boys tend to clump in the back of the auditorium, and when I talk about what a boy might feel like if sex goes badly for him, I can see them sliding to the edge of their seats. I talk about the "bonding" hormones that are released during sex in both boys and girls and how these hormones shift the relationship between the sexual partners. I also talk to the boys about why they may feel badly if they have had sex with a lot of partners. I go on to outline the roots of depression and then show them how having multiple partners can lead to depression in young men. As I say these things, I see many young men lean forward. It's as if a light is going on in their minds. Many of them have never heard anyone talk to them about their feelings and sex.

Almost on cue, as I end my talks, handfuls of junior and senior boys come to me and tell me that they have never before heard anyone address their feelings about sex. The relief I see on their faces over the fact that someone finally treated them as thinking, feeling people is priceless. I wish that every mother could see their son's responses. Boys *need* to talk about their feelings. They feel deeply about sex, they want romance, and they worry about the decisions they are making about both. They fall in love, they have regrets, and after a breakup, many boys have as hard a time as girls do—or harder.

In the book *Hooked,* Drs. Joe S. McIlhaney Jr. and Freda McKissic Bush, both obstetricians, beautifully describe a phenomenon in the brain where certain hormones surge during sex. They cite studies showing that during sexual activity, hormones, or neurochemicals, are released in a boy's brain that affect how he feels about sex. Dopamine—referred to as the "pleasure" hormone—surges, communicating that the experience is enjoyable. This is the same hormone that is released if a boy gets an A on an exam or wins a football game. Sometimes a dopamine surge replicates the feeling of being high.

Another hormone, vasopressin, also surges during sex. Vasopressin tells a boy that he is bonding to the partner he's with. When the two hormones are combined, a boy feels that the union is important both physically and emotionally. When it's over, his mind tells him that this good experience should be repeated. Some scientists believe that these hormones ensure preservation of the human species because they keep the male interested in rebonding with the same individual, increasing the chances of pregnancy. Neuroscience affirms what mothers already believe: that our boys are sensitive, emotional people in all manner of ways, including when it comes to sex.

One might think that with the powerful hormone surge that occurs during sex, a boy would never become depressed afterward. But despite the chemical phenomenon, studies also show that boys who are sexually active have higher rates of depression.[9] One startling statistic shows that boys who are sexually active are twice as likely to be depressed as are boys who are not sexually active, and eight times more likely to attempt suicide than boys who aren't sexually active.[10] This seems to fit what I see in my own medical practice, and depression is always complicated, let alone when it is linked to sexual activity. Here's how it can occur in boys.

Depression is fundamentally about losses that a boy feels are never grieved. Over time these losses get "stuck" in the heart, if you will. One loss compounds on the other and they slowly build up. Sex for many boys can involve loss. For instance, if a boy has sex with a girl and she makes fun of him to her friends afterward, he feels hurt. He loses some self-esteem. Many boys believe in their minds that sex should be a certain way or feel a certain way (they may even compare themselves to someone like Brad Pitt or a football hero who they think is really macho). They then have sex, and if they feel that the experience wasn't what it should have been (based on some imagined expectation), the boy blames himself for not being "good enough." Then he feels worse about himself. If a boy has a bad sexual experience, he might think it is his fault that he didn't feel as great as he believes all his friends feel during sex. This could be another type of loss.

And going back to my belief that boys can take a breakup harder than girls, if they've had these experiences—experiences their brain tells them are important and good—knowing they have lost the means to continue having these experiences can cause boys to suffer acutely. A boy may love his partner deeply (particularly if it is his first romance) and if the two are sexually active and then break up, he may feel profound loss. Trust, for instance, can be lost during a breakup. But of course, because they're boys, they rarely talk about their emotions. And given the way their peers and others around them view sex, the idea that sex can lead to *any* negative emotion seems unnatural to a teenage boy. So he buries his feelings; but eventually these buried feelings can lead to depression.

So, what's a mother to do? Studies show that boys who feel comfortable talking to their parents are more likely to postpone their sexual debut and reduce the number of sexual partners they eventually have.[11] Also, boys who feel connected to their parents are less likely to engage in high-risk behaviors: having sex, taking drugs, or drinking alcohol.[12] Many parents believe that sex is not risky if a boy uses a condom, but this isn't so. The medical community at large refers to any sex a teen boy may have as high-risk because condoms don't protect against infections equally. (For more on this subject, see my book *Your Kids at Risk*.)

The bottom line in figuring out what your son will or won't do when it comes to sex is that what you think, how you engage your son, what you believe about him, and the conversations that you have with him really matter. We can't afford to simply shrug our shoulders and hope for the best, because if things go wrong, your son could end up living with emotional scars or a sexually transmitted infection for years to come.

GET OUT OF CHICKEN MODE AND TALK

First, you need to make the decision that you *will* engage your son in conversations about his sexual development, that you will talk to him, and though his decisions will ultimately be up to him, you will figure out how to best influence the direction of his thinking. You will ask yourself, Should I encourage him to have sex as long as it's "safe"? Or should I encourage him to hold off?

From a purely medical standpoint, the longer he waits to start having sex, the less likely he is to end up with an STD. We know that teens who wait to have sex until they are over sixteen years old have a lower number of lifetime partners, which also decreases their chance of contracting an STD.[13] So from the standpoint of disease prevention, it's all about those two things: waiting as long as possible to start and limiting your number of partners. Of course, your son will decide what he does, and when, but giving him the facts can influence his thinking.

Teenage boys are at least somewhat aware there are dangerous waters out there. They all hear about HIV/AIDS and are told to always use condoms. Pediatricians offer to immunize boys ages nine to twenty-six years old against human papillomavirus (HPV) by giving them Gardasil because the American Academy of Pediatrics recommends it for young boys. Personally, though, I feel that it is unethical to give a young man an immunization for a sexually transmitted infection that he is fully capable of preventing in himself, without first telling him what the infection is and how it is transmitted. The larger medical community advocates giving Gardasil because we physicians are trained to believe that since most boys will be sexually active before they're married, we had better protect them from spreading HPV to their partners. And I understand this because as physicians, our ability to get teen boys to put the brakes on where sex is concerned is limited. And many physicians, like many parents, feel that since "boys will be boys" it is their right to be sexually active. But I feel that it is always important to teach them the risks of what they are doing so that they can make more informed decisions.

I will tell you what I do with my own patients. I talk very openly with boys about sex. I give them some of the above data (though a few numbers go a long way with boys) and then I ask what their thoughts are. How do they feel about sex? What do they want? What are their struggles, concerns? Contrary to what you might think, boys answer my questions. Many say that they don't know what they want to do sexually. They feel confused but believe that "all" of their friends are doing it so they should jump on the bandwagon. They worry about sexually transmitted infections and read about them on the Internet but still have questions. In general, they tell me that no one really wants to answer their questions because talking about sex is uncomfortable for many adults. So I always encourage one of their parents to be the point person in the family, the one who will answer questions and be willing to discuss sex with the kids. It doesn't matter if it is mom or dad, but it needs to be someone because boys will find answers.

Moms: Get in the Game Early and Stay There

Once you have decided that you must address this tough topic, you need to know a few "foolproof" techniques that any mother can use to help her son. When you are at the beach with your wonderful three-year-old, make him wear a bathing suit. When he tears his suit off because he likes being naked, tell him that he needs to put his suit back on because his body is private. He should learn at a young age that when he is in public, there are parts of his body that are too special to be seen by others. By telling him that his body is private, he will feel good about himself and realize that he needs to have some "body boundaries." This is the earliest and best way to begin his sex education. You don't need to use medically accurate terminology when describing his body, though if you want to, go ahead. The most important thing to do is to make sure he realizes that modesty and privacy are important, and that it's because his body is good, healthy, and *his*—not that it's embarrassing or bad.

As he grows older, keep teaching him about his body. When he goes off to kindergarten, remind him that he should go to the bathroom alone. Also remind him that only mom, dad, and the doctor are to see the private areas of his body, but if he occasionally does need help with tasks like going to the bathroom, he should only ask his teacher, not his friends, for assistance. This reinforces in his mind that other kids shouldn't be asking to see his private areas. If you know that he may need help, alert his teacher and let your son know that the teacher will be available to help.

Sometime, usually during the second grade, boys will hear about intercourse. If your son has older siblings, he may hear about it even earlier. Mothers often ask what age their son should receive "the talk" from their parents. The best time to do this is when your son's questions about sex become constant. That's an important cue to listen for; it means he's ready to hear some answers. At that point I encourage you to dive in. Take a deep breath and stay in the conversation. Hearing your son ask you questions about sex may make you feel relieved—but also kind of like you've been punched in the stomach. It's good news and bad news. You like knowing that mom has such influence, but you hate knowing because it might mean that you are the one who's going to have to give him the Talk. But don't worry—even if that's the case, it may turn out to be very different than what you expect.

I would have a conversation like this. "Tommy, you may hear things at school about what moms and dads (or dads and dads, moms and moms) do when they love each other. They kiss, for instance. When you hear things that you don't understand, make sure to come and tell me so that I can explain. I know all about grown-up things and want you to get answers from me because sometimes kids get their answers mixed up. Does that sound okay?" This gives your son permission to listen to other kids and also warns him that someone is going to say something about where babies come from that might bother him. When he hears things, he will be less shocked. Remember, there's a kid in every class who has older siblings and who loves to shock his friends. And more important, it identifies you as the "go-to" person whenever he has questions about sex.

Typically, when young boys hear the details they've been curious to learn regarding intercourse, they make faces and act disgusted. Your son may gag, run out of the room, or tell you to stop talking. This is all very normal and doesn't mean that he hates sex or that you're doing something wrong. He just feels a bit overwhelmed. That's okay. Girls do the same thing. When he makes a sour face, you might say, "Tommy, I know this is kind of uncomfortable. I was un-comfortable talking about it at your age, too. Don't worry. I can do the talking, and if you get too uncomfortable, we can stop and talk again later."

As he moves into third grade, stay on the offensive and tell him that he will probably keep hearing odd things about sex at school, soccer practice, or on the playground. Don't expect him to start coming home and freely offering you information; most boys simply don't do this. Knowing that your little boy *is routinely being sent messages about sex* tells you that you may need to initiate the conversation, probably more than once, even after you've let him know you're available to talk. He needs your input even if you think that he's too young to hear details.

In the middle elementary school years, periodically ask him what his friends are up to. When he is in fifth grade, for instance, casually ask him, "Tommy, are any of your friends interested in girls?" If he says no and moves on, let him. If he says yes and you figure he may be interested in girls, probe a bit. "What do your friends do with girls when they're dating? Do they talk at school, go to each other's houses?" The reason this is important is that dating to one boy may mean something completely different than it does to another. Some fifth-grade boys consider dating to be simply writing texts to a girl, while to others it may mean going to movies, etc. If your son seems interested in dating, I encourage you to talk to him about getting to know girls as friends before dating. Tell your son that girls can be wonderful friends to have and that as friends, you get to know them better than if you were dating

In middle school and junior high, your son will have friends who are not even remotely interested in dating, while others may already be sexually active. There is enormous diversity in sexual interest at this age. It's very important to always maintain an attitude of alliance with your son when you talk about his friends, girls, dating, and sex. In other words, make sure that your tone of voice, your inflections, and your body language let him know that you aren't asking because you're suspicious of him doing something wrong; rather, communicate clearly to him that life is tough and that you are on his side. He can know what you agree and disagree with when it comes to these topics, but always make sure that he knows that you aren't asking because he's guilty of something (or will be soon). This is one of the areas where mothers make the most mistakes, in my experience. They speak to their sons as though they are already up to no good and then wonder why their boys won't talk with them.

As I've mentioned before, when he hits age eleven or twelve, you will notice that your son will pull back from you dramatically. When puberty hits, sons withdraw from their mothers because they need to figure out manhood on their own. He will be much less open to talking with you about what's happening in his life. Don't take this personally, but don't back away from him, either. The choices he makes about sex during his teen years are critical to his health on many levels, so you need to figure out a way to keep a finger on the pulse of what's going on in his life. The best way to do this is to watch what his friends are doing, because chances are good that if his friends aren't dating, neither is he. On the contrary, if his friends are dating and having sex, there is a good chance that he is, too. Boys like to keep up with their friends. So routinely ask what his friends are up to and what they like to do. Again, don't ask with a negative or derogatory tone but with one that shows you are sincerely interested.

Since most fifteen-year-old boys don't want to talk to their mothers about sex, once they reach that age you need to take a different approach to the subject. Or if you haven't talked to him about sex before, it's not too late to start, as long as you know what approach has the greatest chance of working. One of the *best* things that you can do is continue to ask timely questions about his friends, girlfriends, activities, etc. and then, when the two of you are both in good moods, assert your hopes and wishes for him. He will probably not respond and might even pretend that he didn't hear you, but say what you need to say. When boys see that their mothers are still interested in parenting and protecting them in a healthy way, they feel loved and they will remember your words. In the movie *The Blind Side,* there is a final scene during which Michael goes to start his freshman year at college. Clearly, his surrogate mother, Leigh Ann Touhy, adores him and wants to continue to help him even as he leaves home. We see the enormous, masculine man saying goodbye to his mother when she boldly asserts, "And Michael, if you get a girl pregnant, I'm going to come down here and cut off your penis." A bit dramatic and overstated, but you get the point. Leigh Ann was telling her son in a crass but effective way that she had a standard for him. She didn't want him to throw his career away because he couldn't control his sexual behavior. After his mother said this, Michael smiled. He knew what she meant, and that was "your life and the future that you will have are very important to me. I believe in your ability to take the high road and stay out of trouble."

We sense in the scene that Michael feels loved after she has said those words to him because he is certain that she cares about him. This is how your son should feel when you gently assert your wishes for him regarding sex. So even when he's sixteen or eighteen years old and headed off to college, let him know how you feel. Don't do it in front of his friends, but quietly, at a time when you have his ear. He'll listen, because words spoken from his mother's heart always make a son feel better about himself.

Stay Positive and Empowering

Imagine that you are a seventeen-year-old young man. You drive a beater car, work hard at school, and play on the varsity basketball team. Your grades are pretty good and for the most part you get along well with your family. After school, you go to practice, then come home, eat dinner, and decide to do your homework on your laptop. But before you get started, you peruse a few music sites. Up pop scenes of Madonna or Lady Gaga writhing on the screen. You scan different pages, then decide to play a quick video game before you get down to business. While you play, you turn on your iPod for some background music. The video game involves shooting enemies in a war zone and rescuing women who are busty and scantily clad. The music in your ears reminds you that you are "sexy and you know it." After fifteen minutes, you decide it's time to begin your homework.

During those fifteen minutes, you were "told" that being sexy is important and that sex is a great thing. This feels good to you. As you begin your algebra, you struggle with the assignment. You always struggle with math. Your teacher tells you repeatedly that you can succeed in math if you just try harder, and deep down, you believe her. Your coach also pushes you because he thinks you might get scouted if you keep working hard. Your parents trust you when you go out on weekends, and tell you that you're a good kid. They *should* trust you because you don't smoke weed or cigarettes like a lot of your friends and you've only had a few beers on a couple of different occasions. Since you are close to your mother in particular, you don't want to drink because you know she'll get very worried if you do.

At every turn in your life, adults are telling you that you can be in charge. You can drive, play well on the court or field, succeed academically, and stay away from drugs and cigarettes and drinking. They believe in you, and this helps you believe in yourself. But when it comes to sex, what do you hear? Popular culture around you seems to indicate that it's great. What do adults say? Do they say it's great? Are they worried about you? Do they believe that it's okay for you to have sex or do they expect that you won't? No one's really telling you much, except singers, actors, and video games. *They* say it's fine. But when it comes to what your mother (and dad) think, you have nothing to go on. As a matter of fact, you get the general sense from adults that you really *can't* control yourself when it comes to sex, because sex is "all teen boys want." At least that's the message a lot of adult role models in your life seem to convey. If you were that seventeen-year-old young man, wouldn't you feel down about these conflicting messages that are coming at you? I would. *That's why your son needs your help.* Because when it comes to sex, boys get the message that their sexual drives will overtake them no matter what they do.

I was told this very fact by Bill O'Reilly on national television several years ago. I was on his evening show discussing teens and sex and he told me that if I (as one who had worked with teens for twenty-some years at the time) expected teen boys not to be sexually active, I was dreaming (I'm paraphrasing). The bottom line, he insinuated, was that teen boys are out of control when it comes to sex.

How would you like to be told that if you were a teen boy? How devastating must it be to be taught that you are capable of controlling every aspect of your life except your sexual behavior? I believe that this is a travesty on several levels.

First, in order for a boy to psychologically develop into a healthy man, he must transition from being dependent to being independent. This important transition happens when he learns self-control—not over a few aspects of his life, but across *all* aspects. If he is taught that a very significant part of himself—his sexuality—is out of his control, this will confuse him and stunt his psychological development. True, we have all seen men in positions of influence (Bill Clinton, Tiger Woods, David Petraeus) hurt their reputations and their families and even lose their jobs because they seemingly cannot control their sexual behavior. But how cruel for a man to be taught that is his only option.

Second, many teen boys simply feel that they have no choice when it comes to having sex as soon as possible. Thirty years ago, this was not true. Boys were taught that they could opt to have sex with a girlfriend, but if they didn't, there was nothing wrong with them. Today, that mindset has changed in high schools all across America. Many teen boys believe that sex is something that they have to get started with early if they are going to be masculine in any way. Whether or not it is a good experience or a bad one doesn't really matter; it's the act of doing it that's important.

Yours is the voice of reason. The voice that tells him that the decisions he makes about sex are his—not anyone else's. We tell our daughters this, time and again—so why do we hold back telling our sons the same? Maybe because deep down we are afraid that they really *can't* control themselves. We need to get over this fear. Don't talk to him as though having sex is a done deal, and so he'd better always carry fifteen condoms with him. When you talk to him about sexual decisions, talk to him as though he is in control. Let him know that yes, he will have very strong sexual feelings and that those feelings are wonderful, but they don't need to run his life.

You, Mom, are the bright beam of positivity in his world. You can be the one to teach him to live against the current of an environment that can't see past his sexual drives and as such defines him in a constricting, narrow way. When you give him a strong sense of empowerment, he will become a son you will be proud of, I promise. Several years ago, one of the largest studies ever conducted on teens, called the ADD Healthy Study (it started out looking at about ninety thousand kids), looked at what influences in a teen's life could help keep them away from sex, drugs, and alcohol. The study found that the number-one factor that kept them on the high road was feeling connected with their parents.[14] When he starts having sex, the messages he's received from you will make all the difference in his world.

Keep It Simple

Many mothers feel that they are ill-equipped to do a good job talking to their sons about sex. But remember that sons want to know what their mothers think, because deep down, they want to please us and to some extent be like us. You don't need to know everything about infections, condoms, birth control, etc.; your son doesn't expect you to be a "sex expert" and in fact, he kind of hopes that you aren't.

The most common question that parents ask me when I encourage them to talk to their sons about sex is "I was really wild as a teen, so what should I tell my son about my experiences?" My response to the question is always the same. "First of all," I say, "this subject isn't about you. It's about him. Second, you can try to tell your son what you did, but chances are excellent that he doesn't want to hear all about that. In his mind, there are two people in the world who are *never* sexually active and his mother is one of them."

What your son wants to know from you is what you believe about *him,* what you want for him, and whether or not you like the man that he is becoming. You want the answers to those questions to be clear and positive. Tell him that you believe that he is strong and he is worth protecting emotionally, sexually, and physically. Teach him that his sexuality is wonderful and complex but that it needs time to develop. Let him know that he should care for his body even better than he would care for his car. Tell him that you want him to be sexually healthy. This means that you don't want infections to be a lasting part of his future. Let him know that if he starts having sex as a teen, the chances are higher that he will be exposed to an STD. Since your job is to help him have a full, long, and good sex life, it might help to put the brakes on when he is young. Whether he is straight or gay makes no difference. He needs to wait because the risks to his emotional and physical well-being are too high to be cavalier with.

It's also important to tell him about condoms, because he will be taught many things at school about them and unfortunately, not all of the information will be accurate. For instance, if you listen carefully to the medical community talk about disease risk and condoms, you won't hear the common vernacular of "safe sex." They will say "safer sex." The fact is that condoms help *reduce* the risk of each sexually transmitted infection differently. This is very important because teenage boys feel invincible anyway and when they are led to believe that all they have to do if they want to have sex is make sure they pop a condom on, they feel that nothing bad can happen to them. This simply isn't true.

Consider a few other things about boys and condom use. A very interesting study found that the longer a boy is in a relationship, the less likely he is to use condoms when having sex.[15] This makes sense if you think about it. The longer a boy is with a partner, the more comfortable he becomes, and since he doesn't see any infections (many don't have symptoms) he feels that it is safe to stop using condoms. I see this frequently with the teens in my practice. In my book *Your Kids at Risk,* I write extensively about the pros and cons of condom use in teens. The bottom line is that boys should know that even with limitations, using condoms is far better than not using them, but they aren't the "silver bullet" that we wish they were.

I feel strongly that boys who are old enough to be having sex need this information. It isn't meant to shame them or cause them to feel that sex is dirty; on the contrary, it is to give them powerful information. If they choose to be sexually active, they will know exactly what they could be getting into. And if they choose to postpone sex, they will know what they are avoiding.

No one told my friend Jake this. As a teen, he went a little crazy. He loved girls and said that when he was between fifteen and eighteen, he had different types of sex with about ten different girls. He said he was never into drugs or alcohol—he just liked having sex. When he was in his early twenties, he quit having casual sex of his own volition.

When Jake was twenty-five, he met Monique, the woman of his dreams. Fortunately for him, she fell hard for Jake and the two were married one year after they started dating. Before they married, Monique called me. She was the same age as Jake and we had known each other for years because when she was in grade school, she had been my patient. She said she needed to talk to me, so I met her for coffee. She told me about Jake's sexual history and said that she really loved him but was worried about what she might contract. I told her that they should both be tested and that the only way to have a healthy marriage was to be totally honest with each other. They did and for a while, everything was fine.

Two years later, Jake and Monique were on a trip and my cellphone rang. It was Monique, in tears. She was hurting terribly in her genital area and didn't know what could be wrong. The symptoms she described sounded like herpes to me, so I told her to go to an urgent-care clinic. She did, and sure enough, she had it. Once she was on medication, she felt much better.

After they came home, Jake called and asked if we could chat. I met him and he broke down in tears. He adored his wife. Why did this have to happen? My heart *ached* for him.

"I know that this is tough," I told him that afternoon. "But you can deal with it. Monique can deal with it. You just need to be sure to get really good medical care and so does she—especially when you decide to have kids."

"Shit," he cried. "Why was I so stupid? I mean, it's one thing for me to have to deal with this—but Monique. She's amazing. The toughest part for me is what I have put her through."

Sadly, Jake's story is far too common. In fact, he had a harder time dealing with the herpes than his wife did, because he had the guilt of bringing it into the marriage. The million-dollar question: Could his mother have helped him avoid this? I wanted to know so I asked him. "Jake," I said, "I have a question and I'd like you to be honest, if you don't mind. You and your mother have always been close, right?" He nodded his head.

"If your mother had encouraged you to wait until you were older, or even married before you were sexually active, would that have made any difference?"

His response was immediate. "Hell, yes. I adored my mother. I still do. But we didn't talk about sex. I mean, she might have told me to make sure I never got a girl pregnant, but that was it. She was a single mom and honestly, she didn't know how dangerous sex had become. And she didn't really know how to talk about that stuff. Funny, though, we talked about everything else."

The problem for both Jake and his mother was that she simply didn't know how risky the sexual landscape was for her son. She told him to always use condoms, but, again, sometimes condoms protect against herpes and sometimes they don't. Condom efficacy is a complicated issue. Teens ask me all the time, "Do condoms work?" The answer depends on a few things.

First, condoms work best at protecting against infections that are fluid-borne, like HIV, gonorrhea, and chlamydia. If the guy uses them every time (and a lot of teen boys don't) and correctly (a lot of times they slip off), then they will do a good job of protecting. With other infections like herpes and HPV, their track record isn't as strong because these infections are transmitted from one person's skin to the other's. Second, we know that the longer a young man has been sexually active, the less he relies on condoms. It seems that the more sex a young man has without getting a girl pregnant or getting an infection, the more invincible he feels. This is not only dangerous; it is based on fantasy, because many infections don't carry symptoms. He may have a disease and not even know it.

So, yes, boys should absolutely wear condoms, but from a practical standpoint, we need to teach them *more* than just being "safe." As I said before, the only way to keep them sexually healthy is to do two things: delay the sexual debut and decrease the number of lifetime partners.

Keep It Light

After reading all of this heavy stuff, you must be saying to yourself, "Keep it light? You've got to be kidding me." But you can do that. Your whole approach to talking to your son about sex, dating, romance, and all that goes along with each should be fun. Yes, there are serious problems out there. Yes, our sons are getting messages constantly that make our skin crawl. But we must never be intimidated by all of this, because teaching him about sex is one of your most important responsibilities as his mom. Once you get past the initial few talks about sex, it really gets easier. That's when the conversations can get lighter.

The wonderful thing about kids (and teens) is that they always want to hear about sex. Really. But they don't want lectures or too many statistics. They want to talk about their lives and their future. And they want to hear how much better life can get as they grow older. Let me tell you a secret that I have discovered in boys: Many believe that the best sex they will ever have will occur before they turn twenty-five. Many feel that once they get past this age, it all goes downhill. That's why I make sure to talk to all my patients about their sexual longevity. It gives them hope.

I have found that if you talk with your son as though all of the troubles associated with sex are real, but that there is no reason they need to be part of *his* world, he will embrace what you have to say much more readily. Since he may ask the hard questions during his preteen years, be accepting and responsive, even if you feel it is too soon. If you don't know the answer to a question, say so. Tell him that you'll find the answer and you can talk about it later. If you keep the conversations light and simple, he will return to them much more quickly. But if he thinks that the conversations are always going to be heavy, he won't want to go near them. I remember once when I was on a spring break trip to the Caribbean with my daughter, a high school senior. I was a chaperone with two other parents and since her class was fairly small, we were able to ride the same bus from one place to another once we arrived. I knew most of the kids in her class and many knew what I did (go around town and talk to kids about sex). One boisterous senior decided to ask a few questions while we were in the bus one day en route to dinner. I was sitting at the front when I heard him yell from the back, "So, Dr. Meg. What's the deal with gonorrhea and guys—why do they get it so much more than girls?"

All the seniors giggled. And then they waited, so I answered his question. Then another question came, and another. Some kids asked silly questions to make light of their discomfort, and we all laughed. But others asked wonderful questions, and by the time we arrived at our restaurant, everyone was having a fun time. We talked about some very serious issues, but when we decided to keep the conversation uplifting, it ended up being uplifting. Once the conversation started, it developed a life of its own. At first, one teen would ask something and I would answer, but after a while, the kids began talking to one another about sex as well as to me.

I have experienced this dynamic on many occasions. Several years ago I was asked to speak to a high school near Los Angeles where the pregnancy rate of the girls was high. Many of the students came from broken homes and drug use was high as well. The week before I arrived, two boys had been killed by school gangs. I will admit I was a bit intimidated, thinking that these students weren't going to listen to some middle-aged doctor mom who wore a navy skirt and pumps. But once I began asking the kids questions, wanting to know their thoughts and feelings, I couldn't get them to stop talking. One young man made a comment about how he and his friends viewed some of the "wilder girls" and suddenly many girls jumped up and rebuked him. The girls couldn't believe what they were hearing. They asked, how could these boys look down on them? Once they began bantering back and forth, the conversation became lively and everyone really got involved.

The only way to get to the point where discussions about sex and dating can be light is to engage our sons early, and then periodically bring up the topic. If the subject becomes familiar, the mystery is dispelled and it gets easier to discuss all manner of topics. And remember, get going before he's eleven, because once your son hits the teen years, sex will automatically be tougher for him to talk about.

Your son's sexuality is one of the most precious possessions that he has. Now that you realize how crucial your role is in shaping it, I encourage you to do what I did when I went into that school in Los Angeles. I felt intimidated, old, out of touch (I had never been in proximity to a gang), and convinced that the kids would reject what I had to say. But I walked into the room anyway. And the time I spent with those students was one of the richest experiences I've ever had. So, walk into the room with your son and start the conversation. Let him know that you are with him for the long haul and that you will always have his back. And ask yourself, how different would your husband, brother, or significant other have been if their mothers had engaged them at an early age and told them to think long and hard about sex? How many women friends have you talked with who have experienced a lot of emotional pain because their own husbands lacked sexual control either before they got married or afterward? Many wives have a difficult time getting over a husband's past lovers, and vice versa. Don't let your son be set up for these problems when he is older.

From where I sit, you have already started the hard work. You have finished a chapter that dealt with many issues you probably didn't want to read about. But now you know what happens in your son's world and from here on out, you also know that you are the one who can make his future better. If you are still a bit nervous, think about this: Where will your son end up if you fail to engage him about the seriousness and the beauty of sex? No one has very positive news for him, so *you* be the bearer of that good news. And I promise, when he is twenty-five, he will love you all the more for it.

CHAPTER 9

Wisdom and Responsibility
Two Great Assets He Gets from You

Wisdom is a curious thing. It is not knowledge or judgment, intelligence, insight, or the willingness to do what is right. Nor is it simply spiritual, given supernaturally by God. It is all of these combined. Wisdom is crucial to good parenting because every parent aspires to be wise and then pass that wisdom on to their children. As mothers, we can give our kids clothing, an education, love, and all sorts of comforts, but when we teach them wisdom, we prepare them to handle anything that life throws at them. Having wisdom helps them draw on many character qualities, such as perseverance, patience, and assertiveness, and use those qualities to overcome challenging moments in their lives. Passing motherly wisdom along to our sons can feel like an elusive, frightening task. What is the best way to do *that,* we wonder? We might even question our level of wisdom, and whether we possess enough to pass it along. But I have listened to thousands of mothers over the years, and one thing I know for sure is that when it comes to your kids, *you instinctively know* what is right and good for them.

Some of a mother's wisdom is a hardwired, intuitive sense of awareness when it comes to her children. We can either choose to grow that wisdom—feed and water it—or ignore it and let it turn stale; it all depends upon our willingness to learn, listen, and pay attention to our maternal instincts. For most mothers, fear is the greatest enemy of wisdom. Fear can inhibit great parenting, especially when we become afraid to do what our hearts tell us to do and we follow the pack instead. When we succumb to the pack mentality, we constantly compare ourselves to other moms. We work harder to buy our sons nicer stuff, get them into better schools, and cook them more elaborate or healthier foods. We create a list in our minds of the things that all "good" moms do, and we work ourselves to the bone getting that list taken care of. The list for a mother with a second-grade boy might look something like this: make sure he gets to school on time, make sure he is in the "fast" reading group (and if he isn't, find him a tutor), get him to at least two sports per semester in order to find out which sport he excels at and to make sure his talent is adequately developed, do his homework with him, pay attention to how well he concentrates while doing it (you must be the first to discover ADHD if he has it), cook him great meals (preferably with organic ingredients), train him to keep his room neat, and if he doesn't, hire a cleaning person (who, by the way, wants you to clean before she comes), and get him to bed on time to ensure that he gets a healthy amount of sleep. When you are done with this list, finish the work that you couldn't finish at the office (if you have a job outside the home—which, by the way, you constantly feel guilty about) and then spend quality time with your husband.

This is what life on the crazy train is like. Every mother has a picture in her mind of herself as the perfect mom and every day she tries to live up to that image. The problem is, perfection is unattainable. All that image does is cause us to go to bed feeling frustrated and angry with ourselves because we fell short of being the mother we were "supposed" to be. This is not wise living and it is not healthy. It is fear-based living. So why do we do it? Because we live in a culture that has perpetuated this unattainable image of the perfect mother. We've seen it presented in parenting books and in articles about good parenting; this is the image our friends and family hold us up to even if they can't attain it themselves; just like for us, perfection is their goal and they perpetuate the myth even as they fail, like us. Review the above list and if it sounds only too familiar, ask yourself why. Why are you on the crazy train? Is it true that you do most of what you do for your son because you are afraid that if you don't, he will turn out badly and you will be perceived as a terrible mother?

I challenge you today to take a hard look at how well your version of the list is working for you and your son. If it is helpful rather than harmful and you can keep up and enjoy life, great. But if you can't—and most of us can't—then listen to that little voice that says *there must be a better way*, the voice that is prompting you to make some changes. Living on the crazy train is bad for mothers, but it's also bad for their sons. It is the opposite of living wisely. I will tell you a secret about boys: They hate it when they feel their moms are performing for them. They want less of the stuff you do *for* them and more of *you*. It really is that simple.

In order to give your son more of *you*, abandon your fears about what you feel you should be doing. Begin listening to your heart and your instincts, because that is where you will find your great wisdom as a mother. Every mother has an innate sense about her children that can guide her, but I can tell you that if you feel anxious, depressed, and exhausted, you will not be able to hear it. On the other hand, if you slow down enough to listen, you will find that the combination of your life experiences as a mother and woman, the intuition you have as a mother and woman, your moral foundation, your judgment and your heart, will lead you to the right parenting path.

It is possible for a woman to be highly intelligent but not wise. A mother can be very well educated, have an excellent job, and not be wise. Conversely, a wise mother needn't have a job, a higher education, an above-average IQ, or much "worldly" experience under her belt; a wise mother is one who is able to utilize her beliefs, her faith, her instincts, and her feelings about her son in order to foster and maintain a nurturing and supportive home environment. The interesting thing about wisdom is that in order to be wise, a mother must have moral clarity, a deep concern for her children, an ability to see herself and the world around her in a critical, honest light, and a willingness to act on her beliefs. And being wise also means be willing to open ourselves to ask God for help, because there are many times that we mothers come to the end of our ropes. We might not know what to do or what to say. We may not be in charge of the decisions that our sons make and we need to recruit help from beyond ourselves—from God.

When my son was in high school, I leaned on God regularly for help. Every time he got in the car and drove somewhere, I prayed for his safety. When he went out with friends at night, I asked God to help him make smart decisions and cover him even if he didn't. Faith to me was an enormous component in trying to be a wise mom.

A wise mother isn't a wimp. She doesn't follow what others are doing just for the sake of conformity. She knows who she is and goes after what she needs to keep herself and her family healthy and happy. A wise mother knows that the best way to care for her family is to ensure that she is emotionally and mentally stable, that she is happy.

Utilizing our wisdom and teaching our sons to be wise is one of the greatest (if not *the* greatest) gifts that we can give our boys. But what if we don't feel wise in a given *situation*? How do we draw on our intuition and use wisdom when we are in the middle of an argument where tempers are flaring? The trick is to *act* wise; wisdom will follow. If you are having a disagreement with a friend or family member, is it better to yell and call names, or to process what the other person has said and then respond in a calm and well-tempered manner? If you follow the second course, your son will see this behavior and learn from it; if you behave the same way when dealing with him, then he in turn will be given an opportunity to reflect, rather than just fight you and rebel.

I have written earlier about identity development in boys and how it evolves. They watch their mothers. They scrutinize our every move, down to the inflections in our voice and our body language, in order to learn how to be. If we have a secure relationship with them, they mimic our behaviors. They try them on and then, if they like them, they begin to internalize those behaviors. In other words, what they see in us often becomes part of them. Kids are drawn to wisdom because they understand that while intelligence may be a respected attribute, it is somehow not as important as being wise. If our sons see us act out of fear, they will learn that life requires them to be afraid.

Sons mimic us from the time they are very young until they are grown men because mimicking is instinctive when they spend so much time with us. If they see us act using calm reflection and demonstrate openness to others, they will learn those attributes and apply them in their own lives.

Responsibility

Aside from acquiring wisdom from us, our boys also need to learn about personal responsibility.

Those two attributes combined can make for a very healthy, happy, and successful life. Responsibility is mainly taught at home; at school, our sons learn how to compete: get the best grades, beat the other team on the playing field, and so on. In fact, school sometimes emphasizes self-improvement at the expense of other people. So as mothers, as the stabilizing force in our families, it is up to us to provide a good lesson to our sons in responsibility. It is, in most cases, the mother who makes sure the safety belt is buckled, insists on a bike helmet, keeps track of various schedules, provides the transportation to school events, and makes sure homework gets done; in other words, we become our son's model on how to shoulder responsibility in everyday life.

Too often today, the culture we live in doesn't support a sense of personal responsibility. I have had grade school teachers tell me that when a child has acted up and they call the parents, the parents often make excuses for the child or get mad at the teacher. The lesson? The child isn't to blame. And children quickly pick up on this message. They learn that it's fine to step on others' toes to get ahead or to have someone else take the heat for their mistakes. Common themes on television and movies these days seem to be learning how to manipulate—people, a company, you name it—in order to get ahead. Many of my teen patients have told me that they can't help themselves when they scream at their parents. Just yesterday I consulted on a thirteen-year-old boy who "rages," according to his mother. When she takes his iPhone away, he kicks doors, screams names at her, and

destroys his bedroom. She wondered if there was any type of medication because, she told me, he just can't seem to help himself. But he
can help himself, and she must show him how.

It is a lack of personal responsibility as well as the anonymity of the
Internet that has led to an increase in bullying today (as I touched
upon in chapter 6). Now mean kids have easier access to their victims
and know that an adult won't see what they do. Kids feel that they
have the right to say whatever they want to any other kid at any time
of the day. Song artists don't help, either, writing violent lyrics encouraging kids to be mean to others. The media and our celebrities
teach our sons that it is easier to blame someone else's faults than
blame themselves, to get defensive rather than own up to their own
errors. Sincere apologies rarely fall from their lips. This is not entirely
their fault; it is endemic of the time in which we live: We have become a culture of finger pointers. So we moms *must* be there to teach
this valuable trait of stepping up and taking ownership of our actions;
we must be the ones to set an example of responsibility for our boys
and then coax them toward it. We must help them understand the
freedom that comes from admitting an offense committed and understanding *why* it was wrong. We must teach our sons how to feel and
react when they mess up and how to appropriately respond to the
consequent embarrassment and shame. How cruel would it be to
renege on this and allow our sons to grow into men who can never
admit wrongdoing (there are many out there living this way); who
can never say, "I'm sorry." These are the most freeing words in the
English language and you can be the one to teach our sons to say
them.

A Powerful Duo: Wisdom and Responsibility

Wisdom and responsibility are a powerful duo because they work
hand in hand. Wise mothers are responsible and responsible mothers
are wise. You can't be one without the other. But passing those attributes along to our children can sometimes feel as challenging as
swimming upstream. That's especially true when what we want for
our sons in general contradicts what we want for them in specific

situations. For example, we want to teach our sons to treat peers as they themselves would like to be treated and to stand up for the underdog, but when they do confront a bully, we don't want them to get in trouble. We want our boys to be respectful, but also to challenge those around them when they see bad things happening. We want them to be like their friends, but to not give in to peer pressure when those friends are drinking or taking drugs. How peculiar it is to encourage our sons to dress like their classmates (we buy them the shoes that all of their friends wear), participate in the same school events, and spend ample time socializing, but then tell them not to bend to peer pressure under any circumstance. How can we tell them to be like their peers one minute but then reject or dismiss what their peers may be doing the next?

If this question seem confusing to you, know that it is doubly confusing to your kids. So what I propose as an answer is that we simply teach our sons how to act wisely. This means teaching them early on in life what is good and bad, right and wrong, healthy and unhealthy. The beautiful part of wisdom is that it forces you off the fence. A mother can't be wise and have no clue as to what she believes at the same time. Wisdom has a wonderful way of dispersing the gray areas of our lives and bringing clarity to the very important issues. That's why teaching our sons wisdom needs to start right from their birth.

At the risk of squeezing a complex entity into a box, I am going to outline what I have come to appreciate as the attributes of wise mothers.

Trust Your Instincts

If we want to raise wise sons, we need to begin from the time they are toddlers. And we can only teach our sons wisdom when we ourselves act wise. This is very important to always keep in mind. That said, what exactly does behaving wisely entail? Let's dissect wisdom for a moment.

As I said before, wisdom emanates from many places and is generated by many forces coming together. First, wisdom comes from the blending of life experience, emotions, knowledge, intuition, and judgment. When we begin our lives as mothers, we have absolutely no parenting experience. There is no internship for mothering. When we first hold our little boy in our arms, we look at him and realize that we don't know him. Whether we carry him in our belly for nine months or adopt him from another country makes little difference. During those first months with him, we need to find out who he is and what he needs. Should we only breastfeed or give him a bottle sometimes? And what about a pacifier—is one okay or not? We want to snuggle with him in our own bed, but is that safe? Books tell us one thing, friends tell us another, and all we long to do is ask our son what he needs, but we can't. And when he cries, what is he trying to say? Is he frightened, mad, or just tired?

As our son grows, we learn what makes him happy. We learn to read his needs, his wants, his fears, and his hurts. We try our best to meet his needs and minimize his hurts but there are times when we have done everything we can and we know that he must learn to soothe himself. This becomes an important lesson later on in life. Being a good mother can hurt at times because we know that in addition to doing things for him that feel good to us, we need to do some things for him that make us feel terrible. For example, many times infants become so tired that they can't sleep. They will fall asleep for fifteen minutes and then awaken and cry. We pick them up and walk with them, and a little later, try to put them down for a nap. The same thing happens. Repeatedly, we try to coax them to sleep, but to no avail. Finally, we have no choice but to put them back to bed and let them cry for a while. And this feels terrible. I know this as a mother who had a child who simply couldn't sleep. I knew what the problem was—she was overtired and unable to sleep. And I also knew the answer—let her cry. But it felt awful every time. Fortunately for me, she cried long and hard a few times and then her sleep issues disappeared, because once she caught up on her sleep, she was able to sleep better the next day (sounds ironic, but this is true).

I hated having my daughter cry but I also realized that there was nothing else I could do. Looking back, I can see that her cries were merely her expression of frustration with being so tired. They didn't mean that I was not meeting her needs; rather, they meant that she was figuring things out (how to soothe herself) on her own. As I acted on my instincts to calm her every night and hold her for hours on end so that she wouldn't cry, I realized that I needed more. I needed to be a smart mother and this meant doing something that was hard for me. Wisdom drove what I needed to do and it wasn't fun. But in the end, she was better off because that was a turning point and she established much healthier sleep patterns.

Lana is a terrific mother, but she had to learn the hard way that it was important to *be wise and trust* her maternal intuition. When her son Pete was nine years old, he was invited to a sleepover at a friend's home. Pete had been in his school for only a few months (they had only recently moved to town), so Lana was comforted by the invitation and glad he hadn't been left out. She wanted him to make good friends because he had been picked on at his previous school, but she was also determined to do whatever she needed to do to ensure that he would not be bullied again. She was a mom on a mission.

Lana called the mother who was hosting the party to introduce herself and to find out what the boys would be doing. The plan was that they would go to a local baseball field to play, come home and have dinner, and then watch a movie and go to bed; the other mother said she wanted all the boys asleep by 11 P.M. All of it sounded great to Lana.

Over the next few days at school, Pete learned that the birthday boy asked his mother if they could watch a Rambo movie that was rated R. Pete knew that his mother never allowed him to watch R-rated movies, but since he really wanted to go to the party, he decided not to tell her. The day before the party, Pete cracked. He didn't like violent movies, because they frightened him. He didn't want anyone to know that he was scared, but he decided that he should tell his mother about the movie because he was feeling increasingly anxious about the party.

When Pete told Lana what the boys would be watching, she felt as though someone had kicked her in the stomach. Why, she wondered, would anyone let their kids watch something so violent and age-inappropriate? If I had been with her, I could have answered. It's because every mother believes that her son is more mature than his friends and that he has a solid head on his shoulders. And there's another reason: Every mother wants to have the home that the other kids want to come to. In order to make that happen, we feel that we need to offer things that other parents won't. I see this all the time with parents of teens.

Lana had a hard time deciding what to do. After much deliberation, she decided to let Pete go to the sleepover anyway. She considered calling the boy's mother and asking if she could show a less violent movie, but Pete begged her not to. He told her that she would embarrass him and all the other boys would find out and think that he was a wimp. She certainly didn't want this to happen, so, against her better judgment, she relented and didn't call. As planned, the boys played baseball, ate dinner, and then settled into their sleeping bags on the floor in front of *Rambo*. Pete was so frightened that he closed his eyes for most of the movie but—as would become apparent later—he watched enough of it. When he came home the following morning, he told Lana that he had a fun time and that he got along well with the other boys. Then the nightmares began.

For the next two months, Pete had such disturbing dreams that he couldn't sleep. Every night he came into his mother's room and crawled into her bed. After two months, they came to see me for help with his sleep issues. Pete was constantly tired at school; his grades were dropping because he couldn't concentrate. And aside from his schoolwork suffering, Pete had become a bear to live with. Fatigue, it turns out, will take down even the healthiest nine-year-old boys.

Lana learned the hard way what were the consequences of ignoring her instincts—and Pete's—because she was afraid. She had worried that if she told Pete he couldn't go to the party, his friends would think he was a loser and Pete would get mad at her. Pete was afraid to watch the movie, but more afraid to speak up about it, in case he was seen as a sissy.

If Lana had trusted her gut and told Pete that he couldn't go to the party, she would have helped Pete in three very important ways. First, he would have been spared the many difficult nights that followed. Her experience as his mother had already let her know that he was very sensitive and couldn't handle violence (most nine-year-old boys can't, but none will admit it). Her heart told her to protect him from trauma. Her intuition told her that letting him go was not smart and that she should keep him away from the party. And her intellect told her that watching any violent movie was wrong. He was too young—as a matter of fact all of the boys were too young. She had the wisdom she needed from the melding of her experience, heart, intuition, and intellect, but she failed to act on it. Why? Because she was afraid. She was afraid to be wise when other mothers were acting foolishly.

Second, she would have offered him an example of what wisdom looks like, acts like, and thinks like. Sure, he probably would have hated her choice at first. He probably would have thrown a temper tantrum, slammed his bedroom door, and called her names. She would have had to endure a few days of a mad, sulking boy, but then life would have gone on.

Finally, she would have taught Pete to follow his own instincts. He knew he didn't want to see the movie, and by mentioning it to her, he was actually offering her the chance to save him by telling him he couldn't go. One day, he would have looked back at the episode and said, "Thank you, Mom." Perhaps not until he was much older, but eventually he would have. The payoff for us mothers, and even for our sons, comes when we are all older. Pete would have come to realize that his mom was wise; he in turn would have internalized her behavior and learned to go against the norm when his instincts told him to, and he would have been better for it.

If she had said no to her son, the truth is that Pete might have been bullied. The other boys might have taunted him in class about being a "mama's boy" or a "wimp" for several days. Of course these words would have hurt, but Lana could have braced Pete for them, telling him to expect them and then to ignore them. This would have been hard, but would it have been harder than enduring the nightmares? I don't think so. If Lana had put her foot down, something great might have started. The mothers of the other boys at the party would have seen her courage and perhaps have done the same thing in other, similar scenarios. Certainly there were many of them who didn't want their sons watching *Rambo*, either, but they also didn't have the backbone to speak up. Lana would have given each of them permission to act accordingly, and who knows how many other troublesome party issues would have been curtailed in the future.

With sad regularity, I hear young mothers ask me for advice when it comes to giving their kids permission to do certain things. Usually, the advice they want pertains to group activities their kids want to participate in. Many kids get invited to parties where inappropriate movies are shown, as Pete did, or where alcohol is served or sex allowed. What really disturbs me is that sometimes these activities are sponsored by other parents. When the parents of your son's peers and friends offer them choices that go against your instincts, always respond according to your gut. Wisdom tends to align with instincts, and going with wisdom will serve your child best in the long run, even if it seems monumentally tough at the time.

Believe in Who You Are as a Mother

The fact that you are your son's mother is no accident. He didn't get your best friend as his mother; he got *you*. So believe in that. You have a synergy and connection with your son that no one else has. You have an understanding of him that no other woman has. Your problem (if you have one as his mother) isn't that you don't know what to do; it is that *you don't believe in yourself;* you feel too apologetic for or uncertain of the person that you are, and you need to learn to stop that. Matthew's mother did, and she was a better and happier mom for it.

When I asked Matthew if he would tell me about his mother, he was thrilled. He grew up with seven brothers. He was fourth in line and adored his mother. He spoke about her as a wise, strong woman. As I listened to the lilt in his voice, I wanted to know what she had done to earn such respect from her son. "She was entrepreneurial in her parenting," he told me. I wasn't exactly sure what he meant so I pressed him. "She was strong and unafraid of what others thought," he said.

"How did you know that she didn't care what others thought?" I asked. A reasonable question, I figured, because after all, though he was speaking with a grown man's perspective now, at the time he had been a young boy. How could he truly have known that his mother didn't care about the opinions of others?

"That's easy," he replied. "My mother was a stay-at-home mom and felt pressure from other mothers to work. She saw other women working and contributing to the family income. Many of my friends' moms had jobs, but she felt very unapologetic for not having a career outside the home. She was proud of being a mom. She was so sure of who she was that she trusted her own instincts and decisions more than anyone else's. She said what she thought and never backed down. I remember once when she allowed me to stay home from school because I had to study. I had a lot of work to do and found that I couldn't concentrate on it while at school. So she let me study at home. She sent a note to school with me the next day simply stating that I had stayed home for the day. The principal called her and told her that just saying that I was home wasn't good enough. She needed to tell him why I stayed home. Clearly, my mom disagreed because the next time I stayed home from school to study, she sent another note to the principal. It read, 'Matthew stayed home from school today. He has an ingrown toenail.'" When recalling this, he laughed as though his mother had written the note just yesterday.

I asked Matthew what the greatest gift was that his mother had given him. He said, "The best gift my mother gave me was knowing who she was. Because she never wavered in who she was, she inspired me to live with a certain rigor, to know who I am and pursue what matters most to me."

Matthew's mother was a genuinely wise woman and her wisdom changed who her son became as a man. We mothers spend so much energy trying to do things for our sons that we forget what really shapes their character: *our* character. Wise mothers know that we need to *do less* for our sons and *be more* to them.

Be Clear About What You Believe and Act on It

I was recently asked to give a lecture to a large group of parents in an affluent community outside a large city. This community also has one of the highest drug and alcohol use rates among teens in the country.

Several months before I spoke, three teens had committed suicide, and the town was reeling. Teachers, parents, counselors, and pastors wanted help and encouragement. My job wasn't to come and tell them what went wrong; it was simply to help them stand back and take a hard look at what forces might be operating in their kids' lives that were pushing them to the brink. I had just finished my lecture on how parents can recognize signs that their teens might be drinking or taking drugs and how to help them stop when one mother in her midforties raised her hand. She was beautifully dressed and extremely articulate. "Dr. Meeker," she began, "I have a fifteen-year-old daughter who is a sophomore at the local high school. On the weekends she wants to go to parties where I know there will be a lot of drinking. What should I do?"

I returned with a question, "What do you want to do?" She looked at me as though that were an irrelevant question.

"I think that drinking is bad. I mean, I don't think she should drink, but what can I do?" she said.

"Keep her home and offer her an alternative activity. Take her to a movie, go shopping, or go out to dinner," I replied.

"No, that would never work. She'd hate me. She'd scream at me. I don't want her to stop communicating with me. I feel that it's important to keep connecting with her. I also think that it's very important to teach her how to drink responsibly before she goes to college. She needs to learn to handle alcohol and pressure from her peers. I don't want her to drink, I guess, but every parent in our town serves alcohol to their teens on weekends because they believe, like I do, that they want their kids to learn to handle themselves in the real world." She was clearly frustrated with her situation, and I wasn't helping!

"I completely understand your thinking, your situation, and your fears," I said. And I did. After all, I had raised four kids. "But here's the real dilemma. First, because she is fifteen and not twenty, it is impossible to train her to drink responsibly. She can't. Her brain isn't ready because she doesn't have the necessary level of cognitive development. Second, all you are doing is increasing her tolerance for alcohol. While she needs two beers to get drunk now, if she keeps drinking, by the time she gets to college, she'll need four or five drinks to get drunk, and eventually she'll leave beer behind and move on to hard liquor. That's what many kids do. Third, you are teaching her that laws don't really matter. She can't drink legally at a restaurant but the laws are different in your home. Is that what you really want her to believe?" I challenged her.

"No, but I don't have a choice. This is the norm in our community. Kids go to parties at parents' homes and drink. Their keys are taken away and then if they need to sleep over, they do," she responded. I could tell that I was losing her. She wasn't going to change her mind. Her daughter, even though she didn't have a driver's license, was going to the parties. Period. Mom had surrendered.

Here was a bright fifteen-year-old girl attending one of the finest schools in America, probably gunning for an Ivy League college, drinking on weekends at her friends' homes with the consent of their parents and hers. Remember, I was asked to come to the community because they had one of the highest rates of drug and alcohol abuse among teens in the country. And the parents were the ones serving them the alcohol! Can you see the twistedness of the situation? Parents *knew* there was a terrible problem but were so confused about what they believed was right for kids and wrong for kids that they were acting completely against their intuition. Interestingly, as I spoke with this mother, I watched the other parents. They listened intently. It was clear they felt exactly as she did. They were all on the crazy train and every parent wanted off, but they also didn't want to be the one to get off first. Well, that was tough luck, because someone needed to be gutsy enough to stop acting out of the fear. Someone needed to be clear about what they believed was right and then do something about it. The problem was, they *weren't* clear on what they believed was right. They had their instincts, which told them they shouldn't allow their kids to drink, but they listened to their fears, which told them that if they said no to their children, they'd lose them. The kicker was that they were losing them anyway.

I went to bed that night with the sick feeling that I had wasted my time, and worse, that nothing that was wrong in the community would ever change. The kids were going to drink and the parents would continue to facilitate it because they were too afraid to stop them. They weren't sure of what they believed and therefore couldn't do what was right for their kids. I felt very sad.

The following day, I spoke at a session for mothers only. A few hundred women had gathered for the breakfast, but I wasn't exactly sure what I could say that I hadn't said the night before. Feeling a bit downcast, I began to speak about the differences between parenting from fear and from strength. I could see that many of the mothers were listening closely. One woman raised her hand to speak. "I completely agree," she began. "I feel intense pressure to let my sons do things which I don't believe are right. So this is what I've done. I collected four other mothers, whose sons are friends with mine, who feel the same. They don't want their boys drinking on weekends, either, so we formed a kind of 'mom squad,' if you will. We decided to take the heat for each other. When one of our sons complains he can't go to drinking parties, we point out that his friends (whose moms have joined with us) can't, either. The boys don't feel alone then."

My heart jumped. I was thrilled to hear what this mother was doing. I asked her to keep talking. "The other thing we do is offer to take the boys to professional soccer or football games on weekends. Or we ask one of the dads to take them fishing or to the movies. Anything, really—we just want them to have good alternatives so they don't feel like the geeks in the class, for not going out and getting drunk every weekend. The great thing is, it's working. Other mothers are doing the same thing. I know that there's always going to be drinking on the weekends, but at least our boys know that it won't be on our watch. And I think that's a good thing."

Yes, indeed that was a good thing. I can tell you that this mother was one tough bird. She realized that she could easily cave and be part of the problem, but she listened to her instincts instead. How could she participate in something that she knew wasn't right, something that was really bad for her son, and still be happy with herself? She couldn't, so she did what wise mothers do—she found support. She figured that all she needed was a few other mothers—maybe five altogether—to stick to their guns, and then perhaps they could tip the balance of the drinking in her town. I left there happy that I had found a new hero, and hopeful that the other mothers would follow her example. I am still watching from afar to see if the drinking among the students in this town changes because of this handful of tough moms.

John Milton discussed wisdom in *Paradise Lost*, and this particular mother's behavior reminded me of what he wrote. She knew that acting from wisdom was a gritty and intensely practical business:

> But apt the Mind or Fancie is to roave
> Uncheckt, and of her roaving is no end;
> Till warn'd, or by experience taught, she learn
> That not to know at large of things remote
> From use, obscure and suttle, but to know
> That which before us lies in daily life,
> Is the prime wisdom; what is more is fume . . . .

Live Responsibly (So That You Can Pass It On to Your Son)

Sisters often blame their brothers for spilling food and brothers often blame their sisters for breaking windows; a child's nature prompts him or her to point the finger and find a fall guy before they get into trouble themselves. The challenge for us mothers is to figure out who is telling the truth! We are so used to one child blaming another that many of us go to the default position of punishing both parties, because finding the guilty party is too tricky. But this is a mistake.

From the time they are very young, our sons need to learn to accept responsibility. Again, this is a hard task for mothers because it goes against what society at large tells us. We may *want* our sons to learn responsibility, but it's really hard in a world where our sons' friends aren't being taught the same thing. Not only do we take our sons in a direction opposite to their nature, but we take them in a direction which differs from that of their friends.

I believe boys and girls are born different, and that some boys are born with an innate feistiness. They tend to demand their own way more often than girls. They may appear to be more selfish than our daughters. They are more physical and enjoy violent sports and activities more than our daughters. Sometimes, they resort to fabricating when they're guilty: Getting caught pulling a sister's hair lends itself to making up a wild tale of how she asked for a new hairdo, but because his fingers were covered with jam, they got entangled. He will insist he was simply trying to untangle his fingers and she decided to yell. If this type of storytelling comes naturally to many boys, what is a good mother to do? How do we break a son's habit of weaseling out of taking responsibility for his mistakes, without breaking his spirit? It's not that hard if you know a few tricks.

Some years ago, I stopped at an in-store ATM to withdraw some cash. My son was about eight years old at the time and he went up to the machine with me. I typed into the machine that I wanted to withdraw sixty dollars from my account. He was learning addition and asked if he could retrieve the money and count it. A good lesson, I thought, because the bills come out in twenties and counting would be easy. I felt like a pretty good mom wanting to help him enjoy a teaching moment.

When the cash was dispensed, eighty dollars came out, not sixty. With a thrilled look on his face, he yelled, "Look, Mom, you hit the jackpot! You asked the machine for sixty and it gave you eighty! Can I have the extra twenty?"

At first, I was excited to see the extra twenty dollars. Who wouldn't be? I felt like I was at a slot machine and had just won. I reasoned that the money could belong to me because it was coming from the ATM—not someone else's account. It wasn't hurting anyone to keep it, really. So I gave my son the extra twenty and then we walked around the store looking for snacks for the car ride. And at that moment I felt a deep pang of guilt. I tried to tell myself that the bill was "lost" and therefore I could keep it. Another pang. I decided to give the money to the store clerk so that he could figure out whom it belonged to. That meant that I had to take it away from my son, who had already decided what he was going to spend it on. I bit the bullet. He cried, "But Mooooohhhhhm, you said I could have it!" I felt guilty again. I had made my cute little trusting boy cry. What kind of mom was I?

He tried to run out of the store to the car where my husband was waiting, but I grabbed his arm. "No," I said. "I'm sorry. I made a mistake. I wanted to keep the money and give it to you but that was wrong. The money doesn't belong to me or you and we need to give it to the clerk." He wailed. People in the store turned around. They might have thought I was hurting his arm, he yelped so loudly.

What made matters worse was giving the bill to the store clerk. When I explained to him what happened, he smiled. He didn't know who owned the machine, either, but he thanked me for "returning" the money. My son watched the man smile. As we walked away, I turned my head and noticed that the clerk was putting the bill in his pocket. My son saw, too. "Mom—you're just not fair," he said as we left the store.

Though the clerk took the money, I believe that what I did was the right thing to do. The important point here is that we mothers need to stay on our toes when it comes to doing what is right and taking responsibility for our actions. Just as we need to offer seven compliments to counter every criticism our child receives (as the adage goes), we need to act seven times more responsibly for every mistake in judgment we make. The peculiar thing about boys is that they remember the times we were wrong more easily than when we were right (just ask your son and he'll tell you about every mistake you have made in detail!). If we want our sons to grow into men who live with integrity and honesty, it must start with us. It is important to take inventory not simply of what we are saying or doing in front of our sons, but also of how much time our sons actually spend with us, so that they have the chance to see us in action. Remember, it is our character that shapes who they become as men, and if they never see us interact with the world, they can't imitate our behavior.

TEACHING SONS TO BE WISE AND RESPONSIBLE

In a culture where being successful trumps being wise, and improving one's status matters more than being responsible, we mothers know that we have our work cut out for us. First we must acknowledge that

teaching our sons to live wisely and imparting on them the importance of being responsible can feel as though we are parenting completely against the grain. I can't deny this. The truth is, most parenting
books tell us that we must teach our sons to have high self-esteem,
and that the best way to do this is to encourage them to beat the other
guy. We hear that it is most important to raise sons who are successful—
regardless of how their success affects those around him. I disagree. I
have learned from watching hundreds of boys grow up that the hap-
piest men are those who learn to watch, think, listen, and consider
the needs of others before making decisions. I have seen that those
who own their behavior—whether that behavior is good or bad—are
the ones who live with a strong and healthy sense of self. Wisdom and
responsibility are the hallmarks of good men and women.

Aside from modeling these characteristics for our sons (as if these
weren't hard enough), we must challenge them to follow us. Sometimes we must tell our sons that the decisions they want to make are
wrong. We must tell them that we are with them as allies, not enemies, and that therefore we will speak our minds and coach them in
the right direction, because we always have their backs, even if it
doesn't seem that way. When boys understand that we are tough because we are on their side, they will respect a lot more of our rules.
Many mothers don't want to implement strong boundaries and speak
up, because they believe that it's the *rules* boys don't like. This isn't
true. Boys will tolerate almost any challenging rule as long as they
understand that our primary motive in enforcing it is to take care of
them and raise them to be strong. If they believe that we are giving
them strict guidelines because we love them, they'll follow. But when
a boy feels that his mother suspects that he's up to no good, or that
he really *is* no good and therefore she needs to oppose him and bring
the hammer down on him, he'll rebel. Boys follow mothers who
believe in them enough to challenge them as men because setting
high standards communicates to boys that we believe they are capable
of meeting or surpassing those standards.

We mothers often make the mistake of believing that if we are nice
and accommodating and don't challenge our sons, then they will stay
close to us and keep the lines of communication open. In fact, the

opposite is often true; unless our sons respect our authority, they will never trust us. When we say yes all the time, fail to challenge them to act wisely, and comply with their demands too readily, they lose respect for us and disconnect. It may be that their own instincts are telling them that the behavior we tolerate from them is dangerous or wrong. How, then, can they trust us to raise them to be strong men?

We must show them that our job as a mother is to teach them to be wise. If your son hates sports and his friends all play soccer, applaud him for knowing his mind and then ask what else he would like to do. Encourage him. Part of him wants to be different—so let him be that way. Boys need to learn boldness in order to forge their own, independent lives, and mothers are usually the first to accept when their sons are different and don't follow the herd.

The best way to teach our sons to be responsible is to show them that we trust them (but the trust *must* be age-appropriate). Find a chore for your son to do and make sure he does it. We have seen that boys feel better about themselves when they have work to do. But in addition to feeling good about themselves, regular chores teach a boy that he is capable of shouldering responsibility, and is capable in general. They teach him that he is reliable and others can depend upon him. This makes him feel valuable and mature, and so he continues to work in order to continue to feel good about himself. It's a cycle of positivity. One mistake we mothers can make is falling into the trap of doing for our boys what they can do for themselves. This is part of what we are taught to do as loving, doting, and conscientious mothers, but you can see how doing too much for our sons robs them of the opportunity to experience the exhilaration of being responsible.

One of the greatest rewards of responsibility is that it makes a boy feel powerful. And boys like power—especially when it comes from within. As boys mature through the teen years, the great theme of transitioning from adolescence into adulthood is exemplified by their accepting ownership for their feelings and actions. Learning to be responsible facilitates this. Boys who have a task or a challenge to complete, and who are told that they can be successful at it entirely on their own, develop feelings of control. Feeling in control is particularly important through puberty, when everything else seems so *out* of control. And when they feel more in control, they learn to rely more heavily on themselves and less on the help of others. They learn their strengths and weaknesses and so understand how to impose boundaries on themselves instead of waiting for mom to do it. So you see, responsibility is central to the process by which boys become men.

Ask Questions

One of the easiest ways we can train our sons to be wise is to ask them questions. For instance, if your son wants to join the Cub Scouts, even though he's already in band and plays soccer and flag football, ask him if he thinks adding another activity would be wise. Challenge him to look beyond what he feels or thinks he wants. Ask him to think for a day or two about what he would be giving up—sleep, downtime at home, dinner with the family. Never ask if he thinks a decision is smart or stupid because, that sets him up to feel like a failure; if he makes the "wrong" decision then he feels stupid. And likewise, using words that sound judgmental is counterproductive. Ask questions in such a way that there is no right or wrong answer, just an opportunity to consider all the options and the effects of his decisions, and then honor the decision he makes.

As he matures, he will learn that seeking out the wise thing to do involves more than intellect and thought. You teach him that being wise means that he has to weigh what he believes is right against what is wrong and that he needs to draw on past experience (had he done the same thing before and gotten burned?). Choosing the wise move also demands that he take into account his instincts as a boy (or man), and it may even press him to seek outside help from God. When I prayed for my son in high school, as I mentioned earlier, I would often tell him because I wanted him to know that I needed help. Faith is an important component of wisdom because boys need (as we all do) to have a place to turn to when they are no longer in charge. Wisdom comes to us through a combination of many different experiences, but there is a strong component to it that is beyond us. When we encourage our sons to seek what is wise, rather than what is smart, they learn to look outward to God for help, not just inward to themselves.

It is also important to ask questions with a scope that goes beyond the direct choice in front of them. For instance, in addition to asking what the wise decision might be, ask questions about his beliefs, experiences, and feelings. If your son doesn't make first string on his soccer team, gently ask him how he feels about it and then listen. Of course you know that he feels badly, but the point in asking is to help him talk about his feelings. Or, for another example, if a classmate breaks the law but didn't get caught, ask your son what he believes should happen to his friend. You do this for two reasons. First, you want to help him learn to think critically, but you also want to help him clarify his own convictions, or lack thereof, in his mind. Keep your questions simple when he is young and add complexity to them as he gets older. Ask him questions about his feelings: *What do you think about your coach letting kids play even though they've broken the rule?* Ask him questions about his beliefs: *Do you believe that God answers our prayers?*

When asking such questions to stimulate critical thinking in your son, I highly encourage you to listen four times as long as you speak. Give him time to figure out his answers. Resist the urge to interrupt or correct him. Your question may lead him to consider an idea for the very first time and he may be using his conversation with you to put the pieces together for himself. He needs space to do that. If you ask a question and the answer your son gives really disturbs you, make yourself hear him out completely, and then, if you want to challenge him, go back one or two days later and reopen the discussion. If you correct him as he's talking, he won't listen. But if he sees that you heard him out and weighed his answers carefully, then considered them and came back with another question—or even a challenge—he will respect your ideas and learn to act as you do. So, ask questions, and listen to his answers four times as long as you speak.

Work Alongside Him

Mothers have the responsibility of caring for our children every day. So it is good when our sons are exposed to our responsibilities. When you have work to do, ask your son to help. Fold laundry or divide your recyclables together. He might fuss at first, but I guarantee that over time, he will thank you. Boys like to contribute, and since you have to work, have him add his skills to yours. And there's an extra benefit to this, which shouldn't be overlooked: When we ask our sons to live life next to us, good things happen. Conversations erupt. Think about the life-changing moments or talks that you had with your mother. Chances are excellent that they didn't happen during a special event—they happened on ordinary days during ordinary activities. So it is important to make sure that your son sees the work that you are doing and then pitches in periodically. Yes, he needs to have his own regular chores that he finishes on a daily or weekly basis, but pull him into your work, too. If he drives, have him go to the store for you. If you are cleaning, ask him to vacuum. In the end, he will feel good about helping you. And remember, since boys bond with others by doing activities together, working together might even make you closer!

Having work will not only teach your son responsible behavior; he will also learn to be more comfortable with himself. Inevitably, he will make mistakes. He won't mow the yard right, he will spill the entire box of laundry soap, or he'll back the car into the closed garage door when moving it to wash it. If you are there, then you can help him learn how to deal with such mistakes. If you take the situation, whatever it may be, in stride and even laugh about it, he will become more comfortable accepting his failures. If he hears you tell him, "Oops, that's too bad you spilled the whole [brand-new] box of laundry soap," and then you help him clean it up, he'll realize it is easier—and better—to accept responsibility for his mistakes. Many times boys won't admit wrongdoing because they fear their parent's response. They are worried their parent will get mad, or worse, perceive them as a failure. This is enormously frightening for boys (and many fear their father's response even more than their mother's). If we treat them poorly when they do make mistakes, they will never want to accept responsibility or admit guilt.

When your son works alongside you, you can teach him not to be afraid to fail. Once he sees that you accept his errors, he will learn to accept them as well. He can admit them, make corrections, and move on.

Invite Him to Pray

What does prayer have to do with teaching our sons to be responsible and wise? Just about everything.

Plato wrote that wisdom is a virtue. In fact, he called it the most important virtue among the four he described: wisdom, temperance, courage, and justice. And Socrates, clearly one of the smartest men of his time, taught his students that no man was wise. He said, "O men of Athens, God only is wise." We can see through those who revere wisdom that it is a mysterious thing and is found in many places. In fact, I think it is fair to say that wisdom appears on two different levels. There is practical wisdom, which mothers acquire from a combination of sources, as previously discussed, and then there is the wisdom that, as philosophers through the ages have said, comes from God. This second type naturally has a spiritual component.

Sons need to know that they have support. Yes, mom and dad are pretty good as far as backup goes, but the truth is, our sons are going to see us make a lot of mistakes. There are times when our failures will rattle them. A son may hear his mother scream at his father or he might watch his father get fired because he made a large error at work. In the confusion of seeing parents fail, sons can temporarily lose their trust in us. So it's good for us, and for them, that they can look to another source for support.

When we make a mistake in front of them, we need to admit fault and we need to tell them that we try hard, but that sometimes we too need help. Tell him you need to ask God for direction on how to live better and how to be a better mom. Then ask your son to pray for you, just as you pray for him.

That can be a life-changing moment for many sons, when a mother admits that she's trying with all her might but isn't doing the job that she really wants to be doing and needs help. In that moment, a son recognizes his mother's humanity. And when he sees his mother as a person who needs help, then he may give himself permission to need help as well. More important, he will find strength in being asked to help her. He won't have to worry about fixing his mother (he knows that he can't) but he can learn to lean on God, who can help her.

Many mothers aren't comfortable praying with sons and that's all right. Simply ask your son to pray for you and if you want to be specific about your requests, go ahead. If you need help with patience, help being less irritable, or even help knowing what to do or say, ask your son to go to God on your behalf. Then watch what happens to your relationship with your son. It will deepen. He will become more compassionate. He will find comfort and become calmer when he prays. It will give him an opportunity to be quiet and to contemplate, which is hard to do in life today.

There is another wonderful side effect to this activity. By asking your son to pray for you (or with you), you teach him how to draw closer to God. You encourage a strong spiritual self in your son and a strengthening of character. Often we think of girls as being more open to faith and spirituality, but this isn't true—a boy can develop a very deep and strong faith. And once he becomes comfortable with prayer, then you can encourage him to ask God for wisdom. Show him why the great philosophers, theologians, and thinkers believed that wisdom comes from sources outside our human selves. Imagine how empowering this idea might be for a boy of seven, thirteen, or seventeen years, one who is struggling with self-doubt, school, or personal issues. Availing him to the power of a loving and good God, a God who is wise and can help him be wise as well, is one of the most profound gifts that any mother can give her son. The book of James says, "If any of you lacks wisdom, he should ask God, who gives generously to all without finding fault, and it will be given to him." James goes on to say what that wisdom looks like: "But the wisdom that comes from heaven is first of all pure; then peace-loving, considerate, submissive, full of mercy and good fruit, impartial and sincere." And the book of Proverbs teaches us that it is "better to get wisdom than gold." As a jewelry fan, I particularly like that one.

These verses cut to the heart of what theologians and philosophers have argued strongly through the ages: that true wisdom can only be given to us by God. The Bible teaches that "fear of the Lord" is the beginning of wisdom. This is a term that can be easily misunderstood, but upon study, we can see that in context, "fear" means profound respect, a pious respect that causes one to turn toward God, not away from Him. Fear, as we commonly understand it, prompts us to flee, but this fear of God does exactly the opposite.

Even if you are not particularly religious, the following excerpt from Tolstoy's brilliant *War and Peace* should make you think. It is a conversation that takes place between a younger gentleman named Pierre, who has admitted that he has no faith in God, and an elderly man Tolstoy calls "the Mason." (He refers to the man as a Mason because he espouses the beliefs of those men in the order of the Masonic Temple.) Pierre becomes confused by what the Mason says as they talk about how one acquires knowledge.

Pierre: "I don't understand . . . how is it that the mind of man cannot attain the knowledge of which you speak?"

Mason: "The highest wisdom and truth are like the purest liquid we may wish to imbibe . . . the highest wisdom is not founded on reason alone, not on those worldly sciences of physics, history, chemistry, and the like, into which intellectual knowledge is divided. The highest wisdom is one. The highest wisdom has but one science—the science of the whole—the science explaining the whole creation and man's place in it. To receive that science it is necessary to purify and renew one's inner self, and so before one can know, it is necessary to believe and to perfect one's self. And to attain this end we have the light called conscience that God has implanted in our souls."

God alone, Tolstoy contends, holds the greatest wisdom. Inviting your son to have a spiritual life opens up access to that wisdom for him because as he prays, he asks God to both hear him and to speak to him. As this exchange occurs, your son develops a deeper inner self and a deeper faith. Prayer helps him to believe in God (as Tolstoy says) and connect with the conscience that God gave him. And prayer binds the two of you closer together. Asking your child to pray for you is admitting that you are not perfect. And this reassures your child because he knows he's not perfect, either.

Teach Him Forgiveness

At the risk of beating the drum too hard, I want to reiterate how potent the peer pressure that mothers face when it comes to raising our sons can feel. We are taught that our sons should be competent, strong winners. We give them medals for running fast and trophies for kicking a ball. This is fine. But when we fail to show our sons that they won't always be winners—that sometimes they will lose and someone else will win—we teach them to live with the illusion that they are never wrong. And if they believe that, they become monsters. Think, how would you like to be married to a man who thought he was always right and never wrong? I wouldn't like it at all.

It's natural that we want to keep our sons from feeling ashamed when they a make a mistake. We want them to have good self-esteem. But self-esteem comes more from being able to accept errors than from feeling "right" all the time. Our sons are going to mess up and they aren't always going to be right, so we can either teach them how to navigate life when they make a mistake, or we can pretend they are never wrong, allowing them to be thrown to the wolves when they get into college or join the workforce. A son who has never learned how deal with being wrong will walk out of his job, leave college, or quit the team when he's criticized. We can easily spot adults who never learned to accept responsibility for their failures—they are the ones blaming everyone else for all the bad things that happen in their lives.

So, while he is young, let him be wrong and teach him to deal with being wrong. If he misbehaves, teach him to admit it and say he's sorry. And then accept his apology with kindness and grace. One of the best ways to show him the power of those words is to find a time to let him see you saying you're sorry to someone else. If he isn't there, share a story with him that shows as much; about a time when you hurt a friend's feelings and what it felt like when you apologized to her.

Often mothers refuse to make young boys say they are sorry because they believe that if the boy isn't sincere and the apology isn't heartfelt, then it shouldn't be given. I disagree. Who among us ever feels completely 100 percent sorry when we admit we are wrong? I have often said I'm sorry while I'm still fuming. We learn to apologize because it is right to do so, not because of the way it feels. Furthermore, feelings follow actions, and when we learn to *act* the right thing, eventually we will *feel* the right way. Apologizing for our failures just makes us nicer people.

Asking you for forgiveness helps your boy learn how to be forgiven and in turn helps him learn to forgive. This is an extremely important tool in being happy. If sons never learn to forgive others, they give power to those who have offended them. Those of us who have been beaten up by life know very well that those who hurt us go on with their lives, and it is we who suffer for it. Our sons will do the same; they will give power to those who have hurt them if they refuse to forgive the offenders. We teach our sons to forgive because it makes them happier and healthier men.

Wisdom and responsibility are two of the most crucial components to a balanced life. As we have discussed, neither of these attributes comes naturally to sons. They must be taught—deliberately and with strong intention. They are hard to teach and some mothers won't do it because it *is* so hard. But strong women fight for their sons. No one else but you knows what is best for your children. You are wired with everything you require and more to usher your son into a disciplined life filled with wisdom and lived with great responsibility. And no worries if you forget your way; God is always there to help grant what you can't get on your own.

CHAPTER 10

Letting Go

(So You Can Get Him Back)

We know from neuropsychology research that a man's brain isn't fully developed until he's in his early twenties.[1] That means that he will still be experiencing malleable cognitive and emotional changes until he reaches about twenty-five. This is good news and bad news for a mom. It's good news because if, for example, you are struggling with a strong-willed, defiant fifteen-year-old, you've got ten years left to rein him in. It's bad news because you've got ten years more of hard work ahead of you. If you're at that stage, part of you is already exhausted and you wonder if you can make it that much longer. Let me encourage you by saying that you absolutely can; you just need to pace yourself. A common problem for zealous, committed mothers is that we parent with so much intensity and enthusiasm when our boys are young that by the time they hit the challenging years of adolescence, we're burned-out. So if you are reading this with a two-year-old son at your knees, heed my advice and relax a bit. You have many years in front of you to get things right.

Take a moment to picture your son when he is twenty-five. What do you hope he's like? If you are like me, you look forward to him *wanting* to spend time with you. How wonderful to have a grown son who calls you and says, "Mom—what are you doing tonight? Would you like to meet for dinner?" In fact, not only does he call, but when the two of you sit down at a restaurant, you have a good time. You talk about his life and hear that he's enjoying his job; that he has good friends and a new romance. He is kind and caring, and he asks your opinion but feels perfectly free to accept or reject it because you have taught him not only to make his own decisions, but to feel secure in doing so. When you leave the restaurant, you kiss him on the cheek. Both of you are happy to have seen each other. Your heart sinks a little at saying goodbye, but not because you yearn for him to be four again. You're satisfied that he is content with his life and feels no compulsion to go back and rework any part of his childhood. Those who live with an incessant inner urge to go back and rework what was broken so that they can create a different outcome didn't have a complete childhood and aren't in a healthy place; but your son doesn't need new outcomes because the ones he got were just fine.

Let's continue with the picture of your son at twenty-five: You want him to respect his colleagues. You want him to be kind but firm, stand on his own two feet, and not have to ask you for financial help. In fact, you hope he feels that your job is done and in the future, he looks forward to helping *you* out if circumstances call for that. You don't feel needy toward him and neither does he feel needy toward you, as he did when he was younger. He enjoys life, is socially active, and has a few good male friends. He knows that you fully accept and admire him for who he is.

The million-dollar question for you in this moment, whether you have a six-month-old or ten-year-old or eighteen-year-old son in your home, is this: How can I raise him to be a great twenty-five-year-old?

First of all, you absolutely can steer him toward being a great adult. Regardless of how challenging he may currently be, there is time to improve your relationship. Time is on your side. To get him there requires focus both on changing your perspective of who you are to him, and on believing in yourself. Once you learn to see yourself as he sees you, learn to parent based on his needs rather than what you think you *should* be doing, and learn to listen to your instincts, you are well on your way to shaping a good man. But there is one final step that you must master in this journey, and that is the art of letting him go.

This is a sensitive process that requires careful thought and intention, and caution must be taken because it can be very easily misunderstood.

Why Letting Go Is Important

One of the healthiest beliefs that we can have as a mother is that ultimately, we are not in charge of our sons. Call it providence, fate, luck, or as I believe, God: Something or someone else holds the life of our sons in their hands. We can't decide when they are born or when they die and we can only partly control what happens to them in between. Most of us live with the illusion that we are far more in control of many aspects of their lives than we actually are. That's why, I believe, the more truthfully we live, the happier we are. Especially when it comes to raising our kids.

The process of letting go of our sons begins the moment they are born. It is at that moment that we realize our helplessness in the face of what we desperately want to do—protect them from all pain and make only good things happen in their lives. But even in those first moments, we recognize that we need to let go of our deepest wishes and understand that we can't always protect them, that we have to let them face the world, and perhaps get knocked around by it. And the letting-go process continues from that moment. We hand them to their fathers to feed. We let their siblings push them on their swing. We let neighbors drive them to school and we let babysitters watch them while we're away. When they go to school, we let teachers show them how to add and subtract. When we tell them they can go out to play, we let other children influence their thinking. We let our sons choose whom to be friends with, and whom to date. When they learn to drive, a stranger teaches them to parallel park. Does he do it right? We don't know. We hope so.

Having children means learning that parenting is 10 percent control and 90 percent letting go. Fortunately for us, there is a gentle, step-by-step approach that we can follow to lessen the pain of the process.

Many of us understand intellectually that boys must grow into men and that along the way they need us to gently push them from the nest. But we also need to realize that letting go is designed for our benefit as well as for our children's. When we let go in a healthy, timely way, our lives become richer and our relationships with our children deepen. But surrendering our sons doesn't always feel natural. I dare say that there are times when it feels downright unnatural. We have been taught that being close to our sons is a good thing, but what, exactly does that mean? As we've discussed in previous chapters, many of us believe that it means we should share our feelings and thoughts and enjoy depending on one another; that's true to a certain extent, but many times we cross the line and our closeness becomes unhealthy. We are also taught that good mothers stay involved in all aspects of their sons' lives—academics, sports, dating, friendships—and all decision making. Again, some participation is good, but mothers shouldn't always be intimately involved with all of their sons' activities. Finally, we have come to believe that we are so important in our sons' lives that our own activities must always revolve around them. They need us, so we must always be available. At certain points in their lives this is true, but many, many times it isn't.

We have come by these beliefs honestly; we want to be great moms and so we ponder the mistakes our own parents made, and vow that we won't make those mistakes with our own children. If our parents were distant, we decide we will be close. If they never showed interest in our activities, we will take pains to do the opposite, regardless of the cost. We attempt to sort through the plethora of available pop-psychology and parenting literature; some is excellent and some is terrible. We talk with friends about how they parent so that we can glean what works and rid ourselves of bad habits. We want to be open and honest. We want to be a great friend to our sons. In fact, I think that there have never been better mothers than we are today. But all of our earnest and good efforts make it that much more difficult to pull back and let our sons go at the appropriate age.

Letting go of control over our son is important for three primary reasons. First, he can't become a man without it. He can get older, but he will stay a perpetual adolescent if the process doesn't happen. Second, you can't have a healthy adult relationship with him if neither of you lets go. Finally, the completion of the process allows each of you to be an emotionally healthier person. I'm sure you have known friends who are so enmeshed in their children's lives it's as though the child has never even left the house. Or you may have been that enmeshed with your mother or father and know firsthand how suffocating it is. This won't happen if you allow the letting-go process to unfold.

We Don't Own Our Sons

John Riccardo grew up in a wealthy suburb of Detroit. As the son of a corporate CEO, John lived a life envied by many. When I asked John about his childhood, I realized that it had been extraordinary, but not because his family was wealthy or had so many opportunities. It was because of his mother.

From the time he was born until he was seven, John's mother was an invalid. Multiple back surgeries forced her to spend her days bound to a hospital bed parked in the living room of their home. Her pain prevented her from participating in John's life the way she might have liked: driving him to school, baking treats for him, and throwing him birthday parties.

When he was seven, John's mother experienced a miracle. John's sister had been to a church event and heard the preacher talk about a person who had terrible back problems. He told the audience that the woman was going to be healed from her pain. John's sister was sure the man was speaking about their mother. She went home and told her mother what the pastor said. John's mother read the Bible and had faith in Christ, but she wasn't particularly charismatic in her faith. Still, she decided to believe her daughter. Maybe the man *was* talking about her. One month later, John told me, God performed a miraculous healing and his mother was playing tennis.

For the next fourteen years, his mother not only lived an active life;

she was heavily engaged in his life, his sister's life, and the lives of others. The great miracle wasn't just in the restoration of her ability to walk pain-free; equally important was the fact that John had a mother who could now walk beside him. Emotionally, she experienced a restoration, which allowed her to be engaged with him, not consumed by her pain. She loved helping others and her kids and with her health renewed, she could *really live*.

I met John through his work as a priest and he agreed to answer some questions for me about his relationship with his mom. At the beginning of our interview, I asked him, "What was one of the most important lessons your mother taught you that helped you become the man you are today?" A thick silence hung over the phone. I wondered, had she taught him too many things? Too few? Or perhaps he couldn't articulate what she taught him? Instead of answering directly, he began telling me about life with his mother.

"When I think of my mother, I think about the word *class*. She had it in every sense of the word. She spoke beautifully; she dressed beautifully. She wasn't stuffy; she was *lovely*. I remember her sitting at the kitchen table reading the Bible every morning. Sometimes she would tell me about what she read; sometimes she wouldn't. Our kitchen table was always covered with things she was reading or working on. But it was also always open for others to sit at. Friends came to see my mother all the time."

As I listened to his middle-aged voice, I could hear the tenderness and adoration he still felt toward his mother. Many of his inflections had a lilt to them. Clearly, this was one special woman.

"Many times I felt, as a kid, that folks would beat a path to my mother's door. As a boy, I watched them come and sit with her. She would listen and talk. And regardless of how they felt when they came to see her, they always left feeling better. She had this ability to help people feel at peace, to feel blessed, if you will. I marveled at what she did for them. Was it what she said to them? The food she offered? I don't think so. She just had a way of helping people of all ages feel better about life. People could sense that she loved them and genuinely cared for them." I could hear his smile. I was so moved by what this man said about his mother, I wondered if my own grown kids could say the same about me. What effect did my kids see me have on my friends? Had I been the kind of woman who helped them feel better about life?

"I need to tell you something about my dad, too," he added. "As a CEO, he traveled a lot. Many days he had to work in Washington, D.C. The amazing thing about him was that he came home every night—even when he had to spend the day in Washington."

"You mean he flew home every night?" I marveled.

"Yup. If he had to work for the week in D.C., he would fly home and fly back the next day just to be with my mother at night."

Now I was thinking about my own husband. Would he do that for me? I decided not to go there.

"My mom was, and is, a woman who prays. She told me from the time I was a little boy that I wasn't hers; that I belonged to God. I wasn't afraid of this. It made me feel safe. She told me that she carried me in her heart and prayed for me constantly. Of course she prayed for my four older siblings as well, but I had a sense that she prayed differently for me." He paused. "Are we close today? I can say this. I believe that there is a mystical bond between a mother and son. Since I don't have a wife, my mother holds a place in my heart that other men may not understand. We continue to pray for one another. If someone in my parish is ill, she prays for them. We are connected spiritually that way.

"I know that I made my mother grow old faster than she should have. While I was at the University of Michigan, I lived a lifestyle that might not have made her proud. But after I graduated, I felt a tug from God to go into the priesthood. He got hold of my heart and began to change me." After John graduated from college, he did go to seminary and became a priest. At that point I asked him something I was afraid to ask, but really wanted to know. "Was it hard for your mother when you went to seminary, knowing that she wouldn't have grandkids from you or see you married?"

"Giving me up to God was a sacrifice and she knew that. She knew that once I became a priest I wouldn't be home for Christmas dinners and many family events. That grieved her. But this is what you need to know: After my mother handed me over to God, something in our relationship dramatically changed. We became closer. There was an intimacy between us that had never been there before. I can't describe it. All I can say is that in surrendering me to God, it's as though she gave God a chance to see we were hurting and He gave us a deeper closeness in return, and I believe that we think of one another more often than most sons and mothers. We carry that closeness today. She writes me, and I tell her about people who need prayer and she prays for them faithfully."

My original question to John now felt trite to me. What had she done to help him become the man he was today? They carried each other in their hearts and the very essence of her life became the essence of his. She taught him how to give people peace without saying a word about it directly to him. Her demeanor and faith, lived right in front of his eyes, shaped him into a great priest. Men and women come to Father John in droves to listen to him and to ask his advice. His parish is bursting at the seams. I think that in large part this is due to his mother.

Letting go of our sons, even if it isn't giving them to God like John's mother did, draws us closer to them in a mystical way. Maybe it's because the letting go rids the relationship of unhealthy neediness. Maybe it's because we learn to live as separate adults who are free to love one another without strings attached. One thing that I have realized for sure, though, is that we mothers must find the courage to be like John's mother. We need to understand, down to the very core of our being, that we don't own our sons. We can't be their everything, nor should we be. In this short life, the best we can do is to love them like crazy, steer them gently but firmly in the direction we think they should go, and then pray our hearts out for them while living our own lives. Then, when they are adult men, we can offer advice (when asked) and encourage them to be strong and independent. Most important, we can tell them that we believe in their ability to succeed on their own—without our help.

What Letting Go Is

Dr. William Pollack, author of *Real Boys* and perhaps the most learned professional on boys in the country, writes that boys need their mothers' love throughout their entire lives. In fact, he asserts, boys who don't have a secure attachment with their mothers are at an enormous disadvantage. "My research shows that the absence of a close relationship with a loving mother puts a boy at a disadvantage in becoming a free, confident, and independent man who likes himself and can take risks, and who can form close and loving attachments with people in his adult life. In their early years as well as during adolescence, I think boys will benefit enormously from spending time in the loving environment created by his mother *and her friends*—the happy nurturing world of women."[2]

In other words, letting go of our sons isn't about pulling our love out from beneath them—rather, it is about transferring responsibility for themselves from our shoulders to theirs. For example, think of the first day he goes to school. If you have passed this milestone then you know that when he goes off to nursery school or kindergarten, your heart goes with him, but your body doesn't. This is what letting go is all about. It is the constancy of love amid all the changes and separations that life brings. As he matures, the process intensifies because he goes farther away—emotionally, mentally, physically—and our love for him deepens. It is the parallel growth of these two phenomena— the growing distance and the deepening love—that makes the letting go feel so tough for each of us. The dynamic of these two phenomena seems paradoxical. Why should it be that our love deepens when our sons distance themselves from us? Quite simply, because when they become independent, we experience the satisfaction of seeing the fruits of our sweat and all the hard work that we invested while we raised them. When we see them mature and succeed, we see the cycle of life as it was meant to be. Unfortunately, because it feels so hard to let go, many of us opt to forgo the process, which creates a very unhealthy situation for both our son and ourselves.

Letting go occurs primarily on two levels. First, we psychologically let our sons gain independence. I think that this is the hardest process for mothers, because it involves separating ourselves from our own need to micromanage, hyperparent, or overcontrol our sons. Early on, such managing is a good thing, because they need that kind of help. Micromanaging a three-year-old is fine. Hyperparenting a child who is being bullied isn't always a bad thing. The trick is to learn when our management is healthy and when it oversteps bounds and hurts our sons. The good news for us is that we have a long time to practice, and if we do catch ourselves overstepping boundaries and driving our sons nuts, we usually have another chance at stepping back and letting them do the decision making. For instance, I have had friends who are so anxious for their sons to date or marry just the right woman that they will play matchmaker. This is a big no-no, because not only does it rarely work; it also usually causes a lot of tension in the mother's relationship with her son. I have to admit, I have been tempted to do this for my own son, and each time I mention having him meet a woman, one of my daughters reminds me to back off. We mothers reason that since we know our sons better than they may know themselves (this may be true), it is our job to make sure they date someone who is a good fit for them. The problem for our sons is that they resent our interference, and they should. As young men, they need to learn to trust their instincts about women, and as their mothers, our job is to encourage them to trust their instincts. When we swoop in and play matchmaker, the message that we send to them is that we can do a better job picking out dates than they can, enforcing the notion that they need us to make such important decisions as much as we want to be needed to make them.

When our sons are born, each of us finds a fresh sense of purpose as we look upon those chubby cheeks for the first time. We begin to understand that we were born to care for and protect that little bundle. That sense of purpose feels wonderful. As he grows, however, it is the relinquishing of that need to be needed, as wonderful as being needed is, that must take place, so that it can be replaced by a fresh relationship with our son. This can be nothing short of traumatic. Some mothers suffer a crisis when they realize that their son, at age thirteen, no longer needs them the way he did when he was five. *What now,* we wonder. *Who am I and where do I go from here?*

Mothers experience this separation at different stages of their boys' lives. Some feel it most strongly when their sons enter first grade, some when their sons leave for college, and yet others when their sons get their first apartment, say at age twenty-three. But most mothers experience emotional tearing at some significant point in their sons' lives. I believe that, as difficult as it is, it's an integral part of the whole parenting plan for us; if we don't experience it, it might mean we're too detached from our sons. Healthy letting go may cause us grief at first, but then we learn to live with a greater sense of freedom. When this happens, we aren't the only ones to feel the terrific effects of this freedom—our son does as well, and it is at this point that our relationship with him strengthens.

The second part of letting go is more concrete than psychological: It is simply the transference of dependence; it is your boy learning to rely on himself rather than you. When he is three we teach him to ride a tricycle. When he is five he goes to kindergarten, and when he is sixteen he drives a car. Year after year, we find ways to teach our son that he can do things on his own, without our help. To many of us, this transfer of dependence feels good because it means less work for us. Even still, we struggle with our deep desire to be needed and perhaps subconsciously refuse to transfer responsibility entirely. For instance, some mothers encourage their sons to hold a job while in high school but won't let them date. Each of us brings our own bias to this letting-go process and we can do some pretty peculiar things because of it. One friend encouraged her son to make enough money to buy his own car and pay his own car insurance, but never asked him to make his own bed or pick up after himself at home. She constantly complained about his being irresponsible and sloppy. There is a great irony in that. Truth be told, she admired his solid work ethic but never enforced it at home because she wanted to feel that he *needed* her to pick up after him. Of course, she probably didn't recognize this inconsistency because her parenting (like each of our parenting) was peppered with her own insecurities and personal history.

The art of letting go is a delicate balancing act. Doing it in a healthy way requires that we first recognize it as a natural part of a strong mother-son relationship. It then requires that we act intentionally. This is tough because it forces us to do some soul-searching regarding our motives in all aspects of our parenting. Do we do things for our sons because we need to (for ourselves) or because it is actually good for our sons? I am the first to admit that much of what I did for my son stemmed from my own desire to feel like a good mom. My mother always did my laundry when I came home from college and I adored my mother. So guess what happens when my son brings home a pile of laundry while visiting during college? Yup. I first separate the colors from the whites, because he never does. When it's clean and dry, I fold everything neatly for him to pack. And even though my son began doing his own laundry when he was fourteen, I still feel like a better mom when I do it while he's home on vacation. You may not do this precise thing, but if we could chat over coffee, chances are great that you, too, do some things for your son that you know you probably shouldn't; you just do them because they make you feel good. I won't tell.

Slipping up here and there is okay, but it is important to recognize that in order for a son to turn into that wonderful twenty-five-year-old man, Mom must confront her feelings and ask herself, particularly as he moves into his teen and young adult years, *Am I doing what I'm doing because it makes me feel like a better mom or because it makes him a stronger man?* If the answer is that it makes him stronger, go for it. If, on the other hand, you sense a twinge of self-serving hidden in your motives, you must give it up. Both you and he will be a lot happier. I promise.

Every once in a while we can accomplish both. We can do what is best for our son and we can feel better about our parenting at the same time, but this is more the exception than the rule. The point is to *always search our motives* for doing what we do with our sons. If we are honest in doing this, it's startling to see how many times we make decisions based on what makes us feel like better mothers, not on what makes our son better men.

What Letting Go Isn't

Because we are painfully human, many of us tip the fine balance of letting go and maintaining control to one side or another. Some mothers suffer in the struggle to release any measure of control over their sons. On the other hand, some mothers let go of their sons far too soon. Often, mothers are pushed to become more emotionally detached by husbands who fear that their son will be a "mama's boy." I have heard fathers say that their son needs to "man up" in the second grade and not cry to his mother over every little thing. But these fathers are wrong.

I will unequivocally say, and I believe that Dr. Pollack would agree, that young boys require emotional closeness with their mothers. No, a mother shouldn't drive a wedge between a son and his father, but the truth is that many mothers offer a level of comfort and security to sons that fathers can't. And many fathers detach themselves from sons because this is all they know. Their fathers probably did the same to them, and while they hated it, they repeat what they know, not necessarily what they know is right. If you find yourself in this situation, I encourage you to do what you can to help your son's father reconnect with your son. The best way to do this is to tell your husband (or ex-husband) that your son needs him and wants a closer relationship. Tell him that, while he may not know exactly how to be close to your son, he can start by simply spending more time with him—even if it means just doing small things like chores together. Remember that men bond through activities while women bond through communication, so all he needs to do is start spending more time with your son, doing things to get the ball rolling.[3] Often fathers feel inadequate and we mothers need to boost their self-esteem and be a source of encouragement to them. Our sons need us to do this because they need stable relationships with their fathers, too.

Numerous studies have shown that when a boy has a secure attachment to his mother, he is psychologically healthier, stronger, and even braver. He will have higher self-esteem, do better in school, and have lower rates of mental and behavioral disorders.[4] As we have seen in the chapter on giving boys an emotional language, letting go of our sons does not mean becoming emotionally detached. Boys need to know that our love for them is strong, unshakable, and always present. Thus, refusing to let our sons cry (regardless of their age), forcing them to figure their emotions out on their own, or abandoning comfort when they are afraid is not only wrong, it is cruel.

When we properly teach our sons how to identify and be comfortable with their feelings and then teach them what to do with those feelings, we help them learn to make sound decisions as they mature and to rely less and less on us to direct them. Letting our sons have strong and independent emotional lives means that they have an emotional repertoire, feel comfortable with it, and can handle their own feelings in a healthy way. Letting go means teaching them to trust their instincts. What it doesn't mean is refusing to tell them how we feel or rejecting or negating their feelings by telling them that they shouldn't have them in the first place (which is what happens when eight-year-olds are told not to cry).

Letting go also means teaching boys to not only act independently but also take responsibility for their behaviors. But in order to do this, it is important not to give them too much independence too soon. When we give them responsibilities that are too much for them to handle, our boys suffer. For a variety of reasons, this typically happens during the teen years. We hear our son's voice change, watch the facial stubble thicken, and start to assume that because he *looks* like a man, he must think like a man. But this isn't so. Especially when you consider that new research shows puberty occurring earlier in boys than ever before; some boys are entering it as young as nine years old.[5] That's third or fourth grade! Not only do these boys have difficulty dealing with bodily changes, their parents have difficulty as well. So, it is extremely important for us to understand that what we see with the naked eye and hear with our ears isn't necessarily reflective of what is happening in our son's brain. We must always match our parenting to his *mind's* development, not to his *body's* development.

Many of us give too much responsibility to our teen boys because of social bias. We tend to worry constantly about our daughters when they are teens, but when it comes to our sons, many mothers worry less. Sons can't get pregnant, and probably won't get assaulted as a daughter might, so we give them more leeway. We make their curfews later (if they even have curfews). We see that they look strong, responsible, and tough and so we treat them as though they are these things. But letting go of our boys in a healthy, timely manner means not giving them free rein to do what they want whenever they want, just because they are boys and we think they can handle it. Sadly, I see this all the time in well-meaning moms who trust their sons because they are generally "good kids." What we fail to remember is that while our son might be a "good kid," he has an acquaintance or two who isn't. And bad eggs love to wreak havoc in the lives of good kids. Lena learned this lesson the hard way.

Lena is a single mother and has three sons, all of whom play soccer. Her oldest, Eddie, was always close to her. His father died of pancreatic cancer when Eddie was eight, and since that time he had felt like the man of the house. Lena even told him that he was, on occasion. One weekend when Eddie was seventeen and a junior in high school, he had a soccer game in town while his two brothers had soccer games away from home, so Lena sat down and discussed the situation with Eddie. She didn't want to leave him home alone, she told me, not because she didn't trust him, but because it might put him in an awkward situation with his friends; they might want to take advantage of a house with no supervision, seeing it as an opportunity to drink or party and forcing Eddie to have to say no to them. But he was a great student and had never given her trouble, so ultimately they decided together that he would stay home alone for the weekend. He promised her that he would be fine.

On that Friday, he invited a friend to stay with him and they watched a movie. Saturday the soccer game came and went and Eddie was excited because his team won. The victory qualified them for the state tournament. He went home Saturday night, put a frozen pizza in the oven, and invited another friend over. By nine o'clock the two were watching a movie when the doorbell rang. Two girls were at the door, one of whom had a crush on Eddie's friend. The girls heard that the boys were home alone and had decided to stop by. Within a half an hour, five more juniors and seniors were at the door because one of the girls had texted her friends and invited them over. She knew Eddie wouldn't mind; nice guys never mind. Within a one-hour period, forty kids showed up at his home, drinking beer, playing pool, and parking on the lawn. At midnight the police were called by neighbors and when they showed up, the kids scattered. The police ran through the house and found kids in every bedroom. They handed out more than ten citations for underage possession of alcohol—even to Eddie, who drank very little. He hadn't brought any of the beer into the house, either, but that didn't matter because it was his house.

When Lena came home Sunday morning, Eddie had cleaned the house fairly well but the living room couch and carpet were stained. The pool table top was torn and the lawn had deep ruts in it from the cars that had parked there. Lena was furious. She was angry with Eddie and all of the kids who had shown up. She phoned every parent of every teen who had come, and she told me that nine out of ten parents defended their kids with statements like "John would never have ruined your carpet" or "Alicia was at her friend's house so I know for a fact that she wasn't there." All told, Lena spent hundreds of dollars and many days cleaning up the mess, but she only received five apologies from her son's classmates and their parents.

So who's to blame? Eddie? Lena? The girl who had the crush or the parents who refused to admit that their children would do any damage? All of them are to blame. Even good, smart, conscientious kids need to be protected. So, first, Lena was to blame for not putting safeguards into place for Eddie and for giving him too much responsibility. Second, Eddie was to blame for allowing the girls in the house. He knew they had cellphones and he knew that when kids get together, they party. Third, the girls were to blame for taking advantage of a nice guy like Eddie. Fourth, every kid who came over is to blame because they acted poorly. Even solid, responsible kids act crazy and disrespectful when they drink beer amid a pack of their partying peers. Finally, every parent who refused to hold his or her child responsible for the damage at Lena's house was guilty. Of course they should have owned up to their kids' faults and helped set things right.

But Lena was the first to blame because she allowed the whole mess to get put in motion. She did so because she was only thinking about how well-behaved her son was, not about how young he was. Yes, her son was a great kid, but being a wonderful and wise parent means recognizing that we're living in a tough world where any kind of kid can get into all sorts of trouble, trouble that can hit our own doorstep in a second. The wise move would have been for Lena to find an adult to stay with Eddie that weekend. If she had had someone who was much older than Eddie stay with him in their home, all of the trouble could have been avoided. Or she could have closed the house and had Eddie stay at a friend's home (provided the parents were home). One simple move like that would have spared all of them a lot of pain.

Lena thought, like most of us mothers would, that since her son was a "good kid" she had nothing to worry about. This might have been true a generation ago, but sadly, it isn't today. Teenagers should *never* be left alone at home for weekends—regardless of what part of the country you live in or where your son goes to school—because the world we live in provides too many temptations for them and for their friends to act in ridiculous, irresponsible ways. Again, I must reiterate that our sons, regardless of their character, GPA, maturity, or good intentions, mustn't be left alone for days. Not because they can't be trusted but because they are surrounded by others who are looking for opportunities to party and will jump when they see one. And there's one more reason. Boys who are left alone repeatedly get very lonely. We often see them as tough and strong but the truth is, many who are left behind by their parents feel anxious when left. Don't let your son experience this.

The Fine Balance: Getting It Right

On the flip side, as dangerous as it is to give our kids too much freedom too soon, the same is true when we stay overly involved in their lives. We need to find the balance between giving them too much room and smothering them.

Several well-respected authors have composed checklists for sons and mothers to help us understand if we're hitting the balance right. For example, Dr. Kenneth Adams, author of *When He's Married to Mom* (ouch), poses the following questions, aimed at the son:

> "Do you often feel preoccupied about your mother's unhappiness in her life?"
> "Are you the most important person in your mother's life?"
> "Are you distant from your father?"

"Do you often escort your mother to social functions, or have you in the past?"[6]

At first glance, these questions can seem innocuous. What's the big deal about a mother going to an event with her son? Or, why shouldn't a son feel as if he's the most important person in his mother's life? Shouldn't we all want our sons to feel that important?

The answer is, no. We want our sons to feel important, but when they feel that they are the center of our lives, that they consume us, we have crossed the line. I have often asked boys in my office about their mothers, and within moments of talking to some of them, I can sense that enmeshment is a problem. That is, the line between where they emotionally end and their mother emotionally begins is blurred. Boys who are enmeshed with their mothers find themselves feeling their mother's feelings and worrying about her needs above their own. Also, they may think that they need to please their mothers or perform well for them in order to keep them happy. But boys can quickly become troubled if they feel that their mothers depend on them too much.

For example, I was recently at a speaking event and a tearful mother raised her hand after I had finished talking about parent-child relationships. "Dr. Meeker," she said, "my husband and I divorced a few years ago when my son was seven. After my husband left, I was worried about my son, and my daughter who was five at the time. My son told me not to worry too much because he would be the 'man of the house.' When I heard him say that my heart broke, but then I told him that he was right. He could be the man of the house. I thought that by saying that, he would feel better about himself. Was I right?"

As hard as it was to cause her more pain, I told her that while her intentions were undoubtedly well-meaning, she had been wrong. Encouraging a son to be something that he is too young to succeed at puts far too big a burden on his shoulders. It sets him up to fail because there's no way he can deliver. And it is not a son's job at that age—nor should it be—to take care of his mother. While this woman's son might have volunteered for that position, he was too young to understand what it would really mean, to be the man of the house, and she should not allow him to try. It would only cause their relationship terrible harm. I told her she needed to take back the reins and tell her son that *she* was in charge, not him, and that he should stop worrying about her. Equally important, she needed to stop leaning on him for support.

You can see how enmeshment creeps up on us when we're trying to do the right thing. Her motives were right and she's no doubt a great mom—but she needed to free him, let go of needing his support, and tell him that it was okay for him to let go of wanting to take responsibility for her.

As our sons mature, we must be tough enough to ask ourselves some hard questions like the ones posed by Dr. Adams. When your son is four, ask yourself, does he have a close relationship with his father? If not, are you what is keeping them apart? If the answer is yes, then you are fostering an unhealthy dependency; good mothers don't isolate their kids from other relationships—especially relationships with the other parent!

When he is seven, ask if he worries about you too much. Many boys in first and second grade worry about their mothers dying, and this is normal. But when they can't let go of their worry about your health or happiness, a red flag should go up in your mind, especially because there are ways a mother can subconsciously feed into this problem. When a mother wraps herself entirely into her children's lives, she begins to blur the boundaries between her kids and herself. Many zealous mothers surrender all their free time to hauling their kids all over the country to athletic events, or spending every night helping them with their homework. This eventually puts a great burden on the son because he begins to feel that *he is his mother's whole world.* He feels that she needs him in order to be happy and this burden is too great for boys.

If your son is older, perhaps married, you can ask yourself other questions, like: Does he ask my advice before asking his wife's? If so, he may be telling you that your opinion is more important to him than hers, and that is dangerous territory. Does he call you for long chats three or four times per week even though he's in college or working? Young men with healthy relationships with their mothers don't lean on them to this degree. If they do, it's because they feel awkward and isolated from their friends or other family, and that isn't the way it should be.

In addition to asking questions about how our sons are doing, we can ask more personal ones concerning how *we* are doing. Dr. Margaret Paul, author of *How to Become Strong Enough to Love,* poses the following excellent guidelines we can use to find out if we are too enmeshed with our sons. Read the following statements below and see how many ring true for you.

- Your children's good or difficult behavior and successful or unsuccessful achievements define your worth.
- Your children are the center of your life—your purpose in life.
- Your focus is on taking care of your children rather than taking care of yourself.
- Your happiness or pain is determined by your children.
- You are invasive—you need to know everything about what your children think and do.[7]

Dr. Paul concludes that if you identify with one or more of these symptoms, you might be enmeshed with your children. So, what do you do if you think you are overly controlling, overly "close," or enmeshed with you son? The most important step you can take is to admit it. After that, I will tell you that it takes work. The good news for you is that once you get going in the right direction, life gets a whole lot better and a lot more fun—for you and for your son.

GETTING IT RIGHT

Let's get down to the nitty-gritty of how to accomplish the process of a healthy letting go. The first rule is to put in place (at least in your mind) a few safeguards. Here are three that I think work well.

Keep the Process Age Appropriate

As your son matures, find ways to give him independence, but always make sure that what you're asking him to do is age appropriate. I frequently tell mothers of two-year-old boys that if their son is alive at the end of the day, they have succeeded as mothers. Anything beyond that is gravy. It seems that the sole focus of toddler boys is to try to find as many creative ways as possible to kill themselves: a light socket to poke a wet finger into, a drapery cord to wrap around his head, or a pot of boiling water on the stove to tip over his little body. I had one two-year-old patient climb on top of the family swing set and then crawl across the top of the monkey bars from one end to the other. He was far more interested in getting as high up as he could than on swinging in his swing. Fortunately, his mother got him down before he fell and broke his arm. Young boys can be walking tornadoes looking for ways to create chaos.

When he is three, teach him to ride a tricycle on his own but never let him go out into the street alone. When he is four, give him a chore to do in the house that isn't dangerous. You'd never let him mow the lawn, but you might have him help you sweep the kitchen floor after dinner. When he is five, you could ask him to feed his baby brother, but make sure you are always in the room when he does. The key to giving him independent activities is to assess what his physical and cognitive skills are, and then gear his responsibilities toward that while keeping an eye on his progress. This can be tough because you may not always know what is an age-appropriate freedom. It might be helpful to ask a friend with an older kid or even a professional. And I recommend that you always err on the side of caution. If you aren't 100 percent sure that your son can handle the task, wait awhile. And when you aren't sure, pick projects or chores with little risk. Showing him how to do his laundry when he is eight may be a challenge, but he's not going to hurt himself or anyone if he doesn't get it right.

As he moves into the middle elementary school years, he'll start to want more independence. He'll want to go to a friend's house to watch movies. He might want to stay with a friend alone while the friend's parents are away. He is moving into a time of psychological growth where he feels invincible. This feeling intensifies as he moves into junior high; he will be so sure that nothing bad can happen to him that he will try to convince you of the same thing. It's your job to remember that he isn't indestructible. And just because your son reaches twelve or fifteen without any damage, that doesn't mean he's invulnerable. You know why the state won't give him a driver's license at thirteen. You know that even though he's got a smart head on his shoulders, he's still perfectly capable of doing really stupid things. So when you are giving him latitude, always ask yourself, *What is the worst thing that can happen to him if he makes a mistake while doing this?* If nothing life threatening or psychologically scarring can occur, then let him try it.

Trust Your Instincts

I've stressed this throughout the book: Mothers need to learn to trust their instincts more! Listen to that small whisper inside you, the one that tells you whether or not trouble is ahead. You know which of your son's friends you trust and which you don't. You know whether or not your son is ready to date, drive, ride a two-wheeler, or spend the night at a friend's house. You may have other parents telling you to not be so afraid. They may tell you that you don't want to be over-bearing or too strict. Don't listen to them. Listen to your heart. Many times, even well-meaning friends speak from their own insecurities or guilt, and you never want your son to have to pay the price for their issues.

If your fourteen-year old son wants to spend the night at a friend's and you know that the parents won't be home, forget what everyone else says. If your gut tells you not to let him do it, don't let him go. Tell him that the reason you don't want him to go to his friend's house unsupervised isn't that you don't trust him; rather, tell him that the temptation for others to come over and make trouble is too great. Then find another way to let him do something independently. You could offer to drive him and the friend to a movie, dropping them off at the theater and picking them up when it's over. Or you could have him invite some friends over and let them play pool in the basement without you hovering over them. If you recruit his opinions, you'll be surprised what he comes up with. The two of you can find creative ways to help him go off on his own, but in a manner that sits well with you.

Sometimes it's hard to know whether it's our instincts we are following or something else. I have known mothers who allow their sons to travel every weekend for hockey or soccer tournaments but insist on staying with them, driving them everywhere and, in short, running the entire weekend. They say that they are simply enthusiastic and interested, but deep down they realize that they are controlling every detail because they don't trust anyone else to take care of their son. These mothers might state with certainty that they act this way because they are listening to their instincts. I disagree.

Our instincts tell us when we're doing the right thing for the right reasons, and they also tell us when we're doing the wrong thing for the wrong reasons. Occasionally we will want to do the wrong thing for the "right" reasons—at least reasons that we have rationalized are right. But if we are honest with ourselves, we will quickly see that doing the wrong thing for the "right" reasons rarely justifies doing them. For instance, if we find out that one of our son's friends bullied him, it would be wrong to post something nasty about the bully on any of his social networking sites. Sure, we may rationalize that the bully deserves it and that since our son won't speak up, we must. But quickly our instincts (I hope!) should stop us from acting, because such a response would serve no one well.

In most situations we encounter with our sons, our instincts tell us how we should respond and what we should do. So when you are faced with a decision that you must make about your son and you feel confused, I encourage you to pull back from the advice of well-meaning friends and listen to what that small voice inside you is trying to say. Sometimes it is quiet, but if you pay attention longer, it will get louder. So many times you know what to do but you won't because you doubt yourself. Don't.

The best way to avoid this is to tell yourself that you understand your son better than anyone else. You know what he can handle and what he can't. When situations arise where you need to give your approval, separate what others are doing from what you feel is best for your son. Then, and only then, make your decision. Finally, if you find yourself seeking advice from another but your answer is really in the question ("My son asked to go to a movie with his friend and I don't approve of the movie. He really wants to go and all the other parents are letting their kids go, what should I do?"), then don't ask it. You already know the answer; the real stumbling block for you is that you fear acting on your instincts. Be strong. Don't parent from fear; do it from your sound thinking.

Check Your Motives

No matter what decisions we make for our kids, it is always important to make sure that our motives are pure. This is one of the safest ways I know to ensure that you are being a good parent. It is no secret that we are living in a culture that advocates selfishness. We are taught from the time we are young girls that we can have it all—we can be what we want, do what we please, and create a great life for ourselves. We learn that we should focus on finding out what makes us happy and then pursue those things. And if we find multiple things, we should pursue them all at the same time. For instance, when I was at a women's college in the 1970s we were taught that we could have a demanding, stimulating sixty-hour-per-week career, raise four kids, and keep strong marriages alive all at the same time. So many of us tried but burned out and became unhappy because we found out the hard way that no human can do everything at the same time. Quite simply, we got tired trying to pursue happiness.

Careers, family, marriage, and hard work are all terrific things, and yes, they lead to happiness. But enjoying happiness in all these doesn't necessarily mean pursuing them all simultaneously.

As far as creating the life that we *really* want, one with no obstacles and constant happiness, good luck! Yes, we can work hard and be successful at many things, but we can't control our fate. It's important to realize that we can be very happy despite not having that kind of power over our lives, that we can enjoy life by working hard and accepting what comes our way. We don't need to control everything. Especially when it comes to our sons. As mothers, our job is to understand that our sons are a gift and that we have the privilege—for a short time—of loving them and providing all the positive things that we can to them. In order to do that, we must sometimes be willing to sacrifice our own desires and needs. Many mothers sacrifice for their sons easily, but for others sacrifice can be hard—particularly because we live in a culture that encourages women to do whatever they feel they must do in order to be happy, regardless of the cost. Selfishness in motherhood doesn't work very well to foster healthy relationships with our kids because kids feel pushed aside and forgotten when a mother acts too selfishly.

Then again, acting like a martyr doesn't help our kids, either. At the other end of the selfishness spectrum are mothers who believe that their only purpose in living is to care for their kids. We all know mothers like this. Mothers who throw themselves on the altar of martyrdom end up taking many down with them because kids don't respond well when they believe that *they are the reason* for their mother's existence. How can they separate from their mothers? How can they ever disagree with their mothers or upset them? Children of mothers with a martyr complex carry a very unhealthy sense of responsibility; if they become independent, they will leave their mothers with nothing to live for. This is far too great a burden for kids to bear.

How, then, do we find that balance between sacrificing for our sons and still maintaining a healthy independence from them, for our own sakes as well as theirs? Paying close attention to our motives for our behaviors with our sons is a great place to start.

Aimee was a full-time mother and loved staying home to be available for her son, Aiden. She drove him on field trips and to football games, made snacks for his team, and volunteered at the school office every other week.

Aiden was her third child and was a "surprise," she said. Her two older children were grown and living on their own and she had many regrets over how she had raised them. "I was young and struggled with depression for many years when they were growing up," she told me. "I was never available for them and I feel so guilty about that. I know that my depression was one of the reasons that neither of them fully reached their potential. Neither has settled down and my oldest son, who is twenty-five, can't find a career. He just floats from one menial job to another. I'm not going to let that happen to Aiden."

To compensate for "failing" her other two kids, Aimee threw herself into parenting Aiden. She made sure that he had an iPhone in case he needed to call her. If he didn't have any organized games on the weekend, she asked if he wanted to have friends over, or she'd take him to dinner and a movie. From the outside, many other mothers envied their closeness.

One day I was talking to Aiden about his father. Were they close, too? What kind of things did he like to do with his dad, I asked. "I don't get to do a whole lot with my dad. For one thing, he works a lot. And my mom's not wild about some of his hobbies so she won't let me go with him when he's doing them. Like hunting. My dad loves to deer hunt. I'd like to go, but my mom thinks guns are dangerous so she won't let me."

This went on until Aiden was thirteen. Then Aimee brought him to me saying that he was "out of control." "He rages," she told me. "Sometimes he screams and yells so loud that I'm afraid the neighbors are going to call the police! And he's broken things—he kicked a hole in the basement door a few days ago. He frightens me."

After talking with Aiden, Aimee, and Aiden's dad, it became clear that Aiden was rebelling only against his mother. Certainly, adolescent temper tantrums are not uncommon, but his explosions were far beyond those. Why? His mother was suffocating him. In her well-intentioned zeal to make his life good, she crossed the line into enmeshment. Making him happy became her life. She ignored his real need to be with his father. She ignored his natural need to separate from her. She parented with a laser focused on Aiden and, though he couldn't articulate what was driving him crazy, he knew that his mother was asking something from him that he simply couldn't deliver.

Aimee believed that she needed Aiden to be happy so that she could make amends for her past parenting "mistakes" (who knew if she really did make mistakes?) with her older two kids. When she and

I got down to the nitty-gritty of what was going on, she found the strength to confront her motives behind her behavior toward her son. She stayed at home to assuage her guilt, not necessarily to be a better mother. She worked at school because she was nervous about being away from him. As she painfully recounted much of what she had done for Aiden over the previous four or five years, she realized it was her sense of need driving her, not a desire to make him a better young man. Admitting this hurt, but it was the only way Aimee was able to make some really necessary changes for the both of them.

Aimee decided to find ways to do things that were beneficial for Aiden *and* for her as well. She got a job at another school so that she could begin to emotionally peel herself off her son. Then she agreed to let Aiden go hunting with his dad. Those two very simple steps alone made enormous improvements in her relationship with Aiden. And guess what happened to his rage episodes? They began to quiet down.

Asking ourselves the tough questions is often the key to better living. In order to figure out your own motives for doing things for your son, here are a few questions to ask yourself.

- Why do I do _____ for him? (put him in a certain school, sign him up for three extracurricular activities per term, buy him expensive clothes, always go with him and his friends on outings . . .)
- Do I do things with or for him in order to fill a void inside me?
- Do I do things for him in order to feel better about myself?
- Do I do what I do with or for my son because it's best for him, or am I getting some secondary gain that may not be healthy?

Sometimes it is easier to reverse the questions and ask things like the following:

- Is doing _____ for him helping him become more independent?
- Does doing _____ for him encourage him to be a better young man?
- Does allowing him to _____ strengthen his character?

By answering these questions when you are deciding on a certain course for your son, you can figure out whether you are acting from your own need or because it is beneficial for your son.

If we can be strong enough to be honest with ourselves, then we are well on our way to great parenting. If you have difficulty uncovering your true motives, ask a friend or spouse for help. If they really love you, they'll help you be honest. And maybe one day, you can return the favor and help them be honest with themselves, too.

Saying Goodbye Means Saying Hello

No mother can truly be close to her son until she sets him free. This is a pain unique to the mother-son relationship. Fathers don't have to let their sons go because psychologically, boys don't feel the need to separate from dad. Because they are both male, as our sons grow older, they develop a different sort of relationship with their fathers. Similarly, we mothers don't need to separate from our daughters the way we do from our sons, and our girls don't feel the need to disengage from us to the same degree. Certainly daughters need to find their own identity and become independent, but, for example, understanding their sexuality doesn't necessitate completely letting go of us. For a son to understand who he is as a man, to have a sense of his masculine sexuality and his masculine self, he needs to distance himself from his mother because staying close to her emotionally during that process feels too confusing and complex.

Similarly, we know that when a man gets married, he needs to sever some ties with his mother or he can't have a healthy marriage. A daughter can stay emotionally close to her mother and have a strong marriage, but this is far more difficult for a son. Talk to a woman who is married to a man who hasn't separated from his mother, and nine and a half times out of ten, you'll find one unhappy wife.

As our sons grow up, we walk them through many stages of letting go. These are all trial runs for the final goodbye, which must take place when he is a young but fully mature man. That time may come when he gets married, moves across the country to take a job, or goes into military service. The circumstance of the "final goodbye" is different for each mother, but we all recognize the moment when it comes. It is that point when we fully realize that we are done. We have sweated, prayed, cried, argued, and spent ourselves to be the best mother that we could possibly be. Some of us arrive at this point with enormous regrets, much like the ones Aimee had about her older children. One thing is certain: When the time comes to fully let go, none of us is ready. It is always painful.

Watching him stand at the front of the church waiting for the love of his life to appear at the door in her white gown, or seeing him board a plane in full military uniform, will always catch a mother off guard. Our little boy no longer needs us. An emptiness that can take our breath away settles in. Our throats close and in those moments we see all the kisses we gave and the moments we yelled when we shouldn't have. We hear his high-pitched giggle, and we remember the sight of his eyes welling up with tears. We realize that life with our son, as we have always known it, is over. It's time to really let him go—to another woman, to his job, to the life that he has chosen for himself. We must let him walk away, whatever it costs us, because we have come to understand that he, God, or something else is fully in charge of his life from here on out. We aren't.

As painful as this is, it is an extremely important rite of passage. Everything inside us will want to hold on to the past, to beg for life to return to the way it always was. But it can't. Time moves forward, not backward, and we need to move with it. We can't let ourselves hold on, because if we do, he will suffer. We want to hold on not for him, but for ourselves, because it hurts us to let go, and we must always remember that. But we must also remember the words of Father John Riccardo. He told me that it was at the moment that his mother gave him to God that he felt something deep and wonderful change in their relationship. He said that from that point forward, they enjoyed a new closeness that they had never experienced before. It was a closeness he knew they would never have had if his mother had not said goodbye to him.

Therein lies the great mystery singular to the mother-son relationship. It really is in the letting go of our sons that we get them back. They return to us as men who are free from our needs and confident in themselves. We have raised them and served them and after that time, a new period of life emerges. Now it is time for them to be men who want, among other things, to enjoy the company of their dear mother. They assume the duty of helping us when we are in need, of watching over us from a distance, of calling just to check in and make sure that we are well and feel loved.

As I have watched my own son grow into a great man, I have felt the gentle shift from being his mother to being his friend. He went through the teen years as most boys do. As a teen, he never wanted me to touch him in public and he distanced himself from me in ways that felt painful—but now as an adult, he lets me hug him wherever we are. And it never fails to thrill me. The great part about the passage of time is that it changes our sons and us, even if we don't want it to. They grow up and we grow older. Affection is no longer peculiar for sons in their twenties, because they see through the lenses of men, not children, and that means that they see us differently. We are smaller in stature than they are. Our arms are thinner than theirs and the discrepancy in our physical strength is glaring. Sometimes when they note this, they become protective over us because they see our frailties. While my son jokes about my weaker thighs and arms, I see that there is also a realization that I am aging.

For my son, this really hit home as he watched my husband and me care for my aging parents during the last few years of their lives. My father had horrific dementia, and during the last five years of his life, he stayed close to us so we were able to help care for him. My son often stayed with my father while I took my mother on errands. When my father died, my son was nineteen, and he grieved deeply. Several months later I fell off a dock and was impaled on a metal rod anchored to the bottom of the lake. I got out of the water and promptly passed out. Within minutes, my son was hoisting me into his arms and helping to get me off to the hospital. My recovery was long and forced me to remain on my back for several weeks. During that time, my son was home on summer break and he took care of me. He lifted me from the couch when I needed to move, he cooked meals, and he made me a "bell" by filling a Ball canning jar with rocks and securing the lid. He told me to shake it when I needed something. (I tried not to take advantage of him by using it too frequently!)

Six months later, my mother passed away, and again, my son grieved. But in the months that followed, I began to see a part of him emerge that was unfamiliar to me. He called more frequently from college. Whereas he used to call with a specific purpose, after my parents died he called just to check in on me. "So how are you doing today, Mom?" he'd ask.

At first it felt peculiar, because I was always the one worrying about him. Did he get back to school safely? Was he making nice friends? Suddenly he was asking if I was happy, and after a while I became used to it. I found myself telling him what kind of day I really was having. I let go of worrying about his response because I knew he could handle my sadness. When he was younger, of course, I kept my fears and sadness hidden because I didn't want to worry him. Now, as a man, that was changing and *he* was initiating the change.

Several years have passed since my parents' deaths and the accident, and my son is now well into his twenties. He still calls me to check in but also fills me in on what is going on in his life. He went to Argentina to study for three months and I missed him terribly, but I also lived with a great sense of peace and pride that he was living his life the way he wanted to live it. I can honestly say that today we enjoy a closer relationship than ever before.

Something quite mysterious happens when a mother lets go of her little boy. She gets back a man—not just any man but one who shares her values, knows her flaws, accepts her weaknesses, and cares for her in a way that no other man can. He is her son and she is his mom.

And that is about as good as life gets.

Acknowledgments

Many great people contributed to *Strong Mothers, Strong Sons* and I am grateful to each and every one. First, I would like to thank my terrific literary agent, Dan Conaway. Thank you for your encouragement, for challenging me, and for keeping me on task. To my good friend and assistant, Anne Mann, you have fearlessly and fastidiously stood by me through many trials and I will always love you for it. To my editor, Susanna Porter, I want you to know how much I appreciate your fine-tuning and editorial wisdom. Marjorie Braman, you are probably one of the most skilled editors on the planet and I thank you for your hard work. I would also like to thank Shannon Litton and Mary Bernard from the A Group. You have always given me timely and professional advice and you are good friends.

To those who have cheered me and supported me along the way, I can never adequately thank you: my sister Beth and my good friends Dave Ramsey, Jim Dobson, and Lisa Lempke. The gift of prayer, without which nothing can be done, has been faithfully given to me by Lori, Jen, Lara, and Jill. You four are the greatest.

And of course, I thank the men who allowed me to see pieces of their hearts. Father John from Our Lady of Good Counsel, you have inspired me like no one else. And to all the other men who spoke to me about their mothers, for the sake of privacy, I will not name you, but you know who you are. May your lives bless all who read these pages.

Finally, to my wonderful family: Walt, I thank you from the bottom of my heart for your love and understanding, and to Mary and Alden, Charlotte and Brandon, Laura and Walter, what would life be without you?

Chapter Citations

Introduction

1. James Dobson, *Bringing Up Boys* (Carol Stream, Ill.: Tyndale House, 2001), p. 34.
2. Ibid.
3. Jay P. Greene and Marcus A. Winters, "Leaving Boys Behind: Public High School Graduation Rates," Manhattan Institute, Civic Report No. 48, April 2006, http://www.manhattan-institute.org/html/cr_48.htm.
4. William Pollack, *Real Boys: Rescuing Our Sons from the Myths of Manhood* (New York: Henry Holt, 1998), pp. 233–38.
5. Ibid.
6. Ibid.
7. Bureau of Labor Statistics, U.S. Department of Labor, American Time Use Surveys, June 20, 2013, http://www.bls.gov/news.release/atus.nr0.htm.
8. Wendy Wang, Kim Parker, and Paul Taylor "Breadwinner Moms: Mothers Are the Sole or Primary Provider in Four-in-Ten Households with Children; Public Conflicted About the Growing Trend," Pew Research: Social & Demographic Trends, http://www.pewsocialtrends.org/2013/05/29/breadwinner-moms/.
9. *America's Children: Key National Indicators of Well-Being, 2013,* Family Structure and Children's Living Arrangements, http://www.childstats.gov/americaschildren/famsoc1.asp.

Chapter 1

1. Fiona Macrae, "Sorry to Interrupt, Dear, but Women Really Do Talk More than Men (13,000 Words a Day More, to Be Precise)," *Mail Online,* February 20, 2013, http://www.dailymail.co.uk/sciencetech/article-2281891/Women-really-talk-men-13-000-words-day-precise.html.

2. Mortimer J. Adler, ed., *The Great Ideas: A Synopticon of Great Books of the Western World,* vol. 1 (New York: Encyclopaedia Britannica, 1971), p. 690.
3. Ibid., p. 962.

Chapter 2

1. Tyjen Tsai and Paola Scommegna, "U.S. Has World's Highest Incarceration Rate," Population Reference Bureau, http://www.prb.org/Publications/Arti cles/2012/us-incarceration.aspx.
2. William Pollack, *Real Boys: Rescuing Our Sons from the Myths of Manhood* (New York: Henry Holt, 1998), pp. 20–51.
3. J. Shedler, *American Psychologist* February–March 2010, Vol. 65: 98–109
4. http://www.fatherhood.org/media/consequences-of-father-absence-statistics.
5. N. Weinfield, J. Ogawa, and L. A. Sroufe, "Early Attachment as a Pathway to Adolescent Peer Competence," *Journal of Research on Adolescence* 7 (1997): 241–65.
6. "Piaget's Definition of Egocentrism in Adolescence," Education Portal, http://education-portal.com/academy/lesson/piagets-definition-of-egocentrism-in-adolescence-examples-quiz.html.
7. Fiona Macrae, "Sorry to Interrupt, Dear, but Women Really Do Talk More than Men (13,000 Words a Day More, to Be Precise)," *Mail Online,* February 20, 2013, http://www.dailymail.co.uk/sciencetech/article-2281891/Women-really-talk-men-13-000-words-day-precise.html.
8. Patricia M. Greenfield, "Inadvertent Exposure to Pornography on the Internet: Implications of Peer-to-peer File-Sharing Networks for Child Development and Families," *Applied Developmental Psychology* 25 (2004): 741–50.
9. Rob Jackson, "When Children View Pornography," Focus on the Family, 2004, http://www.focusonthefamily.com/parenting/sexuality/when_children_use_pornography.aspx.

Chapter 4

1. Sheryl Gay Stolberg, "Researchers Find a Link between Behavioral Problems and Time in Child Care," *New York Times,* April 19, 2001, p. A22.
2. Peter Ernest Haiman, Ph.D., "Effects of Type of Attachment on Child and Adolescent Behavior," http://www.peterhaiman.com/articles/effects-of-type-of-attachment.html.
3. J. Twenge, et. al., "Birth cohort increases in psychopathology among young Americans, 1938–2007: A cross-temporal meta-analysis of the MMPI," *Clinical Psychology Review* 30 (2010): 145–54.

Chapter 6

1. Craig A. Anderson and Brad J. Bushman, "Effects of Violent Video Games on Aggressive Behavior, Aggressive Cognition, Aggressive Affect, Physiological Arousal, and Prosocial Behavior: A Meta-Analytic Review of the Scientific Literature," *Psychological Science* 12, no. 5 (September 2001): 353–59.
2. Ibid.
3. Vital and Health Statistics Series 10, Number 254, U.S. Department of Health and Human Services; Centers for Disease Control and Prevention, National

Center for Health Statistics, Summary Health Statistics for U.S. Children: National Health Interview Survey, 2011 (December 2012): p. 11.

Chapter 8

1. "ISU's Gentile Authors Study Finding Nearly 1 in 10 Youth Gamers Addicted to Video Games," news release, Iowa State University, http://www.public.iastate.edu/~nscentral/news/2009/apr/vgaddiction.shtml.
2. STD Trends in the United States, U.S. Centers for Disease Control and Prevention, http://www.cdc.gov/std/stats11/trends-2011.
3. Ibid.
4. "Most Reported Chlamydia and Gonorrhea Infections Occur Among 15–24-Year-Olds," STD Trends in the United States, 2011 Data for Chlamydia, Syphilis, and Gonorrhea, U.S. Centers for Disease Control and Prevention, March 2013, http://www.cdc.gov/std/stats11/trends-2011, p. 2.
5. Sexually Transmitted Diseases Surveillance, Syphilis, 2006, U.S. Centers for Disease Control and Prevention, http://www.cdc.gov/std/stats06/syphilis.htm.
6. "Most Reported Chlamydia and Gonorrhea Infections Occur Among 15–24-Year-Olds," STD Trends in the United States, 2011 Data for Chlamydia, Syphilis, and Gonorrhea, U.S. Centers for Disease Control and Prevention, March 2013, http://www.cdc.gov/std/stats11/trends-2011, p. 2.
7. D. T. Fleming et al., "Herpes Simplex Virus Type 2 in the United States, 1976–1994," *New England Journal of Medicine* 337 (1997): 1105–60.
8. http://justherpes.com/facts/genital-herpes-statistics-us-hsv2/.
9. Denise D. Hallfors, Martha W. Waller, Daniel Bauer, Carol A. Ford, and Carolyn T. Halpern, "Which Comes First in Adolescence—Sex and Drugs or Depression?," *American Journal of Preventive Medicine* 29, no. 3 (2005): 163.
10. National Longitudinal Survey of Adolescent Health, Wave II, 1996. For analysis of data, see Heritage Foundation report, "Sexually Active Teenagers Are More Likely to Be Depressed and to Attempt Suicide," Center for Data Analysis Report no. 03-04, June 3, 2003.
11. Cheryl B. Aspy et al., "Parental Communication and Youth Sexual Behavior," *Journal of Adolescence* 30, no. 3 (June 2007): 449–66.
12. M. D. Resnick et al., "Protecting Adolescents from Harm," findings from the National Longitudinal Study on Adolescent Health, *JAMA* 278, no. 10 (September 10, 1997): 823–32.
13. Robert Rector, Kirk A. Johnson, Ph.D., Shannan Martin, and Lauren R. Noyes, "Harmful Effects of Early Sexual Activity and Multiple Sexual Partners Among Women: A Book of Charts," WebMemo #303 on Sex Education and Abstinence, Heritage Foundation, June 26, 2003, http://www.heritage.org/research/reports/2003/06/harmful-effects-of-early-sexual-activity-and-multiple-sexual-partners-among-women-a-book-of-charts.
14. Resnick et al., "Protecting Adolescents from Harm."
15. L. Ku, F. L. Sonenstein, and J. H. Pleck, "The Dynamics of Young Men's Condom Use During and Across Relationships," *Family Planning Perspectives* 26 (1994): 246–51.

Chapter 10

1. http://www.childrenshospital.org/dream/summer08/the_teenage_brain.html.
2. William Pollack, *Real Boys: Rescuing Our Sons from the Myths of Manhood* (New York: Henry Holt, 1998), p. 82.
3. "Gender Differences in Bonding and Friendship," MarriageMoment, http://www.marriagemoment.org/2011/01/gender-differences-in-bonding-and.html.
4. Pollack, *Real Boys,* p. 86.
5. Ibid.
6. Kenneth Adam, with Alexander P. Morgan, *When He's Married to Mom: How to Help Mother-Enmeshed Men Open Their Hearts to TRUE Love and Commitment* (New York: Simon & Schuster, 2007).
7. Margaret Paul, *How to Become Strong Enough to Love* (N.p.: Indie Digital, 2011).

Bibliography

Adam, K. and Morgan, A. P. (2007). *When He's Married to Mom: How to Help Mother-Enmeshed Men Open Their Hearts to TRUE Love and Commitment.* Simon & Schuster.

Adler, J. (1996). "Building a Better Dad." *Newsweek,* June 17, 58–64.

Adler, M., ed. (1952). *The Great Ideas: A Synopticon of Great Works of the Western World.* Chicago: Encyclopaedia Britannica.

Allison, P. D., and Furstenberg, F. F. (1989, July). "How Marital Dissolution Affects Children: Variations by Age and Sex." *Developmental Psychology, 25 (4),* 540–49.

American Time Use Surveys. Bureau of Labor Statistics. U.S. Department of Labor. June 20, 2013. http://www.bls.gov/news.release/atus.nr0.hmtl.

America's Children: Key National Indicators of Well-Being, 2013. Family Structure and Children's Living Arrangements. http://www.childstats.gov/americaschildren/famsoc1.asp.

Anderson, C. A., and Bushman, B. J. (2001). "Effects of Violent Video Games on Aggressive Behavior, Aggressive Cognition, Aggressive Affect, Physiological Arousal, and Prosocial Behavior: A Meta-Analytic Review of the Scientific Literature." *Psychological Science, 12(5),* 353–359.

Ang, R. P. (2008, December). "Dysfunctional Parenting Behaviors and Parenting Stress Among Mothers of Aggressive Boys." *Child & Family Behavior Therapy, 30(4),* 319–336.

Ashby, S. L., Arcari, C. M., and Edmonson, M. B. (2006). "Television Viewing and Risk of Sexual Initiation by Young Adolescents." *Archives of Pediatric & Adolescent Medicine, 160,* 375–380.

Aspy, C. B., et. al. (2007). "Parental Communication and Youth Sexual Behavior." *Journal of Adolescence 30, no. 3,* June, 449–66.

Barkley, R. A. (1995). *Taking Charge of ADHD.* New York: Guilford Press.

Beaty, L. A. (1995). "Effects of Parental Absence on Male Adolescents' Peer Relations and Self-Image." *Adolescence, 30(120),* 873–880.

Belsky, J. (2002). "Quantity counts: Amount of Child Care and Children's Socioemotional Development." *Journal of Developmental and Behavioral Pediatrics, 23,* 167–170.

Belsky, J., and Fearon, R. M. P. (2002). "Infant-Mother Attachment Security, Contextual Risk and Early Development: A Moderational Analysis." *Development and Psychopathology, 14,* 293–310.

Benenson, J. E., Morash, D., and Petrakos, H. (1998, June). "Gender Differences in Emotional Closeness Between Preschool Children and Their Mothers." *Sex Roles, 38 (11/12),* 975–985.

Benn, R. K. (1986). "Factors Promoting Secure Attachment Relationships between Employed Mothers and Their Sons." *Child Development, 57,* 1224–1231.

Bickham, D. S., and Rich, M. (2006, April). "Is Television Viewing Associated With Social Isolation? Roles of Exposure Time, Viewing Contest, and Violent Content." *Archives of Pediatric & Adolescence Medicine, 160,* 387–392.

Bonkowski, S. E., Boomhower, S. J., and Bequette, S. Q. (1985). "What You Don't Know Can Hurt You: Unexpressed Fears and Feelings of Children from Divorcing Families." *Journal of Divorce, 9(1),* 33–45.

Brody, L. R. (1985). "Gender Differences in Emotional Development: A Review of Theories and Research." *Journal of Personality, 53,* 14–59.

Brooks, C. (2012, June). "Today's Working Women Still Do More Housework than Men." *Business News Daily.* http://www.businessnewsdaily.com/2758-men-women-work-housework.html.

Brooks-Gunn, J., and Petersen, A. C. (1991). "Studying the Emergence of Depression and Depressive Symptoms During Adolescence." *Journal of Youth and Adolescence, 20(2),* 115–119.

Brown, J. D., L'Engle, K. L., Pardun, C. J., Guo, G., Kenneavy, K., and Jackson, C. (2006). "Sexy Media Matter: Exposure to Sexual Content in Music, Movies, Television, and Magazines Predicts Black and White Adolescents' Sexual Behavior." *Pediatrics, 117,* 1018–1027.

Bush, L. (2004). "How Black Mothers Participate in the Development of Manhood and Masculinity: What Do We Know about Black Mothers and Their Sons?" *Journal of Negro Education, 73(4),* 381–391.

Bushweller, K. (1994). "Turning Our Backs on Boys." *American School Board Journal, 181,* 20–25.

Coles, R. (1986). *The Moral Life of Children.* New York: Atlantic Monthly Press.

Coles, R. (1991). *The Spiritual Life of Children.* New York: Mariner Books.

Commendador, K. A. (2010). "Parental Influences on Adolescent Decision Making and Contraceptive Use." *Pediatric Nursing, 36(3),*147–156.

Committee on Adolescence. (1993). "Homosexuality and Adolescence." *Pediatrics, 92(4),* 631–634.

Covey, S. (2004). *The 7 Habits of Highly Effective People: Powerful Lessons in Personal Change.* New York: Free Press.

Cox, M., ed. (2005). *Questions Kids Ask About Sex: Honest Answers for Every Age.* Grand Rapids, Mich.: Revell.

D'Angelo, L. L., Weinberger, D. A., and Feldman, S. S. (1995). "Like Father, Like

Son? Predicting Male-Adolescents' Adjustment from Parents' Distress and Self-Restraint." *Developmental Psychology, 31(6)*, 883–896.

Diamond, M. J. (1986). "Becoming a Father: A Psychoanalytic Perspective on the Forgotten Parent," *Psychoanalytic Review, 73*, 445–460.

DiIorio, C., Kelley, M., and Hockenberry-Eaton, M. (1991). "Communication About Sexual Issues: Mothers, Fathers, and Friends." *Journal of Adolescent Health, 24(3)*, 181–189.

Dittus, P. J., and Jaccard, J. J. (2000, April). "Adolescents' Perceptions of Maternal Disapproval of Sex: Relationship to Sexual Outcomes." *Adolescent Health, 26(4)*, 268–278.

Dobson, J. (2001). *Bringing Up Boys*. Carol Stream, Ill.: Tyndale House.

Drexler, P. (2009, Nov. 12). "Mothers and Sons: How Close Is Too Close?" *Huffington Post*.

Eagly, A. H., and Steffen, V. J. (1986). "Gender and Aggressive Behavior: A Meta-Analytic Review of the Social Psychological Literature." *Psychological Bulletin, 100*, 309–330.

"The Father Factor: Data on the Consequences of Father Absence and the Benefits of Father Involvement," National Fatherhood Initiative, http://www.fatherhood.org/media/consequences-of-father-absence-statistics.

Feldman, S. S., and Wentzel, K. R. (1995). "Relations of Marital Satisfaction to Peer Outcomes in Adolescent Boys: A Longitudinal Study." *Journal of Early Adolescence, 15(2)*, 220–237.

Fergusson, D. M., Horwood, L. J., and Lynskey, M. T. (1994). "Parental Separation, Adolescent Psychopathology, and Problem Behaviors." *Journal of the American Academy of Child and Adolescent Psychiatry, 33(8)*, 1122–1131.

Fleming, D. T., et. al. (1997). "Herpes Simplex Virus Type 2 in the United States, 1976–1994." *New England Journal of Medicine 337*, 1105–60.

Forehand, R., Neighbors, B., and Wierson, M. (1991). "The Transition of Adolescence: The Role of Gender and Stress in Problem Behavior and Competence." *Journal of Child Psychology and Psychiatry and Allied Disciplines, 32(6)*, 929–937.

Friedman, C., and Downey, J. (1994). "Homosexuality." *New England Journal of Medicine, 331(14)*, 923–930.

Gant, L. M., et al. (1994). "Increasing Responsible Sexual Behavior Among High-Risk African-American Adolescent Males: Results of a Brief, Intensive Intervention." *Journal of Multicultural Social Work, 3(3)*, 49–58.

Gantt, A., and Greif, G. (2009). "African American Single Mothers Raising Sons: Implications for Family Therapy." *Journal of Family Social Work, 12(3)*, 227–243.

Giedd, J. N., et al. (2006). "Puberty-Related Influences on Brain Development." *Molecular and Cellular Endocrinology, 254–255*, 154–162.

Girgus, J., Nolen-Hocksema, S., and Seligman, M. E. (1989, August). "Why Do Sex Differences in Depression Emerge during Adolescence?" Paper presented at the annual meeting of the American Psychological Association, New Orleans, Louisiana.

Gjerde, P. F. (1988). "Parental Concordance on Child Rearing and the Interactive Emphases of Parents: Sex-Differentiated Relationships During the Preschool Years." *Developmental Psychology 24(5)*, 700–706.

Greene, J. P., and Winters, M. A. (2006, April). "Leaving Boys Behind: Public High

School Graduation Rates." Civic Report, No. 48, Manhattan Institute, April 2006, http://www.manhattan-institute.org/html/cr_48.htm.

Greenfield, Patricia M. (2004). "Inadvertent Exposure to Pornography on the Internet: Implications of Peer-to-peer File-Sharing Networks for Child Development and Families." *Applied Developmental Psychology 25,* 741–50.

Greenson, R. (1968). "Dis-identifying from Mother: Its Special Importance for the Boy." *International Journal of Psychoanalysis, 49,* 370–374.

Grossman, F., Pollack, W. S., and Golding, E. (1988). "Fathers and Children: Predicting the Quality and Quantity of Fathering." *Developmental Psychology, 24,* 82–91.

Grossman, F., Pollack, W.S., Golding, E. R., and Fedele, N. M. (1987). "Autonomy and Affiliation in the Transition to Parenthood." *Family Relations, 36,* 263–269.

Guidubaldi, J., Cleminshaw, H. K., Perry, J. D., and McLoughlin, C. S. (1983). "The Impact of Parental Divorce on Children: Report of the Nationwide NASP Study." *School Psychology Review, 12(3),* 300–323.

Gurian, M. (2006). *The Wonder of Boys.* New York: Penguin.

Haiman, P. E. "Effects of Type of Attachment on Child and Adolescent Behavior." http://www.peterhaiman.com/articles/effects-of-type-of-attachment.

Hall, J. A. (1978). "Gender Effects in Decoding Nonverbal Cues." *Psychological Bulletin, 85,* 845–857.

Hallowell, E., and Ratey, J. (2005). *Delivered from Distraction: Getting the Most out of Life with Attention Deficit Disorder.* New York: Ballantine Books.

Halpern, D. F. (1997). "Sex Differences in Intelligence: Implications for Education." *American Psychologist, 52(10),* 1091–1102.

Hedges, L. V., and Nowell, A. (1995). "Sex Differences in Mental Test Scores, Variability, and Numbers of High-Scoring Individuals." *Science, 269,* 41–45.

Herzog, J. (1982). "On Father Hunger: The Father's Role in the Modulation of Aggressive Drive and Fantasy." In S. Cath, A. Gurwitt, and J. Ross (eds.), *Father and Child* (pp. 163–174). Boston: Little, Brown.

Hodges, W. F., and Bloom, B. L. (1984). "Parents' Report of Children Adjustment to Marital Separation: A Longitudinal Study." *Journal of Divorce, 8(1),* 33–50.

Hoffman, M. I., and Levine, I. F. (1976). "Early Sex Differences in Empathy." *Developmental Psychology, 12,* 557–558.

Hoff Sommers, C. (2000). *The War Against Boys.* New York: Simon & Schuster.

Howard, S. (2004). "The Correlation of Defensive Responses Between Mothers and Sons: An Attachment Perspective." University of the Pacific.

Ishikawa, F., Sumie, S., Akiko, O., and Yasuko, S. (2009, October). "Psychosocial Adjustment Process of Mothers Caring for Young Men with Traumatic Brain Injury: Focusing on the Mother-Son Relationship." *Journal of Neuroscience Nursing 41(5),* 277.

Jacklin, C. N. (1989). "Female and Male: Issues of Gender." *American Psychologist, 44,* 127–133.

Jackson, R. (2004). "When Children View Pornography." Focus on the Family, http://www.focusonthefamily.com/parenting/sexuality/when_children_use_pornography.aspx.

Jenning, L. K. (2009, June). "Mother Courage." *Reader's Digest 174(1046),*110.

Johnston, C., Hommersen, P., and Seipp, C. M. "Maternal Attributions and Child

Oppositional Behavior: A Longitudinal Study of Boys with and Without Attention-Deficit/Hyperactivity Disorder." *Journal of Consulting and Clinical Psychology 77(1),* 189–195.

Jordan, E. (1995). "Fighting Boys and Fantasy Play: The Construction of Masculinity in the Early Years of School." *Gender and Education, 7(1),* 69–86.

Kasen, S., Cohen, P., Brook, J. S., and Hartmark, C. (1996). "A Multiple-Risk Interaction Model: Effects of Temperament and Divorce on Psychiatric Disorders in Children." *Journal of Abnormal Child Psychology, 24(2),* 121–150.

Kessler, R., and McRae, J. (1981). "Trends in the Relationship Between Sex and Psychological Distress: 1957–1976." *American Sociological Review, 46,* 443–452.

Kessler, R., and McRae, J. (1983). "Trends in the Relationship between Sex and Attempted Suicide." *Journal of Health and Social Behavior, 24,* 98–110.

Kimura, D. (1992, September). "Sex Differences in the Brain." *Scientific American,* 119–125.

Kindlon, D. and Thompson, M. (2000). *Raising Cain: Protecting the Emotional Life of Boys.* New York: Ballantine Books.

Kraut, R., Patterson, M., Lundmark, V., Kiesler, S., Mukopadhyay, T., and Scherlis, W. (1998, September). "Internet Paradox: A Social Technology That Reduces Social Involvement and Psychological Well-Being?" *American Psychologist, 53(9),* 1017–1031.

Krosnick, J. A., Anand, S. N., and Hartl, S. P. (2003). "Psychosocial Predictors of Heavy Television Viewing Among Preadolescents and Adolescents." *Basic and Applied Social Psychology, 25(2),* 87–110.

Ku, L., et. al. (1994). "The Dynamics of Yound Men's Condom Use During and Across Relationships." *Family Planning Perspectives 26,* 246–51.

Levant, R. F. (1992). "Toward the Reconstruction of Masculinity." *Journal of Family Psychology, 5,* 379–402.

Lever, J. H. (1976). "Sex Differences in the Games Children Play." *Social Work, 23,* 78–87.

Lewin, T. (1997, April 5). "Teen-agers Alter Sexual Practices, Thinking Risks Will Be Avoided." *New York Times.*

Lier-Schehl, H., Turmes, L., Pinnow, M., El-Khechen, W., and Kramer, M. (2011). "Measuring Mother-Child Relationship: A German Instrument for Both Self-Assessment and Assessment by Others (SF-MKI)." *Praxis der Kinderpsychologie und Kinderpsychiatrie, 60(3),* 192–205.

Lifford, K. J., Harold, G. T., and Thapar, A. (2009, December). "Parent–Child Hostility and Child ADHD Symptoms: A Genetically Sensitive and Longitudinal Analysis." *Journal of Child Psychology and Psychiatry* 50(12), 1468–1476.

Maccoby, E. (1990). "Gender and Relationships: A Developmental Account." *American Psychologist, 45,* 513–520.

Maccoby, E., and Jacklin, G. N. (1980). "Sex Differences in Aggression: A Rejoinder and Reprise." *Child Development, 51,* 964–80.

Macrae, F. (2013, February 20)."Sorry to Interrupt, Dear, but Women Really Do Talk More than Men (13,000 Words a Day More, to Be Precise)." *Mail Online.* http://www.dailymail.co.uk/sciencetech/article-2281891/Women-really-talk-men-13-000-words-day-precise.html.

Manning, A. (1997, August 14). "Teens Starting Substance Abuse at Younger Ages." *USA Today*, 8D.

Mannuzza, S., Klein, R., Bessler, A., Malloy, P., and Hynes, N. (1997). "Educational and Occupational Outcome of Hyperactive Boys Grown-Up." *Journal of the American Academy of Child and Adolescent Psychiatry, 36(9)*, 1222–1227.

McIntosh, H. (1996, June). "Research on Teen-age Friendships Dispels Old Myths." *American Psychological Association Monitor*. Washington, D.C.

McShane, K. E., and Hastings, P. (2009). "The New Friends Vignettes: Measuring Parental Psychological Control That Confers Risk for Anxious Adjustment in Preschoolers." *International Journal of Behavioral Development 33(6)*, 481–495.

Mead, S. (2006, June). "The Truth About Boys and Girls." http://www.education sector.org.

Meeker, M. (2007). *Your Kids at Risk: How Teen Sex Threatens Our Sons and Daughters*. Washington, D.C.: Regnery.

Meeker, M. (2008). *Boys Should Be Boys: 7 Secrets to Raising Healthy Sons*. Washington, D.C.: Regnery.

Miller, K. S., and Whitaker, D. J. (2001, August 1). "Predictors of Mother–Adolescent Discussions About Condoms: Implications for Providers Who Serve Youth." *Pediatrics 108(2)*, e28. doi: 10.1542/peds.108.2.e28.

Moilanen, K., Shaw, D., and Fitzpatrick, A. (2010, September). "Self-Regulation in Early Adolescence: Relations with Mother-Son Relationship Quality and Maternal Regulatory Support and Antagonism." *Journal of Youth and Adolescence 39*, 1357–1367.

"Mother–Son Ties Change Over Time, Influence Teen Boys' Behavior." *Science Daily*, August 31, 2011.

National Institute of Mental Health. (2007). "Teenage Brain: A Work in Progress." NIH Publication No. 01-4929. http://www.nimh.nih.gov/health/publica tions/teenage-brain-a-work-in-progress.shtml.

Nelson, D. A., and Coyne, S. M. (2009, February). "Intent Attributions and Feelings of Distress: Associations with Maternal and Paternal Parenting Practices." *Journal of Abnormal Child Psychology 37(2)*, 223–237.

Nolen-Hocksema, S. (1995). "Gender Differences in Coping with Depression across the Lifespan." *Depression, 3*, 81–90.

Nolen-Hocksema, S., and Girgus, J. S. (1994). "The Emergence of Gender Differences in Depression During Adolescence." *Psychological Bulletin, 115(3)*, 424–443.

Nolen-Hocksema, S., Girgus, J. S., and Seligman, M. E. P. (1992). "Predictors and Consequences of Childhood Depressive Symptoms: A Five-Year Longitudinal Study." *Journal of Abnormal Psychology, 101(3)*, 405–422.

Paul, Margaret. (2011). *How to Become Strong Enough to Love*. Indie Digital, 2011.

Peretti, P. O., and di-Vitorrio, A. (1993). "Effect of Loss of Father Through Divorce on the Personality of the Preschool Child." *Social Behavior and Personality, 21(1)*, 33–38.

Pleck, J., Sonenstein, F. L., and Ku, L. C. (1993). "Masculinity Ideology: Its Impact on Adolescent Males' Heterosexual Relationships." *Journal of Social Issues, 49(3)*, 11–29.

Pollack, W. S. (1990). "Men's Development and Psychotherapy: A Psychoanalytic Perspective." *Psychotherapy, 27*, 316–321.

Pollack, W. S. (1992). "Boys Will Be Boys: Developmental Traumas of Masculinity— Psychoanalytic Perspectives." Paper presented as part of a symposium "Toward a New Psychology of Men" at the centennial meeting of the American Psychological Association, Washington, D.C.

Pollack, W. S. (1995, Winter). "Reframing Masculinity: Men, Empathy and Empathy for Men." Paper presented at the Cambridge Symposium, Cambridge, Massachusetts.

Pollack, W. S. (1995, June). "Becoming Whole and Good: A New Psychology of Men." International Coalition/Boys' Schools Symposium.

Pollack, W. S. (1995, August). "Men's Erotic Desires: Love, Lust, Trauma, Sex, Biology, and Psychoanalysis." Paper presented at the 103rd annual convention of the American Psychological Association, New York.

Pollack, W. S. (1996, June). "Boys' Voices: Can We Listen, Can We Respond? Toward an Empathic Empirical Agenda." International Coalition/Boys' Schools Symposium.

Pollack, W. S. (1996). *Boys at Play: Sports and Transformation.* Hunting Valley, Ohio: University School Press.

Pollack, W. S. (1998). "Mourning, Melancholia, and Masculinity: Recognizing and Treating Depression in Men." In W. S. Pollack and R. L. Levant (eds.), *New Psychotherapy for Men.* New York: Wiley.

Pollack, W. S. (1998). *Real Boys: Rescuing Our Sons from the Myths of Boyhood.* New York: Henry Holt.

Pottorff, D. D., Phelps-Zientarski, D., and Skovera, M. E. (1996). "Gender Perceptions of Elementary and Middle School Students About Literacy at School and Home." *Journal of Research and Development in Education, 29(4),* 203–211.

Potts, M. K., Burnam, M. A., and Wells, K. B. (1991). "Gender Differences in Depression Detection: A Comparison of Clinician Diagnosis and Standardized Assessment." *Psychological Assessment, 3(4),* 609–615.

Pruett, K. D. (1989). "The Nurturing Male: A Longitudinal Study of Primary Nurturing Fathers." In S. H. Cath, A. Gurwitt, and L. Gunsberg (eds.), *Fathers and Their Families* (pp. 389–405). Hillsdale, N.J.: Analytic Press.

Public Health Service. (1956). "Death Rates by Age, Race, and Sex, United States, 1900–1953: Suicide." *Vital Statistics Special Reports, 43(30).*

Ravitch, D. (1994, October). "The War on Boys." *Men's Health,* 110.

Resnick, M. D., et. al. (1997). "Protecting Adolescnets from Harm." *JAMA 278, no. 10,* (September 10), 823–32.

Rideout, V., Roberts, D. F., and Foehr, U. G. (2005, March). "Generation M: Media in the Lives of 8–18 Year-Olds." Henry J. Kaiser Family Foundation, 4–19.

Rohde, P., Seeley, J. R., and Mace, D. E. (1997). "Correlates of Suicide Behavior in a Juvenile Detention Population." *Suicide and Life-Threatening Behavior, 27(2),* 164–175.

Roy, K., Dyson, O. L., and Jackson, J.-N. (2010). "Intergenerational Support and Reciprocity Between Low-Income African American Fathers and Their Aging Mothers." In W. E. Johnson (ed.), *Social Work with African American Males.* New York: Oxford University Press, 2010.

Sanders, C. E., Field, T. M., Diego, M., and Kaplan, M. (2000). "The Relationship of Internet Use to Depression and Social Isolation Among Adolescents." *Adolescence, 35 (138),* 238–242.

Sax, L. (2005). *Why Gender Matters.* New York: Broadway Books.

Science Daily. (2007, June 12). "When It Comes to Delinquency, Boys Are Exposed to More Risk, Less Protection."

Segell, M. (1995, March). "The Pater Principle." *Esquire,* 121–127.

Sells, C. W., and Blum, R. W. (1996). "Morbidity and Mortality among U.S. Adolescents: An Overview of Data and Trends." *American Journal of Public Health, 86(4),* 513–519.

Siegal, M. (1987). "Are Sons and Daughters Treated More Differently by Fathers than by Mothers?" *Developmental Review, 7,* 183–209.

Siegel, D. J., and Hartzell, M. (2003). *Parenting from the Inside Out: How a Deeper Understanding Can Help You Raise Children Who Thrive.* New York: Penguin.

Sinha, J. W., Cnaan, R. A., and Gelles, R. W. (2007, April). "Adolescent Risk Behaviors and Religion: Findings from a National Study." *Journal of Adolescence, 30(2),* 231–249.

Slater, M. D., Henry, K. L., Swaim, R. C., and Cardador, J. M. (2004, December). "Vulnerable Teens, Vulnerable Times: How Sensation Seeking, Alienation, and Victimization Moderate the Violent Media Content-Aggressiveness Relation." *Communication Research, 31(6),* 642–668.

Smith, C., and Lundquist, M. (2009). *Soul Searching: The Religious and Spiritual Lives of American Teenagers.* New York: Oxford University Press.

Spokes, E. (2009, May 8). "The Blessings of Boys." *Baltimore Jewish Times,* 17–19.

Stolberg, S. G. (2001). "Researchers Find a Link between Behavioral Problems and Time in Child Care." *New York Times,* April 19, A22.

Tronick, E., and Cohn, J. (1989). "Infant-Mother Face-to-Face Interaction: Age and Gender Differences in Coordination and the Occurrence of Miscoordination." *Child Development, 60,* 85–92.

Tsai, T., and Scommegna, P. (2012). "U.S. Has World's Highest Incarceration Rate." Population Reference Bureau. http://www.prb.org/Publications/Articles/2012/us-incarceration.aspx.

Tyson, P. (1982). "A Developmental Line of Gender Identity, Gender Role, and Choice of Love Object." *Journal of American Psychoanalytic Association, 30,* 61–86.

USA Today. (1997). "Children's Time Spent with Family." Poll.

U.S. Department of Justice. (1997). *Males and Firearms Violence.*

U.S. Department of Justice. (1997). *Victim Characteristics.*

Villani, S. (2001, April). "Impact of Media on Children and Adolescents: A 10-Year Review of the Research." *Journal of the American Academy of Child and Adolescent Psychiatry, 40(4),* 392–401.

Wang, W., Parker, K., and Taylor, P. (2013). "Breadwinner Moms: Mothers Are the Sole or Primary Provider in Four-in-Ten Households with Children; Public Conflicted about the Growing Trend." Pew Research: Social & Demographic Trends. http://www.pewsocialtrends.org/2013/05/29/breadwinner-moms/.

Weinberg, M. K. (1992). "Boys and Girls: Sex Differences in Emotional Expressivity and Self-Regulation During Infancy." In L. J. Bridges (chair), "Early Emotional Self-Regulation: New Approaches to Understanding Developmental

Change and Individual Differences." Symposium conducted at the International Conference on Infant Studies, Miami, Florida.

Weinfield, N., Ogawa, J., & Sroufe, L. A. (1997). "Early Attachment as a Pathway to Adolescent Peer Competence." *Journal of Research on Adolescence*, 7, 241–265.

Werner, N. E., and Crick, N. R. (2004). "Maladaptive Peer Relationships and the Development of Relational and Physical Aggression During Middle Childhood." *Social Development, 13(4)*, 495–514.

Wolak, J., Mitchell, K. J., and Finkelhor, D. (2003). "Escaping or Connecting? Characteristics of Youth Who Form Close Online Relationships." *Journal of Adolescence, 26,* 105–119.

Zachary, G. P. (1997, May 2). "Male Order: Boys Used to Be Boys, but Do Some Now See Boyhood as a Malady?" *Wall Street Journal,* A1.

Zaslow, M. J. (1988, July). "Sex Differences in Children's Response to Parental Divorce: I. Research Methodology and Postdivorce Family Forms." *American Journal of Orthopsychiatry, 58(3),* 355–378.

Index

PHOTO: © SHEA PETAJA

MEG MEEKER, M.D., is the author of *Strong Fathers, Strong Daughters; Boys Should Be Boys; The 10 Habits of Happy Mothers;* and *Strong Mothers, Strong Sons*. She has been a physician practicing pediatric and adolescent medicine, working with children and their parents, for more than thirty years. Dr. Meeker is the mother of four children and lives and works with her husband in northern Michigan.

www.megmeekermd.com

About the Type

This book was set in Bembo, a typeface based on an old-style Roman face that was used for Cardinal Pietro Bembo's tract *De Aetna* in 1495. Bembo was cut by Francesco Griffo (1450–1518) in the early sixteenth century for Italian Renaissance printer and publisher Aldus Manutius (1449–1515). The Lanston Monotype Company of Philadelphia brought the well-proportioned letterforms of Bembo to the United States in the 1930s.